Routledge Revivals

U.S. Military Strategy in the Gulf

First published in 1989, this title explores the nature and dimensions of the U.S. strategy in the Gulf in the formative years that followed the fall of the Shah, the Soviet invasion of Afghanistan and the outbreak of the Iran-Iraq war. It describes the formation of the U.S. Rapid Deployment Joint Task Force and the U.S. Central Command, their force structure and the network of U.S. bases and facilities in the region. The role of pro-Western countries in the wider region, in particular Pakistan, Egypt, Jordan, and Israel, in the formulation of strategy is discussed in detail, along with a more general assessment of the achievements and failures of U.S. strategy in the Gulf towards the end of the 1980s.

In light of the persistent struggle for peace within the Middle East, this is a timely reissue, which will be of great interest to students researching U.S. military strategy over the past thirty years.

U.S. Military Strategy in the Gulf

Origins and Evolution Under the Carter and Reagan Administrations

Amitav Acharya

First published in 1989
by Routledge, Chapman and Hall, Inc.

This edition first published in 2013 by Routledge
2 Park Square, Milton Park, Abingdon, Oxon, OX14 4RN

Simultaneously published in the USA and Canada
by Routledge
711 Third Avenue, New York, NY 10017

Routledge is an imprint of the Taylor & Francis Group, an informa business

© 1989 Amitav Acharya

All rights reserved. No part of this book may be reprinted or reproduced or
utilised in any form or by any electronic, mechanical, or other means, now
known or hereafter invented, including photocopying and recording, or in any
information storage or retrieval system, without permission in writing from the
publishers.

Publisher's Note
The publisher has gone to great lengths to ensure the quality of this reprint but
points out that some imperfections in the original copies may be apparent.

Disclaimer
The publisher has made every effort to trace copyright holders and welcomes
correspondence from those they have been unable to contact.

A Library of Congress record exists under LC control number: 93132743

ISBN 13: 978-0-415-71747-2 (hbk)
ISBN 13: 978-1-315-87133-2 (ebk)
ISBN 13: 978-0-415-71748-9 (pbk)

U.S. MILITARY STRATEGY IN THE GULF:
ORIGINS AND EVOLUTION UNDER THE CARTER
AND REAGAN ADMINISTRATIONS

U.S. MILITARY STRATEGY IN THE GULF

AMITAV ACHARYA

ROUTLEDGE
London and New York

First published in 1989 by
Routledge
a division of Routledge, Chapman and Hall
11 New Fetter Lane, London EC4P 4EE

Published in the USA by
Routledge
a division of Routledge, Chapman and Hall, Inc.
29 West 35th Street, New York NY 10001

© 1989 A. Acharya

Phototypeset in Baskerville by Pat and Anne Murphy,
Highcliffe-on-Sea, Dorset
Printed in Great Britain by
Billing & Sons Ltd, Worcester

All rights reserved. No part of this book may be
reprinted or reproduced or utilized in any form or
by any electronic, mechanical, or other means, now
known or hereafter invented, including photocopying
and recording, or in any information storage or
retrieval system, without permission in writing from
the publishers.

British Library Cataloguing in Publication Data

Acharya, Amitav
  U.S. military strategy in the Gulf: origins and
  evolution under the Carter and Reagan
  administrations.
  1. Persian Gulf countries. Policies of
  United States government, 1968–80
  I. Title
  953
  ISBN 0-415-01004-7

Library of Congress Cataloging-in-Publication Data

  ISBN 0-415-01004-7

Contents

List of Tables and Maps	vii
List of Acronyms	viii
Acknowledgements	xi
Preface	xiii

1	**Evolution of U.S. Interests and Objectives**	1
	Oil, containment, and stability	1
	After the Raj: an area of 'vital' interests	5
	Notes	17
2	**The Shah and the Nixon Doctrine**	21
	The Nixon Doctrine	21
	Oil and the 'twin pillars'	24
	The Shah as regional policeman	26
	The arms pipeline	28
	Notes	33
3	**From Teheran to Kabul, 1979: Gulf Crises and American Reassertion**	37
	Iran and regional stability	37
	The Afghanistan crisis and the Soviet 'threat'	44
	The Carter Doctrine	49
	Notes	57
4	**The Central Command**	63
	From RDJTF to CENTCOM	65
	Force structure	70
	Strategic mobility programs	79
	Notes	85
5	**Bases, 'Facility Access', and Geopolitics**	89
	The access network	92
	Diego Garcia	96
	Somalia	102
	Kenya	104
	Egypt	105
	Israel	107
	The Gulf Cooperation Council States	110
	Notes	116

v

Contents

6 Threats, Contingency Planning, and Response 123

'Non-Soviet' threats 123
Response to the Gulf War: 1980–84 126
Arms sales 134
'Third-party' assistance 141
The 'worst-case' threat 146
The preemptive strategy 150
The power projection balance 154
Escalation: nuclear or horizontal? 159
Notes 161

7 Conclusion 169

Bibliography 177
Index 199

Tables and Maps

Tables

1.1	Estimated Persian Gulf crude oil and natural gas proved reserves	6
1.2	Percentage of world crude oil production by region, 1938–78	7
4.1	Evolution of the RDF Command Organization	66
4.2	U.S. Central Command Force Structure	71
4.3	Selected CENTCOM exercises, 1980–85	78
4.4	U.S. airlift and sealift forces improvements, FY1980–FY1989	82
5.1	RDJTF/CENTCOM military construction funding, FY1981–FY1985	93
5.2	Diego Garcia facilities expansion program, FY1981–FY1985	100
6.1	U.S. security assistance to the Gulf Cooperation Council States	135
6.2	Major identified arms agreements between the United States and the GCC States, 1979–85	137
6.3	The AWACS package, 1981	139
6.4	Congressional Budget Office estimate of U.S. ground force capabilities for the Persian Gulf, first 16 days after mobilization, with and without the RDF	152

Maps

1.1	The Persian Gulf/Southwest Asia Region	xvii
4.1	CENTCOM Area of Responsibility	68
5.1	The RDF 'access network'	94
5.2	Diego Garcia: Island key map	98

vii

Acronyms

AOR	Area of Responsibility
AWACS	Airborne Warning and Control System
CBO	Congressional Budget Office
CENTCOM	(U.S.) Central Command
CENTO	Central Treaty Organization
CIA	Central Intelligence Agency
COMIDEASTFOR	Command Middle East Force
CONUS	continental United States
CRAF	Civil Reserve Air Fleet
CX	cargo experimental
DOD	Department of Defense
FDL	fast deployment logistics
FHE	forward headquarters element
FMS	foreign military sales
FY	fiscal year
GCC	Gulf Corporation Council
IMET	International Military Education and Training
JCS	Joint Chiefs of Staff
JCSE	joint communication support element
JLP	Jordanian Logistics Plan
JTF	Joint Task Force
LAV	light armoured vehicle
MAB	marine amphibious brigade
MAC	Military Airlift Command
MAGTF	Marine Air-Ground Task Force
MAP	Military Assistance Program
mbd	million barrels per day
MPGS	mobile protected gun system
MPS	maritime pre-positioning ships
MSC	Military Sealift Command
NATO	North Atlantic Treaty Organization
NCA	National Command Authority
NDRF	National Defense Reserve Fleet
NSC	National Security Council
NTPF	near-term pre-positioned force
NTPS	near-term pre-positioning ship

Acronyms

OPEC	Organization of Petroleum-Exporting Countries
PACOM	(U.S.) Pacific Command
PDR Yemen	People's Democratic Republic of Yemen
PLO	Palestine Liberation Organization
POL	petroleum, oil and lubricant
RDF	Rapid Deployment Force
RDJTF	Rapid Deployment Joint Task Force
REDCOM	(U.S.) Readiness Command
RO/RO	roll on/roll off
RRF	Ready Reserve Force
SPF	Strategic Projection Force
STRICOM	(U.S.) Strike Command
SWA	Southwest Asia
TOW	tube-launched, optically tracked, wire-guided
UAE	United Arab Emirates
USAF	United States Air Force
V/STOL	vertical/short take-off and landing

To my parents
Shrimati Acharya and Janardan Acharya

Acknowledgements

In preparing this book, I have received valuable guidance and help from many individuals and institutions. Among them, I would like to emphasize the contribution of Dr. Richard Higgott, the supervisor of my Ph.D. dissertation at Murdoch University, Perth, Australia, and currently the executive director of the Australian Institute of International Affairs.

Several scholars and officials in Washington, D.C., were generous in giving me their time for discussions on the subject of the book. They include Mr. James Wootten (Congressional Research Service), Lt. Col. Martin Burke (the Joint Chiefs of Staff), Professor Bernard Reich (George Washington University), Jeffrey Record (Institute for Foreign Policy Analysis), Robert Littwak (Woodrow Wilson Centre), William Lind (advisor to Senator Gary Hart), Steven Gilick (American-Israel Public Affairs Committee), Joshua Epstein (Brookings Institution) and Thomas McNaugher (Brookings Institution). Among the State Department officials, I am particularly indebted to John Brecht (Bureau of Near East and South Asia), A. Peter Burleigh (Bureau of Intelligence), Mark Hambly (Bureau of Near East and South Asia), Patrick Theros (Bureau of Political-Military Affairs), and Col. Robert J. Lawrence (Bureau of Political-Military Affairs). Pentagon officials who helped in my research include Major James A. Reese (Joint Chiefs of Staff), Ronald Zwart (Office of the Secretary of Defense), Lt. Col. Robert Kirkpatrick (Office of the Secretary of Defense), and Sandy Charles (Office of the Secretary of Defense). I also received a briefing from the NATO division of the Office of the Secretary of Defense.

I thank the staff of a number of libraries whose resources I used in the course of my research. These include the inter-library loan department of Murdoch University library; the United States Information Service libraries in New Delhi, Perth and Canberra; the National Library of Australia and the Australian Defence Forces Academy Library in Canberra; the libraries of Congress, the State Department, the Pentagon (Army Library); George Washington University and the American University in Washington, D.C.; and the libraries of the Royal Institute of International Affairs (Chatham House) and the International Institute for

xi

Acknowledgements

Strategic Studies in London. Finally, a fellowship at the Institute of Southeast Asian Studies in Singapore and the encouragement and advice of its director, Professor K. S. Sandhu, enabled me to complete the book. I also gratefully acknowledge the advice and support extended to me by Professor Mohammed Ayoob, Research Fellow at the Institute, during the final stages of preparation of this book. While the assistance of all the above-mentioned individuals and institutions was valuable and in some cases indispensable, the responsibility for the views expressed and any mistakes and inaccuracies in the book is entirely mine.

Preface

In the post-war era, successive U.S. administrations have declared a major stake in preserving access to oil from the Persian Gulf and taken a stand against perceived threats to Western interests posed by the Soviet Union and myriad intra-regional forces. But the commitment and approach to protecting the interests have undergone a process of radical change. In the first two decades after World War II, Washington recognized British colonial authority over the region and relied on it for the protection of Western interests. In the wake of the British withdrawal from the region in the early 1970s the United States, politically and materially constrained by its Vietnam involvement, chose to apply the Nixon Doctrine in the area and promote Iran and, to a lesser extent, Saudi Arabia to manage regional security. Although this approach suffered some erosion in the aftermath of the 1973 Arab-Israeli War and the oil embargo, it continued to be the basic framework for the U.S. regional security posture until the Iranian revolution toppled its main agent: the Shah of Iran. That setback and the Soviet invasion of Afghanistan in December 1979 became a turning point in U.S. strategy. Instead of depending on local surrogates, the United States came to recognize the need to rely more on its own military power to preserve and advance the interests of the Western nations in the face of what was believed to be a growing atmosphere of instability and tension in the area.

The chief outcome of this transition is a new military strategy structured around a capability for rapid intervention in regional crises. Efforts to build the capability were initiated by the Carter administration and pursued more vigorously by its successor. Elements of this rapid deployment force program include, among other things, organization of a 'central reserve' of combat forces with requisite strategic mobility and logistics support, creation of a new unified regional command with the responsibility to plan for contingencies and employ U.S. forces in response to them, and creation of an extensive network of basing and access arrangements involving a number of countries in the region.

The objective of this study is to provide a systematic, comprehensive account of the evolution of the U.S. military strategy in the Gulf after the fall of the Shah. It will address three major

xiii

Preface

questions: how the U.S. strategy in the region originated, what initiatives were undertaken by the United States to build up a capability for rapid intervention in the region, and how the United States planned to use this capability in various contingency situations in the region. A primary objective of the study is to identify the problems and constraints affecting the use of U.S. military power in the Gulf. The study covers the 1979–84 period. Although events in the Gulf have moved rapidly since then, the essence of the current U.S. strategy in the region continues to be built upon the foundations laid during the 1979–84 period, events such as the 'Iran-Contra' affair notwithstanding. It is hoped that this study will provide a useful background to an understanding of current U.S. policies in the region.

The most difficult barrier to the conduct of such a study is the classified nature of much of the official data. This is as much due to the usual considerations restricting public access to military information as to the additional care taken by Washington in deference to the political sensitivities of the pro-Western Gulf States, few of whom desire any publicity over U.S. military options designed to ensure their protection. Thus, reliable information is particularly scarce with respect to the regional access network supporting the U.S. Central Command. Similarly, U.S. officials have provided little, beyond the level of ambiguous generalities, that throws light on the contingency options and the 'force packages' designed to cope with the varied threats.

While this barrier can never be fully overcome, one can gain reliable insights into the U.S. military strategy in the Gulf by surveying the broadest range of publicly available sources: congressional hearings, press reports, interviews with officials involved in policymaking, and articles in major military journals. This book relies extensively on these sources, especially the transcripts of the hearings conducted by various committees of the U.S. Congress dealing with the Persian Gulf. These transcripts are often the only publicly available record of official views and data on the various aspects of the U.S. Gulf strategy. Other official sources used in this study include the annual reports and posture statements issued by the Department of Defense, policy notes issued by the Department of State in addition to its official journal, memoirs of former top officials, public papers of presidents, reports authored by the staff of various congressional committees as well as agencies as the Congressional Research Service and the Congressional Budget Office, and other U.S. government departments and agencies.

xiv

Preface

Personal interviews conducted with a number of State and Defense Department officials have been used to check my judgements and supplement the data available from other sources but, at the insistence of the concerned officials, these interviews have not been specifically cited in the chapters. The names of officials interviewed are mentioned in the acknowledgements.

For the purpose of this book, Persian Gulf countries include Iran, Iraq, Saudi Arabia, Oman, Kuwait, the United Arab Emirates, Qatar, and Bahrain. Since 1979 it has become fashionable in official U.S. circles to use the term 'Southwest Asia'. It underscores the comprehensive nature of the new U.S. regional strategic framework and highlights the participation in it of countries on the periphery of the Gulf, for example, Pakistan, Egypt, Jordan, Kenya. But it should be noted that the central focus of the U.S. regional military strategy is the oil-exporting core consisting of the states bordering on the Persian Gulf. These states are also seen in Western circles as having the greatest potential for instability and, therefore, have received most attention in the U.S. military strategy.

The book begins with an overview of the evolution of U.S. interests and involvement in the Gulf in the post-war era. The emergence of U.S. interests and objectives in the region relating to oil, containment, and regional stability will be discussed in Chapter 1. The historical context leading to the application of the Nixon Doctrine in the area and role of the Shah of Iran in U.S. strategy will be critically examined in the second chapter. Chapter 3 will survey the impact of the Iranian revolution and the Soviet invasion of Afghanistan on U.S. strategic perceptions. Both crises will be analyzed in terms of their 'wider' geostrategic implications — as American policymakers chose to view them in 1979–80. And the evolution of the Carter administration's response to the crises will be examined.

Chapter 4 will focus on the U.S. Central Command and the programs undertaken to improve its capability to intervene in a Gulf crisis. The RDJTF/CENTCOM's force structure, strategic mobility, logistics support, and command organization are the major issues to be discussed in this chapter. Chapter 5 will look at the outcome of the U.S. quest for obtaining the support and participation of friendly regional states, especially access to their military facilities. Since access is primarily determined by the political sensitivities of the host nations and is contingent upon the state of their overall strategic relationship with the United States,

xv

Preface

this chapter will examine the political response of the regional states to U.S. strategy.

Finally, Chapter 6 will investigate how the United States responded, or planned to respond, to actual or potential crisis situations in the Gulf that were seen as a threat to U.S. interests. The RDJTF/CENTCOM's contingency planning for the region took into account all types of possible threats — from minor intraregional crises to an all-out Soviet invasion. While the exact nature of such planning was shrouded in secrecy, one could discern the broad elements of the strategy from unclassified official sources and analyze them in terms of the known variables likely to determine their success or failure.

Included in the discussion will be an analysis of the U.S. policy toward the Iran-Iraq War, the most important 'real world' challenge to U.S. interests in the Gulf since the Iranian revolution. The section on the war will examine issues such as the 'victory for neither side' policy pursued by the United States, and the U.S. tilt towards Iraq. The remaining sections of the chapter will analyze U.S. options for contingencies involving Soviet forces and intraregional threats. This will include a look at issues such as the U.S. security relationships with Jordan and Pakistan as they affect the latter's capability to play a contingency role in the Gulf, the potential role of Britain and France in providing similar help, and the trends in U.S. arms transfers to the Gulf Cooperation Council states, including the sale of the AWACS package to Saudi Arabia in 1981. Finally, this chapter will provide a detailed analysis of U.S. strategic options conceived in the hypothetical context of a direct military confrontation with the Soviet Union in Iran. It will examine the three phases of the planned U.S. response to such a threat. A detailed comparative analysis of Soviet and U.S. (and allied) power projection capabilities, including the likely response time and efficiency of various types of forces, will be presented and the major variables affecting the outcome of a confrontation will be discussed. The possibility of nuclearization and the geographical spread of such a confrontation will be analyzed along with its implications for the U.S. strategy.

xvi

Map 1.1: The Persian Gulf/Southwest Asia Region

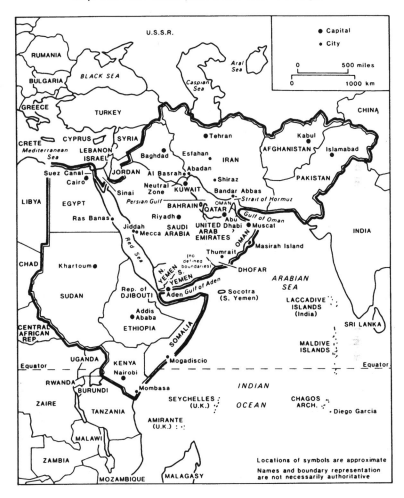

Source: Congressional Budget Office, *Rapid Deployment Forces: Policy and Budgetary Implications* (Washington, D.C., 1983).

1
Evolution of U.S. Interests and Objectives

Oil, containment, and stability

The Persian Gulf region's prominence in U.S. global strategy is a fairly recent phenomenon. Although the United States recognized the importance of the region as part of a land bridge between three continents, its proximity to the Soviet Union, and its increasingly significant contribution to the world supply of petroleum, the Gulf did not become a primary zone in U.S. geographical planning until the 1970s. Unlike the major European powers, the United States did not at any stage have a colonial presence. Much of the early U.S. involvement in the region was in trade or the activities of American Christian missions in education and health.[1] During the inter-war period, U.S. oil companies introduced the first major element of U.S. interest in that region by 1939 with half-ownership of a concession in Kuwait and exclusive concessions in Bahrain and Saudi Arabia.[2] In fact the oil companies were instrumental in bringing the region to the notice of the U.S. government. They sought and obtained the State Department's diplomatic efforts to secure agreement on an 'open door' policy from the British government, which had been accused of discriminatory practices favouring British oil companies in the competition for oil concessions.[3] Yet the Persian Gulf was far from becoming a strategically important region for the United States. The world had not fully shifted from coal as the primary source of energy. Then too, the Gulf was producing only about 8 per cent of the total world oil output and the United States was almost self-sufficient in meeting its oil requirements.

The long-term strategic value of the region's oil resources was

Evolution of U.S. Interests

recognized for the first time during World War II. The war brought into focus the critical importance of petroleum and its by-products as 'foundations of the ability to fight a modern war'.[4] Besides, U.S. energy planners realized that in the post-war period, Persian Gulf oil could serve as a 'well head' for European recovery as well as for U.S. domestic consumption so that depleting indigenous reserves could be saved for future requirements.[5] This realization was clearly reflected in the Roosevelt administration's declaration, in 1943, that the defence of Saudi Arabia was 'vital' to the defence of the United States. The United States extended direct lend-lease assistance to the Kingdom (previously such aid had been given indirectly, through the British) to save it from serious financial trouble caused by the wartime disruption of Saudi oil production.[6] It also proceeded to consolidate the privileged position already enjoyed by U.S. oil multinationals in Saudi Arabia.

The immediate post-war era marked the evolution of two other U.S. interests in the Persian Gulf region: containment of Soviet influence and the preservation of the conservative local regimes. Iran featured centrally in both these developments. The initial impetus for the U.S.-Iranian security relationship came from Iran's young monarch, Shah Mohammed Reza Pahlavi, who during the war had succeeded his father after the latter's forced abdication by the occupying powers, Britain and the Soviet Union. The new Shah solicited American friendship as a counterweight to these two traditional enemies. His efforts received a boost when 30,000 U.S. troops (non-combatant) were deployed in Iran in order to channel U.S. lend-lease supplies to the Soviet Union (the Persian Gulf Command).[7] But the real breakthrough had to await the end of the war and the advent of the Truman administration. The Shah was able to convince the stridently anti-communist Truman administration of Russia's territorial designs on Iran after the Soviets delayed the withdrawal of their troops from Azerbaijan in northern Iran beyond a previously agreed deadline. Suspicious that the Soviets were seeking to carve out a separate state with the long-term objective of its incorporation into the Soviet Union, Truman agreed to ask Moscow to complete the withdrawal. The Azerbaijan crisis came to be regarded as one of the 'opening salvos' of the Cold War.[8]

U.S. interest in Iran as a Cold War partner grew steadily thereafter. Iran found prominent mention in the deliberations over the Truman Doctrine. When briefing congressional leaders on the administration's efforts to combat the communist threat to Greece

2

Evolution of U.S. Interests

and the Middle East, Under Secretary of State Dean Acheson hypothesized that 'like apples in a barrel infected by one rotten one, the corruption of Greece would infect Iran and all to the east'.[9] Saudi Arabia also featured in the containment strategy by agreeing to provide base rights to the United States at Dhahran — an airfield built by the United States to facilitate wartime redeployment of U.S. forces to and from the Far East.[10] But Saudi cooperation was circumscribed due to divisions over the Palestinian issue. Iran, in contrast, lived up to its U.S. designation as the 'strategic prize' of the Near East. It participated in all major Western 'containment' activities in the region, including the Baghdad Pact (later called CENTO). It hosted U.S. military missions (as did Saudi Arabia) and became a major regional recipient of U.S. military aid. The alliance was formalized in 1959 when the two parties signed a Bilateral Security Pact. The pact provided for continued U.S. military and economic aid to Iran as well as an American commitment to take 'appropriate action including the use of armed forces' to assist the Iranian government in case of aggression against Iran.[11]

The third major U.S. interest in the Gulf, regime security in the friendly conservative states, came to the fore at the height of the Anglo-Iranian oil dispute in the early 1950s. The crisis, originating from the Iranian parliament's nationalization of the British-owned Anglo-Iranian Oil Company, was aggravated by the prime ministership of the popular but erratic nationalist leader, Dr Mohammed Mossadeq, in 1951. Mossadeq's refusal to compromise over the issue of nationalization invited a British-arranged boycott of Iran's oil exports and precipitated a grave economic crisis in Iran. Moreover, Mossadeq spurred a political crisis by seeking to undermine the position of the Shah in the domestic power structure. The United States was initially reluctant to take sides, fearing that the alternative to Mossadeq could be a pro-Soviet radical regime in Teheran. But this changed after the domestic position of the Shah came under increasing nationalist attack. After briefly posing as a mediator, the United States expressed decisive support for the monarchy. President Eisenhower turned down an appeal by Mossadeq for economic assistance to stave off imminent bankruptcy of the Iranian state. With his position gravely weakened by the economic crisis, Mossadeq was finally overthrown in a pro-Shah coup in August 1953 to which the CIA provided considerable planning and financial assistance.[12]

Evolution of U.S. Interests

Thus, before the 1970s the three major U.S. interests in the Gulf had been clearly identified and pursued. Yet the Gulf remained somewhat peripheral to overall U.S. strategic planning for the post-war era. The United States was preoccupied with the consolidation of its alliance in Europe. So far as the Cold War was concerned, the distinctive focus was on the Far East, where the United States fought wars in Korea and Vietnam. There were no U.S. moves to establish a major military presence in the Gulf. A very minor exception to this attitude was the decision to station a three-ship (later increased to five ships) flotilla, called the Command Middle East Force, off Bahrain in 1949. The significance of the move, however, was primarily symbolic, to show the U.S. flag in this faraway region. The relatively low priority attached to the Gulf was also reflected in U.S. military aid policy. Even Iran, the centre of U.S. Cold War concerns in the Gulf, was frustrated in its efforts to obtain U.S. military aid at levels the Shah thought appropriate given his country's proximity to the Soviet Union. In the aftermath of the Azerbaijan crisis, the United States delayed action on requests by the Shah for an urgent loan of $40 – $50 million; only a scaled-down amount was subsequently approved. Similarly, Iran was placed in a lower category (Title 3 status) when the United States enacted the Mutual Defense Assistance Program in 1949 to govern its military aid priority.[13] The Shah felt dissatisfied with what he received as reward for his membership in CENTO and his conclusion of a bilateral security pact with the United States (after refusing a Soviet offer to sign a 'non-aggression' pact). As he then wrote, 'although we are deeply grateful for what we have received, I must in candour point out that it fully meets neither our own needs nor those of the Free World in this vital sector'.[14]

A major factor in the U.S. disinclinaton to take a more active interest in the Gulf was its recognition of and regard for Britain's historic role as the Gulf's 'policeman'.[15] The United States considered the Gulf and the Middle East to be within the British sphere of influence and valued the latter's network of treaties with the various tribal sheikhs and rulers and its elaborate regional military presence. Despite occasional differences over issues such as oil concessions, the United States turned to London for advice whenever it considered a major strategic move in the Gulf region. It fully supported the British decision to retain its presence in the Gulf after World War II and India's independence.[16] Even in the aftermath of the Suez fiasco in 1956, Washington encouraged

Evolution of U.S. Interests

British intervention in Kuwait to deter a feared Iraqi attack against the newly independent sheikhdom in 1961.[17] In fact, British expertise in dealing with sources of intra-regional instability came to be more valued as policymakers in Washington, especially the Kennedy administration, came to accept that communist expansion into the Third World would more likely be carried out through subversion rather than direct military attack. The U.S. view was clearly articulated by Defense Secretary Robert McNamara in 1965:

> We are in Europe, we are not in Aden, the Persian Gulf, or the Far East. If Britain quits, the United States for political reasons cannot take her place. Britain's contribution to Western defence is far greater in these places than it could ever be in Europe alone.[18]

It was therefore natural that the British decision to end its presence 'east of Suez' by the early 1970s[19] would force the United States to look for alternative ways to protect its interests in the region. But the British departure was accompanied by a number of other developments, related to oil, trade, finance, and the Arab-Israeli conflict, which brought the Gulf decisively into the centre-stage of U.S. foreign policy in the post-Vietnam era.

After the Raj: an area of 'vital' interests

In the decades after World War II, imported oil had become a critical factor in the economic security and well-being of the Western nations. In 1950 oil accounted for about 30 per cent of the combined energy needs of North America, OECD Europe, and Japan; by 1973 the figure was about 53 per cent.[20] By 1979, 45 per cent of the United States', 55 per cent of the EEC's, and 70 per cent of Japan's energy consumption was in oil.[21] As a result, the world in general and the industrial nations in particular, experienced considerable increases in oil consumption. Between 1950 and 1973 oil consumption in the non-producing nations increased at an average annual rate of 7.1 per cent; the consumption level in 1973 was 35 million barrels per day (mbd) higher than that in 1950. Most of this increase occurred in the OECD bloc, with Western Europe accounting for about 35 per cent, and the North American sector (the United States and Canada) about one-third.[22]

5

Evolution of U.S. Interests

The growing oil consumption in the Western countries meant increasing reliance on imports as their domestic oil production lagged far behind the rate of increase in consumption. Countries previously self-sufficient rapidly became importers. In 1950 the United States was the world's largest producer of petroleum and virtually self-sufficient in meeting domestic requirements. In 1960 it was importing about 16 per cent of its needs. By the time of the first 'energy crisis' in 1973, U.S. import dependence had reached 35 per cent;[23] at the time of the second crisis in 1978–79 it had become 46 per cent. Western Europe and Japan were importing 88 per cent and 100 per cent of their oil requirements, respectively, by 1979.[24]

With the rise in their consumption levels and import dependence, the developed as well as developing nations of the world increasingly turned their attention to the Persian Gulf region. This region contains the only major 'swing' producers which could meet any sudden rises in the global demand for petroleum.[25] The eight Gulf States held, and continue to hold about 55 per cent of the world's total proven crude reserves (see Table 1.1). The Gulf had also become the world's largest oil-producing region. In 1950 the Gulf States produced only about 17 per cent of the total world crude output; in 1975 they were accounting for about 35 per cent of the same (Table 1.2). Much of this output was available for export since the Gulf producers, with low levels of industrialization

Table 1.1: Estimated Persian Gulf crude oil and natural gas proved reserves

Country	Crude oil (billion barrels)	Natural gas (trillion cubic feet)
Bahrain	0.2	8
Iran	55.3	483
Iraq	41.0	29
Kuwait*	67.2	34
Oman	2.7	3
Qatar	3.4	62
Saudi Arabia*	165.3	121
United Arab Emirates	32.4	29
Total, Persian Gulf	367.5	768
World total	670.2	3,034

Source: Department of Energy, Energy Information Administration, *1982 Annual Energy Review*, DOE/EIA-0384(82) (Washington, D.C., April 1983).
*Include one-half of the Partitioned Zone (formerly called the Neutral Zone).

Evolution of U.S. Interests

Table 1.2: Percentage of world crude oil production by region, 1938–78

Continent and country	1938	1950	1960	1970	1975	1978
North America	63.38	54.56	37.24	24.86	19.83	18.50
South America	13.22	16.94	16.47	10.40	6.70	5.83
Europe	13.24	8.72	16.75	16.87	20.30	22.01
Africa	0.08	0.44	1.37	13.25	9.37	10.08
Asia, Middle East	10.08	19.34	28.17	34.23	43.02	42.85
Persian Gulf						
Bahrain	0.42	0.29	0.22	0.17	0.11	0.09
Iran	3.94	6.38	5.02	8.36	10.01	8.58
Iraq	1.64	1.31	4.60	3.40	4.23	4.33
Kuwait	—	3.31	7.73	5.97	3.44	3.07
Neutral Zone	—	—	0.65	1.10	0.93	0.77
Oman	—	—	—	0.72	0.64	0.52
Qatar	—	0.32	0.82	0.79	0.82	0.80
Saudi Arabia	0.02	5.25	5.94	7.75	12.78	14.05
United Arab Emirates	—	—	—	1.70	3.17	3.02
Australia–New Zealand	—	—	—	0.39	0.78	0.73
Total world production	100.00	100.00	100.00	100.00	100.00	100.00

Source: U.S. Congress. House of Representatives. Committee on Interstate and Foreign Commerce. Subcommittee on Energy and Power. *The Energy Factbook.* Prepared by the Congressional Research Service. 96th Congress, 2nd Session, 1980.
Authority: United States Department of Energy.

and small populations, consumed very little of their own output.[26] Thus, by the end of the 1970s, the Gulf region had become the supplier of about two-thirds of total worldwide import requirements.[27]

The Western industrial nations were among those that became most heavily dependent on Persian Gulf oil. For example, in 1980 Western Europe and Japan obtained 57 per cent and 69 per cent, respectively, of their total crude oil and refined products imports from the Gulf. While the United States obtained 'only' 27 per cent,[28] few U.S. economists or policymakers were under the illusion that any damage caused to the European and Japanese economies due to a disruption in the flow of oil would not severely affect basic U.S. economic and strategic interests. Politically, oil shortages could cause severe strains in the Western alliance system; given their greater dependency, Western Europe and Japan would be inclined to pursue unilateral measures to achieve energy security. This pattern became all too evident after the 1973–74 oil crisis, the leading examples being the refusal of almost

7

Evolution of U.S. Interests

all European allies to allow overflight rights to U.S. aircraft carrying equipment and supplies to Israel during the October War, Europe's separate position on the question of Palestinian rights, and attempts by European nations, especially France, to seek 'special relationships' with some OPEC nations.[29] Second, the economies of the OECD nations being closely interdependent, collapse of any segment could not but be seriously damaging to the rest.[30] Third, oil shortages of major proportions would exert an upward pressure on prices in the world market, the effects of which could not be confined outside the U.S. economy. In fact, several studies estimated that a major drop in oil supplies would have serious consequences for the U.S. economy. In 1978 the Congressional Budget Office calculated that a one-year cutback on oil imports of 3 million barrels per day would lead to a U.S. GNP reduction of 2.8 per cent, assuming that the Strategic Petroleum Reserve had been kept at 500 million barrels. If the import loss was 4 mbd for one year, with a Strategic Petroleum Reserve of 250 million barrels, the U.S. GNP would drop 9.8 per cent and the unemployment rate would rise by 3.2 per cent above the rate forecast for 1982.[31]

It should be pointed out here that the world oil market was to undergo a dramatic change following the crises of 1979–80. A sharp fall in demand and a rise in non-OPEC production led to conditions of oversupply, and the oil output in the Gulf region declined from 17.9 million barrels per day (mbd) in 1980 to 10.1 mbd in 1985. In 1985 the Gulf accounted for only about 19 per cent of total world oil output, compared to 30 per cent in 1980.[32] By 1984 oil imports from the Gulf were needed to meet 3 per cent of the United States', 57 per cent of Japan's, and 20 per cent of OECD Europe's oil consumption.[33]

But these trends in the world oil market, which at one stage caused crude oil prices to fall to below $10 a barrel, should not lead to the view that Persian Gulf oil could become strategically irrelevant to the United States. Oil gluts are part of a cycle, and low oil prices could revive the seller's market by rendering a good deal of non-OPEC production economically unviable, especially in the capital-intensive production systems in the West. This trend was evident in 1986 when the oil companies cut their exploration budgets, prompting Vice President George Bush to appeal to the Saudis to 'stabilize' the oil price situation.[34] Moreover, with the projected decline in North Sea and U.S. domestic output, the Gulf should remain the only major source that can meet any sudden

Evolution of U.S. Interests

increase in world oil demand for the foreseeable future. For example, in 1984 the worldwide excess oil production capacity that could come on stream quickly was estimated to be 8 mbd. Of this, all but 3 mbd was located in the Gulf region.[35] According to some estimates, the Gulf will regain its dominant share of the world oil market by 1995, supplying 30 to 45 per cent of the non-communist world's oil requirements.[36]

During the 1970s the Western nations became painfully aware of the vulnerability of their access to oil, especially the vital portion that came from the Persian Gulf. The question of access involves three closely interlinked aspects: continuity of supply, sufficiency of supply, and affordability. In other words, access to oil must be *'continued* access . . . at *reasonable* prices and in *sufficient* quantities' (emphasis added).[37] For the Western nations, trends negatively affecting all three conditions appeared during the 1970s. The decade opened with the governments of the producer nations — their bargaining power considerably enhanced through OPEC — demanding higher prices for their resources, greater overall control over production and pricing, and larger shares in the revenues generated from export. Iran was the leader of negotiations, which achieved a substantial breakthrough for the producers with respect to many of these demands. The Teheran agreement of February 1971, along with similar concessions already gained by Libya, marked the beginning of a rapid end to the dominant role heretofore played by Western multinationals in the world oil market.[38]

On the heels of this trend came a second one, which, spearheaded by another Gulf State, Saudi Arabia, saw the emergence of oil as a potential weapon for the Arab cause against Israel. The first successful deployment of this weapon by a group of Arab producers, led by Saudi Arabia protesting U.S. support for Israel during the 1973 Arab-Israeli War, impressed upon the West that, henceforth, continuity and sufficiency in the supply of Persian Gulf oil would be subject to their Western stand on Palestinian rights.[39] The embargo — which involved a decision by the participants to cease all exports to the United States and the Netherlands, accompanied by a 5 to 10 per cent cut in their oil production — had grave economic consequences for the consuming nations in general and the United States in particular. Through a series of actions related largely, though not exclusively, to the embargo, the producer states raised oil prices from about $3 a barrel in Septmber 1973 to over $11 per barrel by January 1974. For the

9

Evolution of U.S. Interests

United States, the embargo caused a reduction of some 2.7 mbd in imports by January 1974, reducing the total petroleum supply 14 per cent below the anticipated consumption level. A Brookings Institution study later estimated that this, combined with price increases, led to a U.S. GNP loss of about 2.5 per cent in 1973–74, or equivalent to $30 billion at prevalent prices. Indeed, as the Brookings study concluded:

> No event of the period following the Second World War ha[d] so sharp and pervasive an impact on the world economy as the series of shocks to the oil market that followed closely on the outbreak of the Arab-Israeli war on 6 October 1973.[40]

A more subtle peacetime use of the 'oil weapon' also became evident during the 1970s. It consisted of deliberate production cutbacks, often justified in the name of 'conservation', and an expressed unwillingness to raise production levels to ease a tight supply situation unless Arab demands on Palestine were met. Kuwait became a leading practitioner of cutbacks for the sake of conservation, while the Saudis linked their willingness to produce at 'any level that is feasibly possible' to the achievement of an acceptable solution to the Palestinian question.[41]

Apart from embargoes, the oil flow could also be halted by regional instability, invasion, inter-state warfare, and terrorist action. Given the Persian Gulf's history of conflict over ethnic, tribal, and dynastic divisions and territorial disputes, disruption of production and export caused by instability and warfare loomed as a more likely mode of loss of access than embargoes. Concern was also expressed at the possibility of disruption of the oil tanker traffic at the narrow 'chokepoint' of the Strait of Hormuz, through which much of the Gulf oil exports would have to pass.[42] Events during the 1979–80 period substantially added to such concerns. The Iranian revolution confirmed the threat of disruptions caused by domestic instability, while the Soviet invasion of Afghanistan initially led many Western analysts to believe that a subsequent invasion of the oil fields could be imminent. Still later, the Iran-Iraq War demonstrated how inter-state conflicts could undermine production and exports as a result of damages caused to oil wells, export terminals, and tankers.

Apart from its importance in relation to the consumer nations' access to petroleum, the Persian Gulf's role in global politics and U.S. foreign policy concerns came to acquire important

Evolution of U.S. Interests

commercial and financial dimensions. Traditionally, the major U.S. economic activity in the region had been that of the oil multinationals, whose combined capital investments in the Gulf were estimated to be some $3.5 billion in 1974. The replacement value of U.S. company investments in the Gulf oil industry was estimated at some $50 billion in 1972, and annual income from these investments was equal to half the U.S. balance-of-payment deficit at that time.[43] While these stakes were already of immense significance to the U.S. economy, substantial additional opportunities followed the dramatic rise in the oil revenues of the Persian Gulf States as a result of the price increases in the 1970s.

The oil revenues of the six Gulf members of the OPEC — Iran, Saudi Arabia, Kuwait, Iraq, Abu Dhabi/UAE, and Qatar — rose from under $7 billion in 1971 to more than $72 billion in 1974 and $185 billion in 1980.[44] The oil wealth boosted domestic consumer spending and led to ambitious socioeconomic programs by the oil-rich governments, whose countries had remained quite backward and deficient in infrastructure. The combined import bills of the Gulf States plus the two Yemens rose from $8.7 billion in 1973 to $13.5 billion in 1974 (inclusive of arms imports), making the region the 'fastest growing market for [U.S.] goods and services in the world'.[45] In 1973 the State Department told Congress that the Gulf

> is an area which will provide almost unlimited opportunities for the sale of every kind of U.S. good and service. It is an area which is ideally complementary to the high technology and management services that the United States can provide.[46]

U.S. exports to the Gulf rose from $1.2 billion in 1972 to about $11 billion in 1981, despite the loss of the Iranian market.[47] Three Gulf States — Saudi Arabia, Kuwait, and the UAE — together came to be the fifth largest export market for the United States after Canada, Japan, Britain, and Mexico. Saudi Arabia alone became the United States' sixth largest trading partner. The United States was Saudi Arabia's largest supplier, supplying about one-fifth of total Saudi imports.[48] The development schemes spurred by the new oil wealth in the region benefited scores of U.S. businessmen of all persuasions. As the State Department testified in 1975, 'on any given day, hundreds of American businessmen are in the Gulf states actively exploring the possibilities'.[49] Between 1975 and 1979 U.S. companies had won contracts worth $23 billion.[50]

11

Evolution of U.S. Interests

With nascent economies and small populations, the Gulf States could not spend a substantial portion of their oil revenues. Much of this surplus was recycled to the West, especially to the United States. The official foreign assets of the Gulf States were estimated to be over $140 billion in 1980.[51] Exactly how much of this had found its way to the United States could not be definitely known. The U.S. Treasury Department figures for the portfolio investment by the Gulf States, which put it at some $35 billion by 1977, did not include funds placed through third parties or deposits at foreign branches of U.S. banks. In a 1978 report, the American Jewish Committee claimed that three Gulf States, Saudi Arabia, Kuwait, and the UAE, held about $55 billion in investments in the United States and the foreign branches of U.S. banks.[52]

These investments could be a double-edged instrument. On the one hand, they offered substantial benefits to the U.S. economy. By augmenting capital availability in the U.S. money market, the petrodollar inflow reduced the need for government borrowing from the private sector and kept interest rates lower. This in turn helped to boost overall economic activity. By investing in the United States, the Gulf States also helped to keep the U.S. dollar stronger against other major currencies.[53] On the other hand, huge petrodollar holdings could be a threat — giving the Gulf States some sort of a 'money weapon' with which they could manipulate the international financial system and engage in speculative acquisitions in the United States. As a 1978 CIA report on 'Saudi Arabia Foreign Investment' stated: 'Temporary dislocation of international financial markets would ensue if the Saudi Arabian government ever chose to use its accumulated wealth as a political weapon.'[54] American Jewish groups charged that petrodollar investments gave the Arab countries undue influence over U.S. foreign policymaking. While such charges were dismissed by U.S. officials, the financial power of the Gulf States, especially that of Saudi Arabia, was none the less viewed by the U.S. government as a new factor in global politics, and its safe management became a key aspect of U.S. policy toward the Gulf. From 1974 U.S. officials began speaking of a new regional policy objective: 'to assist and encourage the countries of the region to recycle their surplus revenues into the world economy in an orderly and undisruptive manner'.[55]

Events since the British withdrawal also affected the politico-strategic elements of the U.S. interest in the Persian Gulf. These elements, while possessing an importance of their own, became

Evolution of U.S. Interests

more central to U.S. regional concerns given their bearing on the flow of oil. The United States became more concerned with the problem of preserving the conservative status quo in the region after the British withdrawal led to the independence of a number of mini-states — Qatar, Bahrain, and the sheikhdoms that made up the United Arab Emirates. The British military presence in the region had 'frozen' many of its tribal, ethnic, dynastic, and territorial disputes. As independent entities, the ability of the Gulf States to withstand any recurrence of these disputes was in some doubt.[56] Meanwhile, U.S. interest in ensuring their survival had become stronger as a result of a number of perceptions. Apart from being the largest oil producers, they shared the U.S. concern for growing Soviet influence and Soviet-sponsored radicalism in the region. Their policies with respect to the flow of oil were more moderate than those of the revolutionary regimes. The conservative Arab states were more inclined to use a 'carrot approach', by agreeing to be more sympathetic to the oil import requirements of the Western countries in return for their greater political support for the Palestinian cause, rather than the 'stick' approach (i.e. embargoes etc.) advocated by radical states.[57] Moreover, the United States was concerned that regimes succeeding a monarchy through coups or revolutions might prove to be either neutral with a bias against the West or openly pro-Soviet. In the Gulf, the overthrow of the Hashemite monarchy in Iraq had earlier confirmed this trend; the revolution in Iran at the end of the 1970s became a far more decisive proof.

While grappling with the issue of domestic stability in the Gulf States, the United States was soon faced with another major development: the entry for the first time of the Soviet navy into Indian Ocean waters. Occurring in March 1968, only two months after Harold Wilson's announcement of the British withdrawal, the Soviet move sparked off alarm in the West, with some analysts predicting that a Pax Sovietica might replace the Pax Britannica in the waters of the Indian Ocean and the Persian Gulf. In April 1968 Assistant Secretary of State for the Near East Lucius Battle told the House of Representatives Foreign Affairs Committee, 'the temptation on the part of the Soviets to fill a vacuum or at least manoeuvre in troubled waters is very great'.[58] The commander of the U.S. Strike Command told the same committee later that the Soviet action reflected 'an age-old strategy, not new but increasing in intensity and activity, of penetration of the Middle East . . . particularly the oil-rich areas of the Persian Gulf'.[59] Such

13

Evolution of U.S. Interests

perceptions became more entrenched as the Soviets gained footholds in Iraq, Somalia (later Ethiopia), and South Yemen, prompting fears in the United States of a Soviet 'geopolitical offensive', with the Gulf region supposedly a prime target. The Soviet invasion of Afghanistan at the end of the decade was seen as the climax in this sequence, prompting the formulation of the third presidential doctrine (the previous two being the Truman and Eisenhower doctrines) expressing the U.S. concern for Soviet influence and activities in the Middle East, and the first specifically addressed to the Persian Gulf.

For the United States, another major development during the 1970s was the emergence of a third major politico-strategic interest based upon a perceived linkage between Gulf security, Western access to oil, and a solution to the Arab-Israeli conflict. Previously, the Gulf had been accorded a somewhat secondary place in the U.S. perception of the Arab-Israeli equation. This in itself was a reflection of the relative strategic importance of the Gulf in terms of the military and economic capacity of the regional states. The most powerful Gulf State, Iran, was not Arab and its rivalry with Iraq, the next most powerful state, considerably reduced the latter's capacity to devote attention and resources to the Arab-Israeli conflict. Saudi military strength was hardly significant, while the smaller Persian Gulf States were still controlled by the British. Moreover, the economic capability of the Gulf States was as yet insubstantial.

But the situation began to change following the dramatic jump in the oil revenues of the Gulf States. The major oil-producing countries of the Arabian Peninsula, State Department official Joseph Sisco recognized in 1975,

> have become the principal financial support for the Arab states more directly involved in the Middle East conflict . . . their views [on the Arab-Israeli issue] are very important, and they are regularly consulted by the Arab parties to the [peace] negotiations as well as by the Palestinians.[60]

If the United States was to secure a settlement ensuring Israel's right to exist, which is a significant U.S. interest in the region in its own right, then it had to seek the cooperation of this relatively moderate segment of the Arab hierarchy. The United States also realized that the continued stability of the Gulf, upon which Western access to oil depended, was not 'immune to the virus of

14

Evolution of U.S. Interests

the Arab-Israeli conflict'.[61] The continuing stalemate of Palestinian autonomy had become the major source of indigenous radicalism and Soviet influence in the region.[62] In addition to these two developments came the successful use of the 'oil weapon' during the 1973 Arab-Israeli War. Until then, U.S. policymakers had assumed that the Arabs could not 'drink' their oil and that the various political divisions within the Arab bloc would prevent any successful employment of the oil weapon. The embargo proved them wrong. The Saudi leadership of the embargo, despite King Faisal's previous assurances ruling out such options, was indicative of the new Arab solidarity. By 1973 the Gulf States had acquired the necessary economic capacity to withstand a halt to their oil exports for a relatively long period of time. Thus the oil weapon could no longer be taken lightly.[63]

The connection between Persian Gulf security and a mutually acceptable solution to the Arab-Israeli conflict came to be recognized, despite Henry Kissinger's initial efforts to conduct Middle East peace negotiations, 'independent of any oil pressures'.[64] A solution to the Arab-Israeli problem, Kissinger himself acknowledged in 1975, was in 'the fundamental national interest of the United States', not only 'because of our historical and moral commitment to the survival and well-being of Israel', but also 'because of our important interests in the Arab World — an area of more than 150 million people sitting astride the world's largest oil reserves', and 'because continuing instability [in the Arab-Israeli zone] risks a new international crisis over oil'.[65] Later the Carter administration embraced this perspective, by stating that its Camp David peace initiative was 'intimately tied in with the Persian Gulf stability' and 'with energy supplies for our country'.[66]

To sum up, as a result of these developments relating to oil, trade, finance, fear of Soviet-inspired or locally generated instability, and the greater role played by the Gulf States in the Arab-Israeli conflict, the Persian Gulf came to be recognized by the United States as an area of major importance in political, economic, and strategic terms. In 1972 Joseph Sisco, the Assistant Secretary of State for Near Eastern and South Asian Affairs, had noted the 'spectacular . . . transition of the gulf from . . . a position of international significance primarily as part of the British "lifeline" to India to a position of significant strategic and economic importance to many industrial countries'.[67] Eight years later, Sisco's successor under the Carter administration, Harold Saunders, described U.S. interests in the Gulf as 'longstanding,

Evolution of U.S. Interests

major and interrelated', which in the decade since the British withdrawal had 'changed little in nature but have grown in importance'. He listed the factors affecting U.S. interests in the Gulf as follows:

> The area's strategic location and its significance to maintaining a global strategic balance;
>
> The significance we place on the sovereignty and independence of these countries as part of a more stable world;
>
> The world's vital need for the region's oil; and
>
> The importance of these states in international finance and development and as markets for our goods and technology.[68]

U.S. interests and policy objectives in the Gulf, which flowed from these factors, were reiterated by Defense Secretary Harold Brown in 1980:

> To insure access to adequate oil supplies;
>
> To resist Soviet expansion;
>
> To promote stability in the region; and
>
> To advance the Middle East peace process, while insuring — and indeed, in order to help insure — the continued security of the State of Israel.[69]

The increased importance of the Gulf meant greater care and seriousness in devising policy options to advance Western interests. The U.S. approach following the British withdrawal evolved in two distinct stages. The immediate phase, lasting until 1979, was to promote local states, especially Iran, as the guardians of Gulf security and protectors of Western interests in the region. This policy was consistent with the Nixon Doctrine, but was endorsed and pursued by the Ford and Carter administrations until the downfall of the Shah in early 1979. In the wake of the Iranian revolution and the Soviet invasion of Afghanistan, the United States switched to a policy of greater reliance on its own power and influence centering around an elaborate and long-term build-up for the projection of military power into the region.

Evolution of U.S. Interests

Notes

1. For an account of early U.S. activities in the Persian Gulf regions, see Bernard Reich et al., *The Persian Gulf* (McLean, VA: Research Analysis Corporation, 1971); David E. Long, *The Persian Gulf: an introduction to its peoples, politics, and economics* (Boulder, CO: Westview Press, 1978): 133–8; Joseph J. Malone, 'America and the Arabian Peninsula: the first two hundred years', *Middle East Journal* (Summer 1976): 406–24.

2. J. C. Hurewitz, *Diplomacy in the Near and Middle East: a documentary record: 1914–1956*, vol. 2 (New York: Octagon Books, 1972): 238.

3. Robert B. Krueger, *The United States and international oil: a report for the Federal Energy Administration on U.S. firms and government policy* (New York: Praeger, 1975): 39–48; Barry Rubin, *The Great Powers in the Middle East, 1941–1947: the road to Cold War* (London: Frank Cass, 1980).

4. Secretary of Defense James Forrestal, cited in William B. Quandt, *Saudi Arabia in the 1980s: foreign policy, security and oil* (Washington, D.C.: The Brookings Institution, 1981): 47.

5. Michael Stoff, *Oil, War and American Security* (New Haven, CT: Yale University Press, 1980): 111.

6. Hurewitz, *Diplomacy in the Near and Middle East*, vol. 2, p. 239; Krueger, *The United States and international oil*, pp. 46–49.

7. George Lenczowski, 'U.S. policy towards Iran', in Abbas Amirie and Hamilton Twitchell (eds), *Iran in the 1980s* (Teheran: Institute for International Political and Economic Studies, 1978): 353–4.

8. For details of the crisis, see George Lenczowski, *Russia and the West in Iran, 1881–1948: a study in big power rivalry* (Ithaca, NY: Cornell University Press, 1949): Chapter 11; Garry R. Hess, 'The Iranian Crisis of 1945–46 and the Cold War', *Political Science Quarterly* (March 1974): 117–46.

9. Cited in Lenczowski, 'U.S. policy towards Iran', p. 357.

10. Hurewitz, *Diplomacy in the Near and Middle East*, vol. 2, pp. 323–9.

11. Amin Saikal, *The rise and fall of the Shah, 1941–1979* (Sydney: Angus and Robertson, 1980): 56–57.

12. For details of the Anglo-Iranian oil crisis, see R. K. Ramazani, *Iran's foreign policy 1941–1973* (Charlottesville, VA: University Press of Virginia, 1975): Part Two. Details of the CIA involvement are given by the leading participant in the operation, Kermit Roosevelt, in *Countercoup: the struggle for the control of Iran* (New York: McGraw-Hill, 1979).

13. Ramazani, *Iran's foreign policy*, pp. 154–7; C. D. Carr, 'The United States–Iranian relationship, 1949–1978: a study in reverse influence', in Hossein Amirsadeghi (ed.), *The security of the Persian Gulf* (London: Croom Helm, 1981): 58.

14. M. R. Pahlavi, *Mission for my country* (London: Hutchinson and Co., 1961): 314.

15. For discussions of Britain's historic involvement in the region, see J. B. Kelly, *Britain and the Persian Gulf, 1795–1880* (New York: Oxford University Press, 1968); B. C. Busch, *Britain and the Persian Gulf, 1894–1914* (Berkeley, CA: University of California Press, 1967); Philip Darby, *British defence policy east of Suez, 1947–1968* (London: Oxford University Press, 1973); Malcolm Yapp, 'British Policy in the Persian Gulf', in Alvin

Evolution of U.S. Interests

J. Cottrell (ed.), *The Persian Gulf States: a general survey* (Baltimore, MD: Johns Hopkins University Press, 1980): 70–100.

16. David E. Long, 'The United States and the Persian Gulf', *Current History* (January 1979): 28.

17. Peter Mangold, *Superpower intervention in the Middle East* (London: Croom Helm, 1978): 84

18. Cited in Kim Beazley and Ian Clark, *The politics of intrusion: the superpowers and the Indian Ocean* (Sydney: Alternative Publishing Cooperative, 1979): 6.

19. For a critical account of the factors involved in the British decision to withdraw, see J. B. Kelly, *Arabia, the Gulf, and the West* (London: Widenfeld and Nicolson, 1980): Chapter 3; D. C. Watt, 'The decision to withdraw from the Gulf', *Political Quaterly* 39 (1968): 310–21.

20. Congressional Research Service, *Project Interdependence: U.S. and world energy outlook through 1990* (1977): 677.

21. Congressional Research Service, *Petroleum imports from the Persian Gulf: use of U.S. armed force to ensure supplies* (1982): 2.

22. Congressional Research Service, *Project Interdependence*, p. 677.

23. Henry A. Kissinger, 'Energy — the necessity of decision', in Richard P. Stebbins and Elaine P. Adam (eds), *American foreign relations 1975: a documentary record* (New York: New York University Press, 1977): 63.

24. Congressional Research Service, *Petroleum imports from the Persian Gulf*, p. 2.

25. For analytical surveys confirming this fact, see U.S. Congress, Office of Technology, *World petroleum availability, 1980–2000: a technical memorandum* (1980): 36–45; Bridget Gail, 'The world oil crisis and U.S. power projection policy: the threat becomes a grim reality', *Armed Forces Journal International* (January 1980): 25–30.

26. For example, in 1980 the eight Gulf States produced 18.2 mbd of crude oil and consumed about 1.4 mbd. Department of Energy, *1982 Annual Energy Review* (1983): 77.

27. Department of Defense, *United States military posture for FY1982*: 2.

28. U.S. Congress. House. Committee on Appropriations. *Military construction appropriations for 1984*, Part 5: 358.

29. Chris L. Jefferies, 'NATO and oil: conflict and capabilities', *Air University Review* (January–February 1980): 35–46.

30. 'Persian Gulf oil and the economic effects of disruptions', report prepared by Office of the Assistant Secretary of Defense, International Security Affairs, appended to House Committee on Appropriations, *Military construction appropriations for 1984*, Part 5: 343–62.

31. Congressional Budget Office, *The economic impact of oil import reductions* (1978): 14. See also U.S. Congress. House. Committee on Foreign Affairs. *U.S. security interests and policies in the Persian Gulf. Report of a staff mission* (1981): 84.

32. *Oil and Gas Journal*, December 22, 1980: 7; *Oil and Gas Journal*, December 30, 1985: 66.

33. U.S. Congress. Senate. Committee on Foreign Relations. *War in the Gulf* (1984): 35.

34. *Guardian Weekly*, April 13, 1986: 15.

Evolution of U.S. Interests

35. U.S. Congress. Senate. Committee on Foreign Relations. *War in the Gulf* (1984): 35.

36. *International Herald Tribune*, June 9, 1987: 6.

37. U.S. Congress. House. Committee on International Relations. *The Persian Gulf, 1975: the continuing debate on arms sales*: 9.

38. For details, see Saikal, *The rise and fall of the Shah*, p. 116.

39. For a detailed chronology of the embargo, see Jordan J. Paust and Albert P. Blaustein, *The Arab oil embargo* (New York: Oceania Publications, 1977): 4 – 8.

40. Information on the economic effects of the embargo, including analysis of the Brookings Institution Study, is taken from W. H. Donnelly et al., 'Global oil and energy implications of the Iranian revolution', in U.S. Congress. Joint Economic Committee. *Economic consequences of the revolution in Iran* (1979): 114 – 17.

41. Alice Rivlin, 'The world oil market in the 1980s: implications for the United States', in Larry A. Berg, L. M. Baird and E. A. Varanini (eds), *The United States and world energy sources* (New York: Praeger, 1982): 37; Thomas Stauffer, 'The political uses of Arab oil', in Ronald G. Wolfe (ed.), *The United States, Arabia, and the Gulf* (Washington, D.C.: Center for Contemporary Arab Studies, Georgetown University, 1980): 32 – 33.

42. See for a discussion, R. K. Ramazani, 'The Strait of Hormuz: the global chokepoint', in Larry Bowman and Ian Clark (eds), *The Indian Ocean in global politics* (Nedlands: University of Western Australia Press, 1981): 7 – 10; Gerald Blake, 'Flashpoint through which Middle East oil must pass', *Geographical Magazine* (October 1980): 50 – 52.

43. R. M. Burrell, *The Persian Gulf, The Washington Papers*, no. 1 (Beverley Hills, CA: Sage, 1972): 4.

44. *The Middle East and North Africa, 1982 – 83* (London: Europa Publications, 1982): 124.

45. U.S. Congress. House. Committee on International Relations. *The Persian Gulf, 1975: the continuing debate on arms sales*: 13.

46. U.S. Congress. House. Committee on Foreign Affairs. *New perspectives on the Persian Gulf* (1973): 154 – 5.

47. Ibid., U.S. Congress. House. Committee on International Relations. *The Persian Gulf, 1975: the continuing debate on arms sales*, p. 13; International Monetary Fund, *Direction of trade, 1983.*

48. Obeh Aburdene, 'U.S. economic and financial relations with Saudi Arabia, Kuwait, and the United Arab Emirates', *American-Arab Affairs* (Winter 1983 – 84): 77 – 78; R. El Mallakh, 'U.S. economic ties with the Gulf Cooperation Council and Egypt', in David H. Partington (ed.), *The Middle East Annual* (Boston, MA: G. K. Hall and Co., 1983): 182.

49. U.S. Congress. House. Committee on International Relations. *The Persian Gulf, 1975: the continuing debate on arms sales*, p. 13.

50. Richard Preece, 'The future role of Saudi Arabia', in U.S. Congress. Joint Economic Committee. *The U.S. role in a changing world. Political economy: major issues for the 96th Congress* (1979): 533.

51. U.S. Congress. House. Committee on Foreign Affairs. *U.S. interests in, and policies toward, the Persian Gulf* (1980): 355.

52. U.S. Treasury Department data can be found in U.S. Congress. House. Committee on Government Operations. *The operations of Federal*

Evolution of U.S. Interests

agencies in monitoring, reporting on, and analyzing foreign investments in the United States, Part 2: OPEC investments in the United States (1979): 221. For an analysis of the Jewish Committee report, see John K. Cooley, 'The U.S. economic role in the Middle East and North Africa', in U.S. Congress. Joint Economic Committee. *The U.S. role in a changing world economy* (1979), p. 495.

53. 'Arabs are the dollar's best friends, like it or not', *Far Eastern Economic Review*, May 25, 1979: 54–60.

54. U.S. Congress. House. Committee on Government Operations. *The operations of Federal agencies*, Part 2 (1979): 349.

55. U.S. Congress. House. Committee on Foreign Affairs. *The Persian Gulf, 1974: money, politics, arms and power*, p. 73.

56. See for this line of thinking, *The Gulf: implications of British withdrawal*, Special Report Series no. 8 (Washington, D.C.: Center for Strategic and International Studies, Georgetown University, 1969); David Holden, 'The Persian Gulf: after the British Raj', *Foreign Affairs* (July 1971): 721–35; R. M. Burrell, 'Problems and prospects in the Gulf: an uncertain future', *The Round Table* (April 1972): 209–19; R. P. Owen, 'The British withdrawal from the Persian Gulf', *World Today* (February 1972): 75–81.

57. *Department of State Bulletin* (October 1980): 42.

58. *Middle East Record* 4 (1968): 73.

59. *Middle East Record* 5 (1969–70): 463.

60. U.S. Congress. House. Committee on International Relations. *The Persian Gulf, 1975: the continuing debate on arms sales*, p. 8.

61. *Department of State Bulletin*, September 4, 1972: 242.

62. Testimony by Harold H. Saunders, Assistant Secretary of State for Near East and South Asia, before House Committee on Foreign Affairs. *U.S. interests in, and policies toward, the Persian Gulf* (1980): 352–4.

63. Faud Itayim, 'Strengths and weaknesses of the oil weapon', in *The Middle East and the international system*, Part 3. *Security and the energy crisis*, Adelphi Papers no. 115 (London: International Institute for Strategic Studies, 1975): 1–7. For a sceptical view of the oil weapon in later years, see Douglas J. Feith, 'The oil weapon de-mystified', *Policy Review* (Winter 1981): 19–39; William R. Brown, 'The oil weapon', *Middle East Journal* (Summer 1982): 301–18.

64. *Department of State Bulletin*, April 14, 1975: 467. For a discussion of factors leading to his inability to do so, see R. K. Ramazani, *Beyond the Arab-Israeli settlement: new directions for U.S. policy in the Middle East* (Cambridge, MA: Institute for Foreign Policy Analysis, 1977): 8–11.

65. Cited in Emile A. Nakhleh, *The Persian Gulf and American policy* (New York: Praeger, 1982): 86.

66. *Public papers of the presidents of the United States: Jimmy Carter, 1980–1981, Book 1* (Washington, D.C.: U.S. Government Printing Office, 1981): 511.

67. *Department of State Bulletin*, September 4, 1972: 241.

68. U.S. Congress. House. Committee on Foreign Affairs. *U.S. interests in, and policies toward, the Persian Gulf* (1980): 338.

69. *Department of State Bulletin* (May 1980): 63.

2

The Shah and the Nixon Doctrine

The Nixon Doctrine

In the 1970s U.S. policy toward the Persian Gulf was focused on its efforts to promote Iran as the prime regional actor defending security and Western interests in the area. This policy owed its origins to several factors, the most important of them being the shape of U.S. global strategic posture in the wake of the Vietnam War. The war prevented the Nixon administration from giving any serious consideration to the idea of replacing the British with U.S. forces. Apart from the realization that such a move might be rejected by the Congress and the American public at large, no additional forces were available for assignment to the Gulf region, due to continuing operations in Southeast Asia.[1] Instead, the administration sought to respond to the British withdrawal within the framework of its new geopolitical doctrine announced by President Nixon at Guam in 1969. The Nixon Doctrine incorporated the following principles:

The United States will keep all its treaty commitments.

We shall provide a shield if a nuclear power threatens the freedom of a nation allied with us, or of a nation whose survival we consider vital to our security and the security of the region as a whole.

In cases involving other types of aggression we shall furnish military and economic assistance when requested and as appropriate. But we shall look to the nation directly threatened to assume the primary responsibility of providing the manpower for its defense.[2]

The Shah and the Nixon Doctrine

Although the original inspiration of the Nixon Doctrine had nothing to do with security issues in the Gulf, it was soon evident that this region would become the first, and as it turned out, the most serious, test of America's new geopolitical mood. For the Gulf was not only the place where the United States needed to come up with a new security posture, it also met the quintessential requirement for operationalizing the Doctrine: the willingness and ability of a local state to assume the responsibility for regional security on the West's behalf. That state was Iran.

The Shah's desire to play the role of a regional leader was not new, but had previously been viewed with scepticism by the United States. His domestic power base had been considered too shaky to permit such a role. The Eisenhower, Kennedy, and Johnson administrations had all told the Shah to devote his attention to his internal political problems rather than to foreign and military affairs.[3] By the end of the 1970s, however, the Shah's domestic position seemed to have improved, largely as a result of the socioeconomic reform program he proudly termed the 'White Revolution'. In addition, his 'detente' with the Soviet Union permitted him to devote more attention and resources to the Gulf region.[4] When Britain announced its decision to withdraw from the Gulf, the Shah made no secret of his intention and ability to become a regional security manager. Advising the United States to 'physically keep out' of the Gulf (although not from the Indian Ocean, since that was 'quite another matter'),[5] he at the same time claimed that Iran could provide the Gulf States 'as much protection as the British forces in the area today'.[6] To enhance Iran's ability to do so, he planned to build a 'balanced and significant defence force of her own', with the 'moral support, assistance, of our friends, the greatest of them being the U.S.'.[7]

The United States was more than willing to comply with this desire. Iran, as Joseph Sisco put it, had 'both the will and the capability' to play a 'major role in providing for stability in the gulf and the continued flow of oil to consumer countries'. Iran's preparedness to 'offer assistance to the smaller gulf states should they wish it' was also recognized.[8] Henry Kissinger later stressed that Iran's desired role was not only consistent with U.S. strategic objectives, it was also 'achievable without any American resources, since the Shah was willing to pay for the [American] equipment out of his oil revenues'.[9] The Deputy Assistant Secretary of Defense, James H. Noyes, later wrote that Iran's role was preferable since a direct American role 'would have become an

The Shah and the Nixon Doctrine

acutely divisive force in the Arab world', and conflicted with 'Saudi Arabia's and Iran's growing sense of national stature'.[10] After reviewing its options, the Nixon administration reached the following decision: first, that the United States would not replace Britain; second, that a symbolic U.S. military presence in the form of the five-ship U.S. Command Middle East Force (COMIDEASTFOR) would be retained; and third, that the governing framework of U.S. policy in the Gulf would be to encourage and assist Iran and Saudi Arabia to take up the primary responsibility for regional security.[11] American policymakers left no doubt as to which state in this 'twin-pillar' system was to play the predominant role. It was 'Iran in particular', stressed Sisco, that the United States expected to be 'in the forefront' of Persian Gulf security management.[12]

With the encouragement and approval of the Nixon, Ford, and Carter administrations, the Shah dominated the U.S. strategic framework for the region until the revolution in 1979 toppled his regime. While he ruled, American policymakers were generally appreciative of his regional security posture. The policy of reliance on him was considered to be a major U.S. foreign policy success in the post-Vietnam era. The Shah was seen to be domestically strong and his foreign policy was deemed to be both responsible and fully compatible with U.S. interests in the region. His quest for military power was viewed to be worthy of American support. Yet in the wake of the Shah's sudden downfall, much of the prevailing assessment of the U.S. policy changed. With the benefit of hindsight, many critics now saw the backing of Iran under the Nixon Doctrine as short-sighted and based upon dangerously misconceived assumptions regarding the Shah's domestic and regional position.

But it would be a mistake to view the widespread disillusionment with U.S. Gulf policy within the Nixon Doctrine as entirely a by-product of the Iranian revolution. To be sure, the revolution sharpened the controversy surrounding the policy. In the debate in the U.S. over 'Who lost Iran?' one group blamed the Nixon–Kissinger policy, while another held the Carter administration's human rights policy and its failure to back the Shah responsible for the U.S. debacle in Iran. But the limitations of the 'twin-pillar' policy had become quite recognizable even when the Shah was firmly saddled as Iran's undisputed leader and the Gulf's powerful 'policeman'. This can be ascertained from an analysis of the three principal issues on which its credibility rested: access to oil,

Oil and the 'twin pillars'

Being the 'pillars' of U.S. policy did not prevent Saudi Arabia and Iran from imposing their political and economic conditions on the Western access to oil. While Saudi Arabia was a 'moderate' on prices, it was the driving force behind the political restrictions on the flow of oil. The Shah received praise, as Kissinger put it, for having refuelled U.S. 'fleets without question' and having 'never used his control of oil to bring political pressure' — including his refusal to join 'any oil embargo against the West or Israel'.[13] But his leading role in OPEC negotiations resulting in steep price hikes earned him the title of 'hawk' and inflamed passions in official Washington circles. The Shah followed up his victory at the Teheran negotiations by nationalizing Iran's oil industry in 1973. The United States saw this as a bad precedent for its interests elsewhere in the region. The Shah took the view that the international oil companies had for long 'defrauded' the producing nations 'of their just economic benefits'.[14] In the United States, however, resentment against the Shah's oil policy became quite serious.[15] Critics of U.S. arms sales to Iran scored a major point by arguing that American generosity in giving Iran freedom to buy any weapon it liked had not been reciprocated by the Shah in the form of moderation on oil prices.[16] Unless such moderation was forthcoming, 'high' officials of the Ford administration were reported to have pressed the Secretary of State, the United States should reconsider its massive arms sales program to Iran.[17]

The United States sought to dissuade Iran from its hawkish stand on oil prices through diplomatic pressures and discreet hints of an arms cutoff. But dealing with Saudi Arabia and its 'oil weapon' was far more problematic. Frustrated U.S. policymakers hinted at a more drastic step if embargoes were pushed too far. The Secretary of State, Henry Kissinger, made it known that military action would be a possibility if there was 'some actual strangulation of the industrialized world' as a result. His views were 'fully endorsed' by President Ford, while Defense Secretary James Schlesinger contended that it was 'indeed feasible to conduct military operations' against Persian Gulf producers.[18]

The Shah and the Nixon Doctrine

There was, of course, some attempt by the administration to reassure the nervous oil producers, who were told that military action would be a very last option against the more extreme provocations. 'Strangulation is the key word', said President Ford, while adding that force would not be used 'to bring a price change'.[19] In addition, the producer nations could derive some comfort by realizing the constraints on the feasibility of a U.S. attempt to seize their oil fields. Although some civilian analysts, among them Robert Tucker and Miles Ignotus (pseudonym for a 'Washington-based professor'),[20] agreed with Schlesinger, an authoritative study by the Congressional Research Service, entitled *Oil fields as military objectives: a feasibility study*, disagreed. It expressed doubts whether U.S. intervention forces could seize the oil fields intact (Saudi oil fields were selected as a case study), repair damaged installations rapidly, operate them without the help of the owners, and finally ship the petroleum to the consumer nations. Its conclusion:

> In short, success would largely depend on two prerequisites:
> — slight damage to key installations
> — Soviet abstinence from armed intervention.
> Since neither essential could be assured, military operations to rescue the United States (much less its key allies) from an air-tight OPEC embargo would combine high costs with high risks wherever we focused our efforts. This country would so deplete its strategic reserves that little would be left for contingencies elsewhere. Prospects would be poor, with plights of far-reaching political, economic, social, psychological, and perhaps military consequence the penalty for failure.[21]

Yet neither this nor the official reassurances could remove the anxiety of the oil-producing states who took the threat seriously. The 'oil-grab scenario' permanently entered the lexicon of U.S. Persian Gulf policy. With it, the limitations of the 'twin pillar' approach in ensuring continued access to Persian Gulf oil became quite evident. It is not rash to assume that some of the groundwork for the shift in U.S. policy towards an alternative posture — a direct intervention capability — was laid as a result of internal Pentagon planning to prepare for an 'oil grab'.

The Shah and the Nixon Doctrine

The Shah as regional policeman

The Shah's performance on the regional security front, unlike that with respect to oil prices, received considerable praise in U.S. government circles. Some of it was well deserved. The Shah's abandonment of Iran's longstanding claim on Bahrain removed a major uncertainty over the future of the island-state. The Shah dropped his earlier opposition to a group of tiny Persian Gulf nations joining a federation — the United Arab Emirates — which would enhance their stability. His success in negotiating a number of agreements with his Gulf Arab neighbours, demarcating their continental shelf boundaries, was praised by the United States as 'concrete evidence of [Iran's] desire for cooperation'.[22] Pursuing a formula of 'domination through seduction', the Shah launched a campaign — focused on high-level diplomacy, trade, cultural exchange, and economic cooperation — to improve relations with his fellow monarchs in the region.[23]

He also achieved a major breakthrough in reducing tensions with Iran's traditional and most formidable local rival: Iraq. Through Algerian mediation, the Shah and the Iraqi President, Saddam Hussein, reached an accord in March 1975 that settled their bitter historical dispute over the Shatt-al-Arab waterway — the confluence of the Tigris and Euphrates rivers forming the Iraqi–Iranian border.[24] Under the terms of the agreement, Iraq agreed to the Iranian demand for demarcating the boundary along the median line and in return received an Iranian pledge to end its support for the Kurdish insurgents demanding autonomy from the Iraqi state. The compromise was beneficial to both sides. The Shah won for his country a major nationalist demand, and the overall reduction in tensions in the northwestern frontier helped him to devote greater attention elsewhere in the region. Iraq, on the other hand, benefitted from the weakening of a serious threat to its integrity, which had also prevented the full exploitation of oil reserves in the insurgent areas.[25]

The Shah's regional role also involved his support for the status quo throughout the region against the forces of indigenous 'radicalism' and external 'subversion'. The most notable example was Iran's military intervention in Oman to support Sultan Qabus against the Soviet- and Chinese-backed Dhofar rebellion. Between 1972 and 1977, Iranian counter-insurgency troops, their number varying between 300 and 3,000, backed by artillery, helicopters, and strike and reconnaissance aircraft, were involved in extensive anti-insurgent operations.[26] The Dhofar campaign gave the untested Iranian military valuable field practice and the Shah a reason for pride in his role as 'regional policeman'. To the east, Iran provided logistics and (possibly troop) support to the Pakistani government against the Baluchi insurgents,[27] while Iranian aid was offered to Afghanistan to lessen its dependence on Moscow and secure the abandonment of its efforts to carve out a separate 'Pushtunistan' involving parts of Pakistani territory. Outside his immediate geostrategic environs, the Shah's vision extended to Africa, where he campaigned for Western support for Somalia (while himself providing some aid) against its Soviet- and Cuban-backed rival, Ethiopia.

But the Shah's enhanced regional activism was marked by major limitations and failures. In the Persian Gulf in particular, the Shah failed to inspire the confidence of the Arab states whose security he was seeking to enhance. The Iran–Arab divide was based upon ancient and deep-rooted ethnic, cultural, national, and sectarian factors; but matters were not helped by the Shah's occasional heavy-handedness. His seizure of three Persian Gulf islets, Abu Musa and the two Tunbs, from the sheikhdoms of Sharjah and Ras al-Khaima, respectively, was bitterly protested by the Gulf Arabs including Saudi Arabia. The Gulf Arab states were suspicious of Iran's military build-up and resentful of the Shah's ties with Israel.[28] Saudi Arabia was unhappy about Iranian military intervention on 'Arab soil': Oman. Iran, in return, disliked 'Saudi obscurantism and "big brother" posture' toward the smaller Gulf States, which it saw as a threat to its own regional ambitions.[29] Iran and Saudi Arabia also differed often and strongly over the issue of oil prices, which reflected their divergent domestic economic growth rate preferences and absorptive capabilities. But the net outcome was to reinforce the divisions in the 'twin pillar' system. Some members of the U.S. Congress wondered whether the policy was viable. As Chairman Lee Hamilton of the House Near East Subcommittee put it: 'for several years to come, one of our prime challenges in the Persian Gulf will be to avoid any confrontation between our two close friends'.[30]

The 'twin pillar' concept was a clear misnomer, because Saudi Arabia was neither willing nor able to act as a 'pillar' of the U.S. regional security policy in the sense that Iran did. Manpower shortages, its preoccupation with complex territorial disputes with the smaller Gulf States, and King Faisal's greater emphasis on

The Shah and the Nixon Doctrine

domestic modernization limited Saudi ability to play an active role outside its frontiers.[31] But above all, the Saudis were hardly keen about acting under U.S. and Iranian auspices. Against Iran, it was the concern to preserve the 'Arabism of the Gulf'; against the United States it was the concern to preserve the 'Arabism of the Middle East', threatened by U.S.-backed Israel. The Kingdom's initial response to the British withdrawal was marked by a cautious, wait-and-see attitude. When the Shah was busy installing himself as the head of the new security regime in the Gulf, Saudi Arabia, as *The Economist* observed, 'seemed to retreat into itself'.[32] King Faisal's leadership of the 1973 oil embargo drove the Kingdom out of its self-imposed passivity, but even then Saudi diplomacy gave the impression of countering, rather than complementing, Iran's leadership. For example, one of the first hints of a new Saudi interest in Persian Gulf diplomacy, a visit by King Khalid to several Gulf capitals, came soon after the Shah had recalled his Gulf ambassadors to protest the proposed creation of an 'Arabian Gulf News Agency'.[33] The accumulated suspicion of Iran harboured by the Saudi-led Gulf monarchies thwarted the former's efforts, strongly backed by the United States, to form a regional collective security grouping of the conservative Gulf States. After the failure of his early overtures, the Shah backed off, settling for a unilateral security posture.[34]

The arms pipeline

But the Shah's limitations as regional policeman caused far less controversy than the U.S. encouragement and support of the modernization of the Iranian and Saudi military establishments through massive arms sales. Emphasis on arms transfers was inherent in the Nixon Doctrine. As a Pentagon document pointed out in 1970: 'The more rapidly [allied and friendly forces] capabilities can be improved, the sooner it may be possible for the United States to reduce both the monetary and the manpower burden inherent in honoring international obligations.'[35]

The U.S. keenness to sell was matched by the growing appetite for weapons on the part of the Gulf States. Their increased concern with security in the wake of the British withdrawal, the prestige value of armaments, and, in the case of Iran, its assumed regional leadership role, all combined to make the Gulf States the leading buyers of conventional armaments in the world. The

28

The Shah and the Nixon Doctrine

advent of the oil wealth ensured that financial constraints would no longer prevent the Gulf States from buying weapons of greater quality and magnitude, whatever the reason for the purchases.[36] Iran, of course, was the regional state at once most committed to the goal of military modernization, and the largest buyer of American-made weapons. The Shah perceived Iran's military capability as central to its new regional security role, leading to one of the largest and most extravagant military build-ups in peacetime history. Between March 1970 and March 1977, Iran's defence budget rose by 1,100 per cent — from approximately $800 million to $9.4 billion.[37] Defence expenditure as a share of GNP rose from 7.8 per cent in 1970 to 14.6 per cent in 1978, while the value of Iran's annual arms imports (in constant 1978 dollars) rose from $264 million in 1970 (9.6 per cent of total imports) to a peak of $2.6 billion in 1977 (17.7 per cent of total imports).[38]

The impact of such expenditure was reflected in the increasing size and quality of Iran's weapons inventory. Between 1971 and 1979, the size of Iran's armed forces grew from 181,000 to 415,000 personnel, with a similar increase in the number of main/medium battle tanks and combat aircraft. As for quality, in 1971 Iran's inventory included few advanced systems while by 1979 its existing or planned (ordered) inventory included such state-of-the-art systems as F-14 interceptors, Chieftain main battle tanks, F-16 fighter-bombers (on order), E-3 airborne warning and control systems (on order), and Spruance-class destroyers.[39] To facilitate Iranian power projection into the Gulf region, the Shah assembled the world's first operational hover-craft squadron (14 units) at the Kharg Island naval base and acquired a fleet of C-130 transport aircraft. Commenting on the extent of the Shah's military build-up, a U.S. Senate Committee report in 1976 observed: 'Upon delivery between now [July 1976] and 1981 of equipment ordered to date, Iran, on paper, can be regarded as a regional super-power.'[40]

The United States became Iran's largest and most dedicated arms supplier. Following a visit to Teheran in 1972 by Nixon and Kissinger, policy guidelines from the National Security Council to U.S. government agencies read: 'decisions on the acquisition of military equipment should be left primarily to the Goverment of Iran'.[41] U.S. foreign military sales (FMS) agreements with Iran exceeded $20 billion between 1971 and 1978.[42] The Iranian market became a bonanza for U.S. weapon manufacturers, with some, like the Grumman Corporation, being able to finance a portion of the development costs of their new weapon systems from advances made by the Shah's government. At the time of the Shah's downfall, some $12 billion in U.S. military sales was awaiting delivery to Iran over the next five years.[43]

The military modernization of Saudi Arabia and the extent of U.S. involvement in that process matched those in Iran in dollar value, but there were major differences in the type of activity involved. While Iran already had a respectable military establishment that could introduce modern weapon systems more rapidly, the Saudis needed to build a basic infrastructure before going in for advanced systems and thus invested most of their military spending developing it. Accordingly, U.S. military sales to Saudi Arabia, worth over $30 billion between 1971 and 1980, were focused mostly on construction and training. According to one estimate, U.S. 'defense-related' programs in the Kingdom were distributed thus: 60 per cent in construction, 20 per cent in training, and 20 per cent in hardware.[44] Much of the construction activity was managed by the U.S. Army Corps of Engineers, which at the end of the 1970s held projects worth more than $20 billion.[45]

Major Saudi military projects involving U.S. supervision, training, and equipment included: (1) a Saudi Ordnance Corps program — involving the creation of an integrated logistics system for the Saudi Ordnance Corps, improvement of its maintenance facilities and construction of its support facility; (2) a Saudi naval expansion program — a 10-year modernization program involving the addition of some 25 ships, construction of naval bases and provision of training and maintenance; (3) a Royal Saudi Air Force Peace Hawk program — involving the acquisition of the F-5 fighter-bomber, provision of its personnel training and construction of the support infrastructure; (4) a Royal Saudi Air Force Peace Sun program — involving the acquisition of 62 F-15 fighter aircraft and the provision of their training and support infrastructure requirements; (5) a HAWK air defence system — designed to protect major Saudi population centres, military cities, and oil fields from air attacks; (6) a Royal Saudi Army modernization program involving the conversion of two infantry brigades into mechanized formations; and finally (7) a National Guard modernization program — designed to organize and train four mechanized infantry battalions and two headquarters into a strike force.[46]

As arms transfers became a key instrument of U.S. policy towards Iran and the Gulf, controversy was raised over the

The Shah and the Nixon Doctrine

quantity and sophistication of the armaments sold and their potentially negative impact on Iran's domestic stability and the future of U.S. – Iranian relations. Sections within the Congress became increasingly critical of arms sales to the Gulf, and the ensuing debate between the legislative and executive branches undermined the overall credibility of U.S. policy in the region. The administration of the U.S. arms sales program for the Gulf region in general and Iran in particular was riddled with problems. Nixon's 1972 decision on arms sales to Iran was not preceded by any systematic inter-agency consideration, but its net effect was to exempt future Iranian requests from the normal review process. Lack of effective oversight by U.S. government agencies often led to corruption and bribery involving sales negotiated by private U.S. weapon manufacturers. For example, Senate investigations revealed that two top American defence suppliers, Northrop and Grumann, had paid more than \$2 million each in illegal commissions to Iranian agents who assisted the sales of the F-5 and F-4 aircraft, respectively. Corruption charges also led to the fining and jailing of the chief of the Iranian navy.[47]

Another major fallout of the U.S. arms sales program in the Gulf was the increased U.S. presence in the region, especially in Saudi Arabia and Iran. By 1977, defence-related personnel constituted about one-fifth of the more than 30,000 Americans living in Saudi Arabia. In Iran about one-third of the approximately 40,000 resident Americans were similarly associated.[48] Such large American presence was incompatible with the Nixon Doctrine itself, whose primary objective was to *reduce* U.S. military presence abroad. More important, the presence constituted a major source of resentment against the United States within the local population. As a Senate Foreign Relations Committee report, released in 1976, prophetically warned: 'anti-Americanism could become a serious problem in Iran, as it has elsewhere, if there were to be a change in government'.[49]

The quantity and sophistication of the weapons did not accord with the absorptive capability of the recipient states. The Gulf States lacked the requisite manpower, industrial base, and technical expertise to operate much of their inflowing weaponry without substantial help from the supplier state. In 1976 – 77, for example, more than half of Iran's armed force was illiterate, and the Iranian air force was about 7,000 short of its technical personnel requirements.[50] The manpower problem was even more acute for Saudi Arabia, whose native population was far smaller

The Shah and the Nixon Doctrine

than Iran's. A congressional staff study report in 1977 argued that 'The skilled manpower deficiencies in all gulf [sic] countries and the smallness of the manpower base in some countries, especially Saudi Arabia and Kuwait, could serve as grounds for severely limiting arms sales . . .'.[51] Such warnings, however, went largely unheeded.

It was also evident that Iran faced a 'guns versus butter' problem, despite the Shah's claim that the country had ample resources to permit both. Under its Fifth Economic Development Plan, for example, Iran's total outlay on defence constituted 31.1 per cent of its total allocations, compared to only a 2.7 per cent higher allocation for economic development programs.[52] Emphasis on the military sector also caused a diversion of skilled manpower from other sectors of the economy, in which the total available expertise was in limited supply. Apart from the neglect of socioeconomic development, higher defence spending was responsible for a very high inflation rate in the 1976–77 period, and a sharp fall in Iran's capital surplus from $10.7 billion in 1974 to $4.5 billion in 1976. Iran reported a budget deficit of $2.4 billion in 1976.[53]

U.S. support for the Shah's military build-up through weapon sales was exploited by the Iranian political opposition. Abol Hassan Bani Sadr, a leading dissident who was to become Iran's president under Khomeini, once argued that the Shah was an American puppet who would sacrifice the 'economic health, social welfare and cultural integrity of the nation' in order to 'continue to rule within the framework of American strategic objectives'.[54] Iranian critics of U.S. arms sales to the Shah viewed it as a symbol of U.S. endorsement of the Shah's domestic repression, which, according to the 1974–75 report of Amnesty International, involved 'the highest rate of death penalties in the world, no valid system of civilian courts and a history of torture which is beyond belief'.[55] Such criticism helped undermine the Shah's domestic legitimacy and was to be a major factor in the popular revolt against the Shah in 1978–79.[56]

It should be noted that such controversy over arms sales did not undermine the basic support for the Shah from the Nixon, Ford, and Carter administrations. Kissinger remained a loyal friend of the Shah and strongly endorsed his role in U.S. strategy in the Gulf. The only serious effort to restrict the flow of weapons to Iran was made by James Schlesinger, Defense Secretary under Nixon and Ford between 1973 and 1975.[57] But the Carter administration, which came to office promising to champion human rights

32

The Shah and the Nixon Doctrine

and curb arms sales to the Third World, continued to comply with the Shah's requests for more U.S. weapons.[58]

The fall of the Shah in 1979 following widespread popular unrest spearheaded by virulently anti-American leaders highlighted the risks of dependence on autocratic local regimes as a foreign policy option. America's 'one-pillar' strategy in the Gulf had led to the erosion of the domestic legitimacy of its surrogate regime. The Shah's perceived subservience to the U.S. strategic design had alienated many sections within the Iranian population and bred popular antagonism against the United States which was closely identified with his regime. With the Shah gone, US–Iranian relations lurched from crisis to crisis. To these crises, and the Soviet invasion of Afghanistan, the United States responded by moving towards a posture that it had consciously chosen to abandon a decade earlier.

Notes

1. Henry Kissinger, *The White House years* (London: Weidenfeld and Nicolson, and Michael Joseph, 1979): 1264.

2. Ibid., pp. 224–5.

3. Gary Sick, *All fall down: America's fateful encounter with Iran* (London: I. B. Tauris & Co., 1985): 345; see also the text of an internal State Department policy paper, 'Current internal situation in Iran', dated February 11, 1961 and declassified recently. Text in Y. Alexander and A. Names (eds), *The United States and Iran: a documentary history* (Frederick, MD: University Publications of America, 1980): 315–21.

4. R. M. Burrell, 'The Indian Ocean: an Iranian evaluation', in Alvin J. Cottrell and R. M. Burrell (eds), *The Indian Ocean: its political, economic and military importance* (New York: Praeger, 1972): 86; Hossein Amirsadeghi, 'With Russia and America: the Shah's balanced alignment', *New Middle East* (November 1971): 10–11.

5. *Middle East Record* 5 (1965–70): 487.

6. Cited in Shahram Chubin and Sepehr Zabih, *The foreign relations of Iran: a developing state in a zone of great power conflict* (Berkeley, CA: University of California Press, 1974): 238.

7. *Middle East Record* 4 (1968): 83–84; *Middle East Record* 5 (1969–70): 486.

8. *Department of State Bulletin*, September 4, 1972: 244.

9. Kissinger, *White House years*, p. 1264.

10. James H. Noyes, *The clouded lens: Persian Gulf security and United States policy* (Stanford, CA: Hoover Institution Press, 1979): 54.

11. *Department of State Bulletin*, September 4, 1972: 243–4; U.S. Congress. House. Committee of Foreign Affairs. *New perspectives on the Persian Gulf* (1973): 6–10, 38–44.

The Shah and the Nixon Doctrine

12. *Middle East Record* 5 (1969–70): 464.

13. Kissinger, *White House years*, p. 1262.

14. William H. Sullivan, *Mission to Iran* (New York: W. W. Norton and Co., 1981): 118.

15. Barry Rubin, *Paved with good intentions: the American experience and Iran* (Harmondsworth: Penguin Books, 1981): 172.

16. Robert E. Hunter, 'Arms control in the Persian Gulf', in Andrew J. Pierre (ed.), *Arms transfers and American foreign policy* (New York: New York University Press, 1979): 116.

17. *New York Times*, November 12, 1976: D1, D9.

18. Kissinger made the statement in an interview with *Business Week*, December 23, 1974. The text of this interview and of related statements by President Ford and Defense Secretary Schlesinger cited in this section are reproduced in U.S. Congress. House. Committee on International Relations. *Oil fields as military objectives: a feasibility study* (1975): 77–82.

19. Ibid., p. 77.

20. Robert W. Tucker, 'Oil: the issue of American intervention', *Commentary* (January 1975): 21–31; Miles Ignotus, 'Seizing Arab oil', *Harper's Magazine* (March 1975): 45–62. For dissenting views, see Earl C. Ravenal, 'The oil-grab scenario', *The New Republic*, January 18, 1975: 14–15; Bard E. O'Neill, *Petroleum and security: the limitations of military power in the Persian Gulf*, Research Directorate Monograph 77–4 (Washington, D.C.: National Defense University, 1977); 'The oil crisis: is there a military option?' *The Defence Monitor* (December 1979).

21. U.S. Congress. House. Committee on International Relations. *Oil fields as military objectives* (1975): xi, 75–76.

22. *Department of State Bulletin*, September 4, 1972: 244–5.

23. R. K. Ramazani, 'Iran's search for regional cooperation', *Middle East Journal* (Spring 1976): 173–86; Alvin J. Cottrell, 'Iran, the Arabs and the Persian Gulf', *Orbis* (Fall 1973): 978–88.

24. For a history of the Shatt-al-Arab dispute, see Tareq Ismael, *Iraq and Iran: roots of conflict* (Syracuse, NY: Syracuse University Press, 1982).

25. *Strategic Survey, 1975* (London: International Institute for Strategic Studies, 1976): 86.

26. For a discussion of the Dhofar rebellion and Iran's role, see John Duke Anthony, 'Insurrection and intervention: the war in Dhofar', in Abbas Amirie (ed.), *The Persian Gulf and Indian Ocean in international politics* (Teheran: Institute for International Political and Economic Studies, 1975): 287–303.

27. *Iran: a country study* (Washington, D.C.: American University, 1978): 399–400.

28. Edward Kennedy, 'The Persian Gulf: arms race or arms control?' *Foreign Affairs* (October 1975): 24–25.

29. Amir Taheri, 'Policies of Iran in the Persian Gulf region', in Amirie, *The Persian Gulf and Indian Ocean*.

30. U.S. Congress. House. Committee on Foreign Affairs. *New perspectives on the Persian Gulf* (1973): vi.

31. Emile A. Nakleh, 'Future directions of U.S. policy in the Arabian Peninsula and the Gulf: prospects and reflections', in Envor M. Koury and Emile A. Nakhlet (eds), *The Arabian Peninsula, the Red Sea, and the Gulf:*

34

The Shah and the Nixon Doctrine

strategic considerations (Hyattsville, MD: Institute of Middle Eastern and North African Affairs, 1979): 94.

32. 'Shah to the rescue', *The Economist*, October 11, 1969: 43.

33. David Lynn Price, *Oil and Middle East security, The Washington Papers*, no. 41 (Beverly Hills, CA: Sage Publications, 1977): 58.

34. Chubin and Zabih, *The foreign relations of Iran*, Chapter 7; 'Gulf Security: for whom, against whom?' *The Middle East* (November 1977): 63–7.

35. Cited in Geoffrey Kemp with Steven Miller, 'The arms transfer phenomenon', in Pierre, *Arms transfers and American foreign policy*, p. 52. For studies of the Nixon Doctrine's implications for security assistance, see Lewis Sorley, *Arms transfers under Nixon: a policy analysis* (Lexington, KY: University of Kentucky Press, 1983).

36. U.S. Congress. House. Committee on International Relations. *United States arms policies in the Persian Gulf and Red Sea areas: past, present and future* (1977): 5–6.

37. U.S. Congress. Senate. Committee on Foreign Relations. *U.S. military sales to Iran* (1976): 13.

38. Arms Control and Disarmament Agency, *World military expenditures and arms transfers, 1970–1979* (Washington, D.C.: U.S. Government Printing Office, 1982): 62.

39. *The military balance* (London: International Institute for Strategic Studies), for 1970–71, 1979–80.

40. U.S. Congress. Senate. Committee on Foreign Relations. *U.S. military sales to Iran* (1976): viii. See also Richard Burt, 'Power and the Peacock Throne', *The Round Table* (October 1975): 349–56.

41. U.S. Congress. House. Committee on International Relations. *United States arms policies in the Persian Gulf and Red Sea areas* (1977): 135.

42. Bernard Reich, 'The United States and Iran: an overview', in U.S. Congress. Joint Economic Committee. *Economic consequences of the revolution in Iran* (1979): 8.

43. Andrew J. Pierre, *The global politics of arms sales* (Princeton, NJ: Princeton University Press, 1982): 142–56.

44. U.S. Congress. House. Committee of Foreign Affairs. *Saudi Arabia and the United States* (1981): 48.

45. U.S. Congress. House. Committee on International Relations. *United States arms policies in the Persian Gulf and Red Sea areas* (1977): 28.

46. U.S. Congress. House. Committee of Foreign Affairs. *Saudi Arabia and the United States* (1981): 48–51.

47. Rubin, *Paved with good intentions*, pp. 163, 172–3.

48. U.S. Congress. House. Committee on International Relations. *United States arms policies in the Persian Gulf and Red Sea areas* (1977): 12.

49. U.S. Congress. Senate. Committee on Foreign Relations. *U.S. military sales to Iran* (1976): x.

50. *Iran: a country study*, p. 409.

51. U.S. Congress. House. Committee on International Relations. *United States arms policies in the Persian Gulf and Red Sea areas* (1977): 8.

52. Saikal, *The rise and fall of the Shah*, pp. 157–8.

53. *New York Times*, February 4, 1976: 1, 6.

54. *New York Times*, December 11, 1978: A23.

The Shah and the Nixon Doctrine

55. Rubin, *Paved with good intentions*, p. 176.
56. See, for example, Theodore H. Moran, 'Iranian defense expenditures and the social crisis', *International Security* (Winter 1978–79): 178–92.
57. Sick, *All fall down*, pp. 15–17.
58. Ibid., p. 25.

3

From Teheran to Kabul, 1979: Gulf Crises and American Reassertion

The year 1979 was a watershed for U.S. position and policy in the Persian Gulf region. The year brought in a series of upheavals, beginning with the overthrow of the Shah in Iran and ending with a massive Soviet invasion of Afghanistan. Never before in its relatively short but eventful association with the region did the United States have to confront challenges more disruptive of Western interests. Further, the Iran and Afghanistan crises were not thought to be isolated events, but rather were considered as examples of a general pattern of conflict and instability afflicting the entire region. Iran was viewed as a symbol of the unsettling consequence of the rapid modernization of the Persian Gulf societies. In Afghanistan, many Western observers found a demonstration of what some had earlier characterized as a Soviet 'geographical offensive' in the regions of Africa and the Middle East. Between them, the events in Iran and Afghanistan helped close an era in U.S. policy in the Gulf. After the shockwaves they generated, the foundations of another were laid.

Iran and regional stability

As catalysts of the transition in America's regional role, events in Iran were more decisive than in Afghanistan. In Iran, the United States suffered one of its greatest setbacks in the Middle East region. The replacement of a staunchly pro-Western ally by a rabidly anti-American regime had far-reaching and diverse implications for the U.S. position in the region.

Economically, it meant the loss of a reliable source of oil and a

37

Gulf Crises and American Reassertion

major market for U.S. goods and services. The Iranian market, one of the largest export markets for the industrial world among developing countries, was by 1978 worth over $3 billion annually to the United States. Iran was the world's fourth largest oil producer and second largest oil exporter. It exports amounted to 5.2 mbd before strikes and unrest among the oil field workers seriously disrupted production and brought exports to a standstill. In all, the disruption in Iranian exports amounted to a loss of about 8 per cent of the world's total trade in petroleum in the first nine months of 1979. Sparking off panic in the international oil market, the Iranian shortfall was instrumental in escalating oil prices by a huge margin (from $12.81 per barrel in December 1978 to $23.50 in October 1979).[1]

The political and strategic consequences of the revolution were equally negative for the United States. Prior to Ayatollah Khomeini's return to Teheran, the ill-fated interim regime of Shapur Bakhtiar (appointed by the Shah) pledged to abandon the Shah's pro-Western regional security posture. Iran's security concerns, said Bakhtiar, would from then on be restricted to the defence of 'our own coast and our own country'.[2] Among other things this meant the withdrawal of Iranian troops from Oman, where they had assisted Sultan Qabus in curbing the Dhofari rebels. Bakhtiar also announced the scaling down of Iran's military build-up in order to make it conform to 'the limits of our possibilities and our resources'.[3] Iran cancelled its order for about $12 billion worth of military equipment from the United States that was due for delivery within the next five years.[4] The new regime also ended Iran's longstanding participation in the U.S. strategy of 'containment' by formally withdrawing from CENTO. The Iranian departure led to the dismantling of two electronic listening posts that the United States maintained in northern Iran for monitoring Soviet missile tests.[5]

The fall of the Shah threatened U.S. diplomacy in the Arab-Israeli conflict. Iran quickly halted all oil exports to Israel and broke off diplomatic relations with that state. While the Shah was one of the rare regional leaders to have openly supported the Camp David peace process, Islamic Iran was vocal, at least initially, in its backing for the PLO. A Palestinian delegation visited Teheran soon after the Islamic regime was established, and the PLO was granted full diplomatic recognition. Iran's strong support for the Palestinians might have been a blow to whatever hopes the United States still entertained of eliciting a favourable

Gulf Crises and American Reassertion

Saudi response to Camp David. The Saudis had been embarrassed by Iran's stand on Palestine and could not afford to look less Islamic on the Egyptian-Israeli peace treaty.

The Carter administration was also concerned about the damaging implications of the revolution for U.S. credibility as a security partner to the other pro-Western regional states. This concern had an important domestic aspect. In the inevitable and heated controversy concerning 'who lost Iran' that ensued, many critics contended that the administration's pressure on the Shah to improve his human rights record had spurred Iranian opposition to open revolt in the first place. Worse still, they maintained, was Carter's failure to back the Shah adequately once the agitation gained momentum.[6] This was alleged to have undermined the confidence of the pro-Western Arab states in U.S. determination and ability to counter threats to their security.[7] The Carter administration's handling of the Iranian crisis was seen as a blow to the United States in its geopolitical competition with the Soviet Union, which in contrast was perceived to be pursuing an aggressive course in consolidating its strategic gains in and around the region.

Iran's internal turmoil, worsened by the intense power struggle between its three principal domestic factions — the clergy, the Marxist groups (Mujaheeden-i-Khalq, Fedayeen-i-Khalq, and the pro-Soviet Tudeh Party), and the National Front — presented another source of concern for the United States. The clergy's execution of several thousand officials of the former regime led to the disintegration of the Iranian military, already weakened by large-scale desertion during the final days of the Shah's regime. With the central authority in shambles, Iran's ethnic minorities repeated a familiar historical pattern of unrest, demanding autonomy and secession. Serious ethnic strife occurred involving the Kurds, the Arabs, the Turkomens, and the Baluchs.[8] This, in turn, prompted U.S. fears of a Soviet move to exploit the situation to its advantage.[9] The possibility of direct Soviet military intervention in Iran soon became a focus of U.S. military contingency planning for the Gulf region.

The Khomeini regime's intense antagonism towards the United States frustrated the Carter administration policy of damage limitation in Iran. The administration had initially sought to establish functional ties with Iran by approving the shipment of 1 million barrels of heating oil to Iran and even holding talks on the delivery of military equipment ordered by the Shah.[10] But

Gulf Crises and American Reassertion

attempts at a reconciliation quickly proved to be futile as the clergy steadily consolidated its hold over Iran's domestic power base and revealed its intense hatred of the United States. Anti-Americanism was not only the legacy of America's long support for the Shah's oppressive rule, but also a unifying element binding competing constituents of the Islamic revolution. The Khomeini regime was not about to give up that important advantage by negotiating a reconciliation with the United States.

The hostage crisis that erupted on November 4, 1979, when more than 60 Americans were confined in the U.S. embassy by militant 'student' revolutionaries, dealt the final blow to the Carter administration's efforts to come to terms with the Islamic regime. The move by the Iranian revolutionaries was prompted by a fundamental mistrust of the United States — an element of which was an apprehension that the latter might engineer a repetition of the 1953 coup to put the Pahlavi regime back on the throne. But once the hostages were taken the crisis was used by the fundamentalist clergy to expose and discredit the moderate faction (represented by leaders such as Prime Minister Mehdi Bazargan and President Abol Hassan Bani Sadr) who were more inclined to restore functional ties with the United States. The continued detention of hostages became a unifying symbol of the revolution's humiliation of the hated superpower. The Carter administration's obsession with the release of the hostages, leading to the ill-fated rescue mission in 1980, thus played into the hands of the fundamentalist elements and probably itself prolonged the crisis. The crisis also aggravated the decline of U.S. standing in the region. Coming after the demonstrated impotence of U.S. power to save its closest regional ally, the failure to secure a prompt release of the American hostages only complicated U.S. efforts to salvage its regional interests and restore its sinking credibility.

The Carter administration perceived the Iranian revolution as the symptom of a 'wider strategic crisis' afflicting the entire Middle East.[11] After the Shah had fallen, U.S. apprehensions about regime stability in the Persian Gulf focused on the remaining conservative, generally pro-Western rulers of the Arabian Peninsula. To Washington, the revolution was a reminder of their vulnerability to a host of internally generated pressures and challenges including the impact of modernization, Islamic fundamentalism, dynastic rivalry, and territorial disputes.[12]

The spectacular rise in oil revenues and the consequent 'interrelated growth trends in the economy, technology, education,

Gulf Crises and American Reassertion

urban lifestyles, and mass media exposure'[13] in the Gulf societies have unleashed a number of unsettling effects. Modernization has eroded the principal 'legitimizing values' — Islam, tribe, and extended family — that have historically sustained the legitimacy of the centralized and feudal decision-making systems in the Arabian Peninsula. Modernization is resented by the older and traditional sector of the population, which blames it for destroying Islamic values and life styles and replacing them with a culture permeated by alien values and ideas. This in turn reinforces resurgent trends in Islam.[14] Against this background, the Iranian clergy's leading role in the campaign that overthrew a powerful and modernizing monarch within a single year had its message to elements in other Gulf societies resentful of the pro-Western outlooks and modernizing policies of their own regimes.

If the message had failed to get across to the Arab population of the Gulf, Khomeini's Iran sought to correct that situation by launching an enthusiastic campaign to export it. Iran's clergy viewed this campaign as a potent instrument in its efforts to prevail over the disparate ideological factions challenging the clergy's domination of the post-revolutionary polity. An additional factor behind this drive was the Islamic republic's insecurity in the face of what its leaders feared were attempts by external powers to subvert its existence. To best guarantee the survival of an Islamic regime in Teheran, the Iranian clergy apparently felt, it was necessary to create an Islamic political environment in its neighbourhood.[15] Thus, Iran launched a campaign, including a series of provocative radio broadcasts complemented by the activities of pro-Khomeini religious and political groups in the Middle East, to discredit the Gulf monarchies and the Baathist regime in Iraq.

The presence of a large number of Shi'a Muslims within the population of the Arab Gulf States, especially in Bahrain and Iraq, helped the Iranian drive. In all the Sunni-ruled Gulf States, Shi'ites are among the most economically and politically disadvantaged. Their susceptibility to the Khomeini campaign was evident in Shi'i demonstrations which occurred in Bahrain in April 1980; in Kuwait in September and November 1979; and in Saudi Arabia's Eastern Province in November 1979 and February 1980. Another development, not linked to Khomeini's influence but suggesting, even more ominously, that the impact of Islamic resurgence might not be confined to the Shi'i sect alone also occurred in Saudi Arabia. On November 20, 1979, a group of some 500 armed men seized the Grand Mosque in Mecca. The

Gulf Crises and American Reassertion

group was protesting what it called the un-Islamic policies of Al-Saud. Its leader had in his earlier writings attacked corruption in the Kingdom and declared that the Al-Saud should no longer be regarded as leaders of Wahhabism. The insurrection lasted until December 4, producing hundreds of casualities on both sides, before Saudi forces, allegedly assisted by French commandos, flushed out the perpetrators.[16]

Apart from the Islamic challenge, several other factors complicate the security milieu of the Gulf States. The seeds of tension between the political aspirations of the growing middle class and the archaic form of government in the Arabian Peninsula pose a threat to political stability. Radical opposition groups, espousing a variety of ideologies ranging from Marxism to democratic republicanism, challenge the authority of the sheikhs and kings. Groups such as the National Front for the Liberation of Saudi Arabia, National Front for the Liberation of Bahrain, and cells of the Arab Nationalist Movement, though without significant popular support, are none the less security challenges that the Gulf regimes have had to contend with.[17] Another source of potential social and political unrest in the region is the presence of large numbers of foreigners in the conservative Gulf States. In 1980 there were an estimated 3 million foreign workers in the six Gulf monarchies.[18] Much of the expatriate work force lives in conditions far inferior to that of its fellow native workers, and enjoys few rights. As such, it is considered susceptible to radical and subversive influences from elements either in the native population or the resident non-citizen Arab community. A significant segment of the latter category, about half a million in the entire Arabian Peninsula, are expatriate Palestinians, which have been viewed by the United States and, privately, by the Gulf regimes to be a potentially destabilizing factor.[19]

The Gulf regimes are also vulnerable to dynastic factionalism and rivalries within the ruling families. Forced deposition of rulers by contesting family members have recent precedents in Oman, Abu Dhabi, Qatar, and Sharjah. Latent dynastic competitions have continued to cloud stability of a variety of ruling families, especially in Ras al-Khaima, Qatar, and Kuwait. The political integration of the United Arab Emirates has suffered from the rivalry between the Al-Nihayan family ruling over Abu Dhabi and the Al-Muktaum family ruling over Dubai. In Saudi Arabia, the factional competition between the powerful 'Sudairi Seven' (sons of King Ibn Saud and his senior Queen), whose membership

Gulf Crises and American Reassertion

includes King Fahd and the defence minister, Prince Sultan, and the more conservative group headed by Prince Abdallah, the Crown Prince, and the powerful head of the National Guard, have created doubt about the future of the Al-Saud dynasty.[20]

The revolution in Iran sharpened the latent tensions in the Gulf caused by disputes over territory. Leading members of the Khomeini regime revived Iran's irredentist claim on Bahrain, which the Shah had abandoned in the early 1970s.[21] For a time, this created serious concern in Saudi Arabia and Bahrain. Iraq's claim on Kuwait[22] led to Britain's intervention in support of the newly independent sheikhdom in 1961, and Kuwait continues to harbour misgivings about Iraqi intentions on two islands, Warbah and Bubiyan, which Iraq has used in its war with Iran. The Iranian revolution unfroze Teheran's dispute with Iraq over the Shatt-al-Arab waterway which divides them. While a settlement of the disputes had been reached through Algerian mediation in 1975, the Iraqi leaders had felt humiliated by the accord which made them concede the median line, rather than the Iranian bank, as the boundary between the two states. Thus in a move that exemplified the transient nature of territorial settlements in the region, Baghdad denounced and repudiated the agreement when the Iranian state appeared to be falling apart as a result of prolonged internal strife. The border issue[23] along with rising Shi'ite militancy in Iraq inspired by Khomeini's message were two of the major factors behind the Iraqi initiation of the Iran-Iraq War in September 1980, which soon became the principal challenge to U.S. security interests in the Gulf region.

Although many of these sources of regional strife pre-dated the Iranian revolution, the shock waves of the Iranian turmoil reinforced the impression of the Gulf as one of the most volatile and unstable areas of the world. Such perceptions were widely entrenched within the U.S. policymaking establishment before the Soviet Union invaded Afghanistan at the end of 1979. The Soviet invasion greatly aggravated U.S. concerns regarding threats to its interests in the Persian Gulf. But the Carter administration's response to the invasion would probably have been less bellicose had it not been preceded by the spectre of regionwide domestic instability raised by the Iranian revolution. In fact, leading administration officials, such as Zbigniew Brzezinski, were of the opinion that 'Had the Shah not fallen, it is unlikely that the Soviets would have moved so openly into Afghanistan, transforming that neutral buffer into an offensive wedge, bringing the Russians

43

Gulf Crises and American Reassertion

so much closer to their historic target of the Indian Ocean'.[24]

The Afghanistan crisis and the Soviet 'threat'

To the United States, the 'proximity, power and behaviour' of the Soviet Union constitute 'the most dangerous threat' to its interests in the Persian Gulf and the Middle East.[25] Although American concern regarding Soviet influence and activities in the Middle East had been longstanding, it was the Afghanistan crisis and the Carter administration's response to it that spurred a new awareness of the 'Soviet threat' focusing specifically on the Persian Gulf. The Afghanistan crisis also led to an intensified U.S. commitment to countering Soviet power and influence in the region.

The Soviet invasion of Afghanistan, resulting in the overthrow of the relatively independent-minded Hafizullah Amin regime and its replacement by a far more compliant Babrak Karmal, sparked off a major debate in the West about the motives and intentions underlying the Soviet action. Several lines of interpretation were advanced.[26] One school held that the Soviet invasion was part of an offensive 'grand design', constituting another step along a pre-determined course of expansion. Viewing the invasion in the context of earlier Soviet interventions in Africa and the Middle East, this school dismissed suggestions that the invasion of Afghanistan reflected Soviet insecurity against the Islamic uprising in Iran and its possible spillover into its own Muslim population. Rather, as Richard Pipes, a noted advocate of this view, insisted, the invasion was part of a calculated Soviet 'pincer . . . directed toward the Middle East and aim[ed] at cutting off, in the event of hostilities, fossil fuels and minerals without which the economies of America's allies would not be able to function'.[27]

The alternative conception of the Soviet motives in Afghanistan viewed the invasion as essentially a defensive, short-term, local and limited step. George F. Kennan, the most respected adherent to this school, hypothesized that the Soviets might have been 'sucked into it . . . rather involuntarily'.[28] The basic assumption underlying this view was that the Soviets 'were impelled to act by the prospective costs of *not* acting, and *not* by the expected *gains* of their actions'.[29] The proponents of the 'defensive' view argued their case on the following lines. The evident failure of the Amin regime to broaden its control and contain the growing domestic

Gulf Crises and American Reassertion

rebellion against its radical policies had created the possibility that the communist revolution in Afghanistan could have been totally defeated. But the Soviet stakes in Afghanistan — in economic, political, and prestige terms — had become too substantial for them to permit that reversal. Although no hard evidence has surfaced to support the suggestion that the Soviets had engineered the downfall of the Doud regime in April 1978,[30] they had none the less moved quickly to recognize the new communist regime. Moscow undertook a significant expansion of its military and political involvement in Afghanistan. It signed a Treaty of Friendship with the new regime in December 1978 and agreed to provide it with considerable aid over the next five years. Thus the Soviets were forced to intervene because failure to protect such an important client regime from the forces of counter-revolution could have undermined Soviet credibility before other communist regimes while encouraging their internal opponents.

The 'defensive' view further held that the implications of the advent of a non-communist regime in Kabul for the security of its own southern borders needed to be added to the list of Soviet apprehensions. A setback in Afghanistan would have come in the midst of an escalating regional trend toward Islamic fundamentalism sparked off by the Iranian revolution. An Islamic republic in Afghanistan, which the Soviets probably foresaw as the likely outcome of a communist defeat, could have greatly increased the possibility that its own large central Asian Muslim population would be aroused to revolt. Soviet insecurity over such a development could have been further enhanced by the alleged Chinese and Pakistani backing of the Afghan rebels.[31]

A third line of interpretation, which rejected the 'grand design' hypothesis but contended that the Soviet motives were not all 'defensive', perceived the invasion as an 'opportunistic' move. According to this view, while the Soviets were worried about the immense costs of losing Afghanistan from their sphere of influence, that alone would have been an insufficient basis for military action if they had also not perceived in it great opportunities to advance their interests in the wider regional context. As former State Department official Joseph Sisco stated, the Soviets, 'pursuing a policy of tactical opportunism, assessed correctly' that a takeover of Afghanistan 'would put them in a good position to exploit the instability that exists in the area . . . to our disadvantage'.[32] There already existed an exploitable situation of chaos and turmoil in Iran. Further opportunities could be created by encouraging the ethnic strife in Pakistan, especially in Baluchistan. And the Soviets, perhaps miscalculating, thought that they could achieve their goals with a relatively lower level of military and political risk. The United States was experiencing a severe loss of position and credibility throughout the region, and was not in a position to retaliate strongly against a Soviet move. The Soviets had 'nothing to lose' in terms of their relations with the United States, since the latter was already moving toward a significant dilution of its commitment to detente. A few weeks before the Soviet action, NATO had announced its decision to modernize its intermediate-range missiles in Europe by introducing Pershing II and Cruise missiles. It had become increasingly evident that SALT II would not be ratified by the U.S. Congress. The United States also had normalized its relations with China, a step that would surely have magnified Soviet insecurity.[33]

The Carter administration did not publicly side with any particular viewpoint, although there were clear and major differences among top foreign policy officials regarding the motives underlying the invasion. To Brzezinski, as he later wrote, the invasion was 'part of the current phase of Soviet assertiveness' which in turn was 'symptomatic of the long-term [Soviet] historical drive . . . toward the Persian Gulf', with 'military power supplanting Marxist ideology as its basic, dynamic source'. In May 1979, when there were indications of growing Soviet involvement in Afghanistan, he had briefed the President 'specifically in Molotov's proposal to Hitler in late 1940 that the Nazis recognize the Soviet claim to preeminence in the region south of Batum and Baku'.[34] Secretary of State Vance, on the other hand, leaned more toward the 'defensive' interpretation. He believed the Soviets 'badly miscalculated' the extent of U.S. and international reaction and the resistance offered by the Afghan population to the Soviet occupation.[35] But the focus of the administration's public position was not so much to speculate on Soviet motives, but to emphasize the objective geostrategic consequences.[36]

The military occupation of Afghanistan, the administration contended, drastically altered the strategic balance in the entire Southwest Asian region and, coming after the disintegration of the Northern Tier system following the Iranian revolution, opened up the entire region to direct or indirect Soviet penetration. 'A Soviet-occupied Afghanistan', claimed President Carter, 'is a stepping stone to possible control over much of the world's oil supplies'. The invasion, by bringing 'Soviet military forces to within 300

Gulf Crises and American Reassertion

miles of the Indian Ocean and close to the Strait of Hormuz', posed a 'grave threat to the free movement of Middle East oil'.[37] Moreover, staging from bases in Afghanistan, Soviet combat aircraft could now attack U.S. warships operating near the Persian Gulf and neutralize U.S. carrier-based aviation. Soviet fighters would for the first time be able to reach the Strait of Hormuz, removing a significant constraint on Soviet power projection into the Gulf region.[38]

A Soviet position in Afghanistan, said Harold Brown, would enable Moscow 'to apply pressure, be it military, political, or internal insurgent, to Iran and Pakistan and the littoral states of the Persian Gulf and the Arabian Sea'.[39] Whether a desire to exploit local instabilities had originally gone into Soviet calculations or not, the Soviets would now be in a position to take advantage of the ethnic strife in Iran and Pakistan in order to make further inroads to the region and threaten Western interests.[40]

Thus, the significance of the Afghanistan crisis, as that of the Iranian revolution, came to be judged in the context of its wider geostrategic implications. Among the issues that aroused much speculation in the West was the question of Soviet designs on the region's oil resources. Two theories were advanced. One view held that the Soviets were about to undertake an aggressive interest in Persian Gulf oil owing to their own prospective energy shortage. The most important basis for such predictions had come from the CIA which, in a series of reports during the second half of the 1970s, had forecast that the Soviet Union, the world's largest producer of petroleum, could become a net importer of that resource after the mid-1980s.[41] Although the Agency's forecast was challenged by other analysts, including the Defense Intelligence Agency, and the Agency itself subsequently came up with a less pessimistic prediction, much of the Western speculation about the future direction of Soviet Persian Gulf policy continued to focus on the prospect of a Soviet energy crisis.[42] Given the grave domestic and foreign policy implications of a loss of export capacity, which would deprive Moscow of its single most important source of hard currency and hurt its leadership of the Warsaw Pact, the Soviet Union might not bear a domestic oil crisis passively. Thus, as Admiral Stansfield Turner, the then CIA director, told the Senate Energy and Natural Resources Committee:

To ease the problem, Moscow will no doubt make an intense

Gulf Crises and American Reassertion

effort to obtain at concessional prices from the oil producing countries through barter deals, sometimes involving arms sales. More forceful action, ranging from covert subversion to intimidation, or, in the extreme military action, cannot be ruled out.[43]

The second view of the linkage between oil and future Soviet policy in the Gulf argued that even if the Soviet Union continued to be self-sufficient in meeting its domestic and alliance oil requirements, there were other factors that could tempt it to take possession of the Persian Gulf oil fields.[44] The Soviets, as a House Foreign Affairs Committee report pointed out, could 'use the revenue generated by the sale of oil to revitalize [their] sagging economy while simultaneously continuing to enlarge [their] military power'. Gulf oil could also be used either as an incentive or as a weapon to 'placate or coerce restive client states, and to procure new clients in strategically important areas of the world'. Above all, the Soviets could use their control of Persian Gulf oil to exploit the divisions within the Western alliance.[45] Given the differential between U.S. import needs and those of its European and Japanese allies, and given the history of allied discord over Middle Eastern political issues that bear upon their access to oil, a Soviet offer to Western Europe or Japan of a secure energy supply could lead the latter to distance themselves from U.S. policies.

Apart from causing concern regarding the Kremlin's motives for expansion into the Gulf, the Soviet invasion of Afghanistan closely influenced U.S. perception of the growing Soviet capability for power projection. Afghanistan, the first post-war instance of a direct Soviet invasion outside Eastern Europe, underscored the possibility that the Soviet Union, which had traditionally relied upon other instruments in its dealings with the Third World, would now increasingly rely on direct military force as an instrument of geopolitical expansion. This would be especially true of countries in close proximity to the Soviet Union; as President Carter put it, Afghanistan was a warning that 'the Soviets will use force to take over a neighbouring country'.[46] In addition, Afghanistan provided a demonstration of the growing reach and sophistication of Soviet projection forces. The massive Soviet airlift to Kabul and the deployment of its airborne units all indicated a level of quality and efficiency unattained during past interventions in Hungary and Czechoslovakia.[47] Moreover, Afghanistan highlighted the flexibility of Soviet intervention options with respect to

Gulf Crises and American Reassertion

the Persian Gulf. Traditionally, the Soviet naval contingent in the Indian Ocean, since its first arrival in 1968, had been seen in the West as the most visible and dedicated instrument of Soviet influence in the littoral region. In the Afghanistan operation, however, the employment of about 100,000 Soviet ground troops and a large number of tanks drew attention to the overland component of the Soviet military threat. The Soviets, should they decide to launch an overland attack on a Persian Gulf State, could draw upon a reservoir of more than 20 ground divisions stationed in the Transcaucasus, North Caucasus, and Turkestan military districts.[48] Heavily armoured and enjoying good battlefield mobility, these divisions could pose a far more formidable threat than that which could be projected through naval activity alone. In fact, the Soviet navy's ability to play a meaningful combat role could be enhanced if it was deployed in coordination with land forces. The invasion of Afghanistan, as an article in the *U.S. Naval Institute Proceedings* pointed out, marked 'the first time' when the Soviet navy was deployed in the Indian Ocean 'as a defensive flank for the Soviet Army'.[49] Coming on the heels of a major Soviet effort to enhance the sustainability and strikepower of its seaborne military instrument, this combination was seen in Western military circles as an ominous development.

The American response: Carter Doctrine

Washington's response to the Iran and Afghanistan crises had two aspects. The first related to crisis management, comprising a number of short-term measures to cope with setbacks unfolding in rapid succession. These included economic sanctions and diplomatic efforts at the UN aimed at punishing the offending sides — Khomeini's Iran for holding American hostages and the Soviet Union for invading Afghanistan; increased naval deployment to demonstrate American 'resolve' to friends and enemies; and diplomatic missions to the Gulf to reassure the pro-Western regional states of continued U.S. commitment to their security and stability. The second aspect was the fashioning of a long-term military strategy to replace the defunct 'twin-pillar' doctrine as the basic framework for U.S. policy in the Gulf. This involved increased emphasis on building a direct U.S. force projection capability to deal with possible contingencies in the region. With the Shah gone, the Carter administration decided to 'rely more heavily on

49

Gulf Crises and American Reassertion

our own military capability' to protect Western interests in the region.[50]

The first major hint of a new direction in the administration's Persian Gulf strategy came in February 1979 when Defense Secretary Brown was sent to the Middle East to reassure key regional allies of America's continued commitment to their security. In discussions with Saudi leaders, Brown raised the possibility of increasing U.S. military assistance to the region, enhancing the U.S. naval presence in the Indian Ocean, and building up a force for crisis intervention.[51] Upon returning to Washington, Brown announced that the oil flow from the Gulf was 'clearly part of our vital interests' which would be defended 'with whatever means are appropriate, including military force where necessary'.[52]

Further evidence of the administration's plans to pursue a more assertive role in the region came when it overreacted to the Yemeni crisis in March. Even though there was considerable doubt regarding the seriousness of reported South Yemeni incursions into the North, the President waived the requirement for congressional oversight in rushing approximately $400 million worth of military equipment to North Yemen.[53] At the same time, the aircraft carrier *Constellation* was dispatched to the Arabian Sea, and a fleet of Airborne Warning and Control System (AWACS) planes were deployed to Saudi Arabia to strengthen Saudi air defences.[54]

A crucial policy session to determine the administration's Persian Gulf strategy was held in the third week of June, in the form of two successive White House meetings attended by all top foreign policy and defence officials including Carter, Vance, Brzezinski, Brown, Energy Secretary James Schlesinger, and Joint Chiefs of Staff Chairman General David Jones. The meeting reviewed the implications of the unfolding events in Southwest Asia and debated proposals for an appropriate response. In his memoirs, Brzezinski recalls the lines advocated by different participants:

> At one point in that debate, Schlesinger argued forcefully that American military presence in the Indian Ocean – Persian Gulf area should 'balance' the Soviets, and when Vance and Christopher reacted negatively, I not only backed Schlesinger, but stated that in fact our objective ought to be military preponderance, since the area was vital to the United States while not of equal significance to the Soviets.[55]

These deliberations led to agreement on the following measures:

Gulf Crises and American Reassertion

(1) preparation of a list of military deployment options to the Gulf by the Pentagon; (2) exploration of the feasibility of a permanent Indian Ocean naval fleet; (3) regular deployment of land-based aircraft to friendly countries in the region; (4) increased military sales to the region; (5) closer cooperation with the pro-Western regional states on security; and (6) movement on the Palestinian issue.[56]

The idea of an Indian Ocean fleet (to be called the Fifth Fleet) as a long-term measure to protect Western interests in the Gulf and other Indian Ocean littoral regions had been under consideration for some time. The Pentagon advocated that such a fleet 'would be tangible evidence that we have a vital national interest in the Gulf and we are prepared to do what is necessary, including the use of military force, to defend our vital interests there'.[57] Noted naval strategists such as the former Joint Chiefs of Staff Chairman, Admiral Thomas Moorer, and Alvin J. Cottrell argued that 'a formal fleet designation' be given to 'whatever U.S. naval presence is retained in the region' because that would be 'important for regional perceptions'.[58] Such arguments appeared to find favour in the Carter administration in the wake of the Horn of Africa crisis in 1978, which led to the abandonment of U.S.–Soviet talks on Indian Ocean naval arms limitation.

But a Fifth Fleet could not be assembled without withdrawing ships from other existing fleets. The Pentagon realized that any major and long-term detachment of units from the Sixth or Seventh Fleets would reduce their ability to respond to contingencies in other areas, such as a NATO alert in the Mediterranean or a contingency in the Western Pacific. In addition, Navy officials understood from recent experience that any large-scale Indian Ocean presence would be expensive and logistically extremely demanding.[59] If the Fifth Fleet was to be a credible instrument of power projection, then a carrier would have to be homeported in the region. But the Pentagon found that 'about five years and about $800 million would be needed to homeport a battle group'.[60] Moreover, the United States had difficulty in finding a location in the Indian Ocean that could offer adequate facilities for the ships, air wing, and about 15,000 military and enlisted personnel involved in homeporting a carrier. Against this, the existing arrangement for Indian Ocean deployments — in the form of naval task forces (Task Force 70) reporting to Commander, Seventh Fleet and the U.S. Pacific Command — had worked satisfactorily. The Fifth Fleet proposal was subsequently dropped.[61]

Gulf Crises and American Reassertion

Instead, U.S. policymakers decided that the time had come to bring rapidly into reality an idea that had been quietly evolving within the Pentagon and the National Security Council for the past two years. This idea was contained in a Presidential directive (PD-18) signed by Carter in 1977. This directive, in turn, grew out of a 'broadly gauged review of the U.S. – Soviet strategic balance' commissioned by Brzezinski in the early days of the Carter administration and conducted by Professor Samuel P. Huntington of Harvard University.[62] The findings of the study were distilled into a Presidential Review Memorandom (PRM-10) with appropriate inputs from the military establishment. One of the major recommendations of PRM-10 related to the Persian Gulf, which it identified 'as a vulnerable and vital region, to which greater military concern ought to be given'.[63] Exactly what form of concern was contemplated was later recalled by General P. X. Kelly, the first Commander of the Rapid Deployment Joint Task Force:

> PRM-10 discussed the forces required beyond those necessary for NATO. Included were Army and Marine Corps land-combat forces, together with naval and tactical air forces, and strategic mobility forces with the range and payload to minimize our dependence on overseas staging and logistical support bases. This, in essence, was the rapid deployment force.[64]

The PRM-10 was made into official policy in the form of Presidential directive 18, which ordered the formation of a 'deployment force of light divisions with strategic mobility independent of overseas bases and logistical support' and 'moderate naval and tactical air forces which could be used in the Middle East, Persian Gulf, Korea or elsewhere'.[65] Although PRM-10 and PD-18 were classified documents, broad outlines of what they contained were available from official statements and press leaks. One report, published in *Inquiry* magazine, disclosed that PD-18 had called for the creation of a 'rapid reaction mobile force for quick strikes in Third World crises' which could consist of approximately 100,000 troops, including two army airborne divisions and a Marine amphibious brigade, backed by two to four aircraft carriers and up to three Air Force wings. In the article, Brzezinski was quoted to the effect that where appropriate, this force could be used in a 'preemptive' mode (because 'who gets there first had command of

Gulf Crises and American Reassertion

the situation') to contain escalation of minor contingencies.[66]

Despite its inclusion in a Presidential directive, however, the rapid deployment concept had been received in the policymaking establishment with little enthusiasm. During inter-agency discussions of PRM-10 and PD-18, the State Department argued that regional security issues such as in the Persian Gulf/Indian Ocian region could better be dealt with by negotiating a naval arms limitation agreement with the Soviets.[67] Indeed, in September 1977, Brzezinski himself issued a memorandum requesting the Secretary of Defense to monitor and limit the pace of construction at Diego Garcia in accordance with progress in the U.S.–Soviet Naval Arms Limitations Talks.[68] Also, the Pentagon was then attaching more emphasis to the European theatre and NATO, and as a consequence 'the creation of . . . a contingency force was naturally placed on the back burner'.[69]

Until the Iranian revolution, the only progress attained in implementing the proposed deployment force was 'several detailed staff studies' on comparative U.S.–Soviet capability for limited contingencies. Although these studies later had 'considerable influence'[70] in shaping the rapid deployment programs undertaken after the fall of the Shah, they were not decision documents of any importance.[71] In a related development, responding to the secret 'consolidated guidance' issued by the Secretary of Defense in 1978, the Army had begun to plan for a 'Unilateral Corps' (the name stressing its independence from NATO or other alliance commitments). This initiative was intended to bring the Army's light divisions as well as other service units as a 'go anywhere' force for limited contingencies. But when the outgoing Army Chief, Bernard Rogers, revealed this project in late June 1979, he concluded that it had not gone beyond the initial planning stage.[72]

The fall of the Shah was a major turning point in the evolution of the rapid deployment concept. It needs to be stressed that it was the Iranian revolution, and not the Soviet invasion of Afghanistan, which provided the decisive impetus for the realization of the deployment force conceived in PD-18. In fact, by the time the Soviet invasion took place, most of the planning for the Force was at an advanced stage: specific force assignments had been decided upon, headquarters identified, and official statements announcing the creation of the force made.[73]

In mid-September 1979, the new Army Chief of Staff, General Edward Meyer, asserted that the Unilateral Corps was 'well on its way toward reality'.[74] But U.S. officials soon began referring to

Gulf Crises and American Reassertion

the new contingency force as the Rapid Deployment Force (RDF). It also became clear that the RDF would not be an exclusively Army outfit,[75] and its mission would be primarily focused on the Persian Gulf. Most of its constituent units would be based in the United States in peacetime. To facilitate its deployment to the Gulf during a contingency, the Carter administration launched two major initiatives. First, in December 1979, President Carter proposed a new fleet of maritime pre-positioning ships (MPS) and intercontinental airlifters (CX).[76] Second, a serious effort to secure access to regional military bases and facilities began. The need for such access had been acutely felt when the naval forces operating in the region were found to be experiencing serious logistical difficulties. One immediate response was to expedite improvements to the Diego Garcia naval support facility in the Indian Ocean, but even this was not thought to be enough. Moreover, the administration felt that access agreements with regional countries would be concrete evidence of its new assertive regional posture. In late 1979 the National Security Council debated and approved proposals to initiate negotiations with several regional states for additional access.[77] In mid-December a high-level negotiating team was sent to Oman, Kenya, Somalia, and Saudi Arabia 'to feel out how those nations would receive some offer or initiative of U.S. presence'. The Saudis refused but the others, according to the Pentagon, gave a 'very positive response' to the U.S. quest. Encouraged, the Pentagon followed up with a survey team in early January to look at 'all facilities that have potential military usefulness' in Kenya, Somalia, and Oman. Based on selections from its findings, legal and negotiating teams began working on the final agreements, which despite some setbacks with respect to Oman and Somalia, resulted in signed agreements with all three states in the June–August 1980 period.[78]

As the momentum in developing the various capabilities for the RDF accelerated, the Carter administration felt the need to issue a strong policy statement announcing its new approach to protecting Western interests in the Gulf. The Soviet invasion of Afghanistan proved to be the key factor behind this. The invasion added to the already strong domestic feelings about the 'decline' of U.S. power. The Carter administration's domestic stock, despite a brief recovery in the aftermath of the hostage crisis, was seriously threatened by accusations of indecision, *naïveté* and lack of firmness in foreign policy. There was growing opposition to the policies of detente, emphasis on human rights, and other tenets of Carter's

54

Gulf Crises and American Reassertion

'moralistic' foreign policy. The mood in the country, in short, was for a reversal of the so-called Vietnam syndrome.[79] In addition to these pressures, Brzezinski believed that if the United States was to defend its Persian Gulf interests, then only a forceful 'public commitment' would be 'capable of generating the necessary budgetary support and the other decisions that are needed to implement' it.[80] Thus was conceived the rationale for the Carter Doctrine, announced in the President's State of the Union address on January 23, 1980:

> Let our position be absolutely clear: An attempt by any outside force to gain control of the Persian Gulf region will be regarded as an assault on the vital interests of the United States of America, and such an assault will be repelled by any means necessary, including military force.[81]

The Carter Doctrine was received with mixed feelings in the United States. A Harris opinion poll found that by a 75 to 18 per cent majority, the American public supported the application of the Doctrine 'if the Russians try to take over control of the Persian Gulf'.[82] There were a few dissenting voices, like that of Senator Edward Kennedy, who saw the 'unilateral and unlimited American commitment' embodied in the Doctrine as 'hazardous' and 'ineffective'.[83] But overall, Congress supported the commitment. Even some of the strongest critics of the Vietnam War, such as Senator Frank Church, took a different position on the Gulf and favoured use of force to protect Western access to Persian Gulf oil.[84]

Criticism of the Doctrine related not to the stated necessity of military force to protect U.S. interests in the Gulf, but to whether the Carter administration had the will and ability to back the Doctrine with the requisite level of force. The President was accused of 'speaking loudly while carrying a small stick'. The RDF was branded as a paper tiger. Republican presidential aspirant Senator Robert Dole called the Carter Doctrine a 'bluff' that the Soviets would be likely to call 'as little more than an attempt at intimidating propaganda'.[85] Democrat Senator Henry Jackson asked: 'is it wise to send that kind of signal to the Soviet Union when there may be a real question whether our doctrine is credible?'[86]

It was also alleged that the Carter Doctrine had not been preceded by careful and adequate inter-agency planning. After

Gulf Crises and American Reassertion

retiring as Under Secretary of State for Political Affairs, David Newsom claimed that the Doctrine 'grew out of last-minute pressures for a presidential speech'.[87] The Doctrine was also criticized for being vague about what threats would spur a U.S. military intervention in the Gulf and at what level such a response would be provided. The absence of any reference to non-Soviet threats was seen as an important loophole. As a House Foreign Affairs Committee member, Stephen Solarz commented, the Carter Doctrine, by drawing the line against the Soviet threat, was 'stating the obvious, but the primary threat to our interest comes in by the way of internal subversion, political instability . . . the Carter doctrine is not really responsive to that threat'.[88]

The Carter administration rejected such accusations. The Doctrine, senior Carter officials held, was not the idle or empty commitment its critics alleged. Defense Secretary Brown, while admitting the problems involved in countering Soviet power in the Gulf, asserted: 'the United States has forces that can be moved into that area quickly. And I would urge that no one underestimate our capabilities.'[89] Carter later wrote that the Doctrine was a 'carefully considered statement, which would have been backed by concerted action' and to this end he was 'resolved to use the full power of the United States'.[90] In his memoirs, Brzezinski revealed that escalation options — both vertical (nuclear weapons) and horizontal (spreading the war to other theatres where the United States would have an advantage) — would have been considered if a Soviet conventional threat proved too overpowering.[91]

The administration pointed to all the measures being undertaken, or planned, that would substantially increase the capability of the RDF as a warfighting force. These improvements, the Pentagon contended, would make a Soviet invasion of the Gulf both costly and risky even if the RDF could not match the full weight of the offensive soldier for soldier or tank for tank. In his final report to Congress as Secretary of Defense, Brown outlined the administration's Persian Gulf military strategy:

the presence of significant combat forces (e.g. carrier battle groups and amphibious forces);

designated RDF combat forces with training, equipment, and doctrine suited to likely contingencies (e.g. mountain and desert warfare);

support forces tailored for Southwest Asia and structured

Gulf Crises and American Reassertion

for time-phased deployment;

mobility capabilities for both inter-theatre and intra-theatre movements;

overflight rights, as well as access to and improvement of enroute bases and facilities, in order to support large-scale airlift and sealift operations;

access to and improvement of regional airfields and ports to permit large-scale deployments in time of crisis;

pre-positioning of stocks at regional facilities or on maritime pre-positioning ships; and

secure land, air, and sea lines of communication by which to deploy and resupply our forces.[92]

Upon entering office the Reagan administration not only endorsed the Carter Doctrine, it also stated much more explicitly that the U.S. commitment to defend its Persian Gulf interests included possible military action against internally generated threats as well. It was also to devote more money and effort to boost the capability of the RDF.[93]

Notes

1. Bernard Reich, 'The United States and Iran: an overview', in U.S. Congress. Joint Economic Committee. *Economic consequences of the revolution in Iran* (1979): 10–14; Fereidun Fesharaki, 'Revolution and energy policy in Iran: international and domestic implications', in Hossein Amirsadeghi (ed.), *Security of the Persian Gulf* (London: Croom Helm, 1981): 259; Congressional Research Service, *Iran in crisis* (1979): 9–10.
2. *New York Times*, January 4, 1979: A1, A11.
3. Ibid.
4. *New York Times*, February 4, 1979: A16.
5. Reich, 'The United States and Iran', p. 16.
6. One of the most forceful critics was Henry Kissinger. See his interview with *The Economist*, February 10, 1979: 32.
7. James E. Akins, 'Saudi Arabia, Soviet activities, and Gulf security', in Z. Michael Szaz (ed.), *The impact of the Iranian events upon Persian Gulf and United States security* (Washington, D.C.: American Foreign Policy Institute, 1979): 105.
8. For information on the minority problem in Iran, see Nikki R. Keddie, 'The minorities question in Iran', in Shirin Tahir Kheli and S. Ayubi (eds), *The Iran–Iraq War* (New York: Praeger, 1983): 85–108.

Gulf Crises and American Reassertion

9. Prepared statement of Harold H. Saunders, Assistant Secretary of State for Near East and South Asia. U.S. Congress. House. Committee on Foreign Affairs. *U.S. interests in, and policies toward, the Persian Gulf* (1980): 11.

10. Congressional Research Service, *Iran: Executive and Congressional reactions and roles* (1981): 2–3.

11. *New York Times*, January 1, 1979: 3.

12. A major part of this concern related to Saudi Arabia. A classified CIA study, leaked to the press in January 1980, was reported to have warned the Carter administration that the Al-Saud regime's survival 'could not be assured beyond the next two years'. Intra-dynastic squabbles were cited as a major factor. For reference to this study, see Joe Stork, 'Saudi Arabia and the U.S.', *Merip Reports* (October 1980): 29.

13. Michael C. Hudson, *Arab politics. The search for legitimacy* (New Haven, CT: Yale University Press, 1977): 126. See also John Duke Anthony, *Arab states of the Lower Gulf: people, politics, petroleum* (Washington, D.C.: Middle East Institute, 1975). For an official U.S. perception, see *Department of State Bulletin* (October 1979): 44–50; U.S. Congress. House. Committee on Foreign Affairs. *U.S. security interests in the Persian Gulf. Report of a staff study mission* (1981): 9; *Department of State Bulletin* (October 1980): 5.

14. 'Islamic resurgence' (some scholars use the term Islamic 'revivalism' or 'reassertion') has been the subject of an extensive body of literature. For a historical treatment, see W. C. Smith, *Islam in modern History* (New York: Mentor Books, 1957); for contemporary interpretations, see Mohammed Ayoob (ed.), *Politics of Islamic reassertion* (London: Croom Helm, 1981); M. Kramer, *Political Islam, The Washington Papers*, no. 73 (Beverly Hills, CA: Sage Publications, 1980); Bassam Tibi, 'The renewed role of Islam in the political and social development of the Middle East', *Middle East Journal* (Winter 1983): 3–13; R. Hrair Dekmejian, 'The anatomy of Islamic revival: legitimacy crisis, ethnic conflict and the search for Islamic alternatives', *Middle East Journal* (Winter 1980): 1–2; David L. Price, 'Islam and the Arabian Peninsula', *RUSI anmd Brassey's Defence Yearbook 1981* (Oxford: Brassey's Publishers, 1980): 79–88; James A. Bill, 'Resurgent Islam in the Persian Gulf', *Foreign Affairs* (Fall 1984): 108–27.

15. *Islam and revolution, writings and declarations of Immam Khomeini*, translated and annotated by Hamid Algar (Berkeley, CA: Mizan Press, 1981): 286–94.

16. Jim Paul, 'Insurrection at Mecca', *Merip Reports* (October 1980): 3–4; A. Hottinger, 'Who held the Grand Mosque Hostage?' *New York Review of Books*, March 6, 1980: 35–36.

17. U.S. Congress. House. Committee on Foreign Affairs. *U.S. security interests in the Persian Gulf. Report of a staff study mission* (1981): 31; Michael M. J. Fischer, 'Competing ideologies and social structure in the Persian Gulf', in Alvin J. Cottrell (ed.), *The Persian Gulf States: a general survey* (Baltimore, MD: Johns Hopkins University Press, 1980): 521–6; Fred Halliday, *Arabia without sultans* (Harmondsworth: Penguin Books, 1975): 425–65; 'The Arabian Peninsula opposition movement', *Merip Reports* (February 1985): 13–15.

18. *The Times* (London), September 16, 1985: 14.

Gulf Crises and American Reassertion

19. Herman F. Eilts, 'Security considerations in the Persian Gulf', *International Security* (Fall 1980): 100–101; John K. Cooley, 'Iran, the Palestinians and the Gulf', *Foreign Affairs* (Summer 1979): 1017–34.

20. John Duke Anthony, 'The Persian Gulf in regional and international politics: the Arab side of the Gulf', in Hossein Amirsadeghi (ed.), *Security of the Persian Gulf* (London: Croom Helm, 1981): 173–4; 'The Gulf: survey', *The Economist*, December 13, 1980: 27. David L. Price, *Oil and Middle East security, The Washington Papers*, no. 41 (Beverly Hills, CA: Sage Publications, 1977): 15–22; Valerie Yorke, *The Gulf in the 80s* (London: The Royal Institute of International Affairs, 1980): 37; U.S. Congress. House. Committee on Foreign Affairs. *Saudi Arabia and the United States* (1981): 17–22.

21. For a historical account of the Iranian claim on Bahrain, see Hussein Al-Bahrana, *The legal status of Arabian Gulf States* (Manchester: University of Manchester Press, 1968): 167–95; Robert Litwak, *Security in the Persian Gulf: sources of inter-state conflict* (London: Gower Publishing House, 1981): 41–48.

22. For a history of the Iraqi–Kuwaiti dispute, see Al-Baharana, *The legal status*, pp. 250–8; Litwak, *Security in the Persian Gulf*, pp. 25–33; Will D. Swearingen, 'Sources of conflict over oil in the Persian Arabian Gulf', *The Middle East Journal* (Summer 1981): 323.

23. Daniel Pipes, 'A border adrift: origins of the conflict', in Tahir Kheli and Ayubi (eds), *The Iran–Iraq War*, pp. 12–21.

24. Zbigniew Brzezinski, *Power and principle: memoirs of the National Security Advisor, 1977–1981* (New York: Farrar Straus and Giroux, 1983): 356.

25. The Joint Chiefs of Staff, *United States military posture for fiscal year 1984*: 7.

26. Congressional Research Service, *U.S. –Soviet relations after Afghanistan* (1980): 3.

27. Richard Pipes, 'Soviet global strategy', *Commentary* (April 1980): 37.

28. 'Opposing views: how real is the Soviet threat?' A debate between George F. Kennan and Richard E. Pipes. *U.S. News and World Report*, March 10, 1980: 33. For other examples of this view, see Geoffrey Warhurst, 'Afghanistan — a dissenting appraisal', *RUSI* (September 1980); Raju G. C. Thomas, 'The Afghanistan crisis and South Asian security', *Journal of Strategic Studies* (December 1981): 415–34; Geoffrey Stern, 'The Soviet Union, Afghanistan and East–West Relations', *Millenium: Journal of International Studies* (Autumn 1980): 135–46.

29. Dennis Ross, 'Considering Soviet threats to the Persian Gulf', *International Security* (Fall 1981): 164.

30. Congressional Research Service, *Afghanistan: Soviet invasion and U.S. Response* (1982): 5.

31. According to recollections made by former Secretary of State Cyrus Vance, the factor of Islamic contamination was one of the 'two theories . . . advanced within the administration' on Soviet motives in Afghanistan (the other one was the 'opportunistic' view). *Hard choices: critical years in America's foreign policy* (New York: Simon & Schuster, 1983): 388.

32. Testimony by Joseph Sisco. U.S. Congress. House. Committee on

Gulf Crises and American Reassertion

Foreign Relations. *U.S. security interests and policies in Southwest Asia* (1980): 44.

33. According to Vance, this view had wide prevalence within the Carter administration as well. *Hard Choices*, p. 388.

34. Brzezinski, *Power and principle*, pp. 427, 567.

35. Vance, *Hard Choices*, pp. 388–9.

36. *Department of State Bulletin* (April 1980): 12.

37. *Department of State Bulletin* (January 1980): A (special section): *Department of State Bulletin* (February 1980): B (special section).

38. U.S. Congress. House. Committee on Foreign Affairs. *U.S. security interests in the Persian Gulf. Report of a staff study mission* (1981): 8.

39. Testimony, U.S. Congress. House. Committee on Foreign Affairs. *Foreign assistance legislation, fiscal year 1981*, Part 1: 202–203.

40. *Department of State Bulletin* (January 1980): A.

41. The CIA predictions are analyzed in a Rand Corporation study. See Ethan S. Burger, *Eastern Europe and oil: the Soviet dilemma*, P–6368 (Santa Monica, CA: Rand Corporation, October 1979): 6–7.

42. See for example, 'Oil seen spurring Soviet Mideast move', *Aviation Week and Space Technology*, October 1, 1979: 47; Dennis Ross, 'Considering Soviet threats', p. 169; Herbert Meyer, 'Why we should worry about the Soviet energy crunch', *Fortune*, February 25, 1980: 82–88.

43. U.S. Congress. Senate. Committee on Energy and Natural Resources. *Geopolitics of oil* (1980), Part 1: 92.

44. See, for example, Albert Wohlstetter, 'Meeting the threat in the Persian Gulf', *Survey* (Spring 1980): 138–9; Henry S. Rowen and John P. Weyant, 'Trade-offs between military policies and vulnerability policies', in James Blummer (ed.), *Energy vulnerability* (Cambridge, MA: Ballinger, 1982): 308.

45. U.S. Congress. House. Committee on Foreign Affairs. *U.S. security interests in the Persian Gulf. Report of a staff study mission* (1981): 85–86.

46. *Public papers of the Presidents of the United States, Jimmy Carter, 1980–1981*, Book I (Washington, D.C.: U.S. Government Printing Office, 1981): 184.

47. Jiri Valenta, 'From Prague to Kabul: the Soviet style of invasion', *International Security* (Fall 1980): 114–41; 'Soviet Afghanistan move keyed to airlift', *Aviation Week and Space Technology*, January 7, 1980: 15; Kenneth Allard, 'Soviet airborne forces and preemptive power projection', *Parameters* (December 1980): 42–51.

48. Department of Defense, *Annual report to Congress, FY1981*: 114.

49. Kevin B. Jordan, 'Naval diplomacy in the Persian Gulf', *U.S. Naval Institute Proceedings* (November 1981): 30–31.

50. U.S. Congress. House. Committee on Foreign Affairs. *U.S. interests in, and policies toward, the Persian Gulf* (1980): 26.

51. *New York Times*, February 13, 1979: A1.

52. *New York Times*, February 26, 1979: A12.

53. Testifying before the House Middle East Subcommittee, Col. John J. Ruszkiewicz, the then U.S. military attache in North Yemen, alleged that reports of the South Yemeni invasion had been blown out of proportion. U.S. Congress. House. Committee on Foreign Affairs. *U.S. interests in, and policies toward, the Persian Gulf* (1980): 103–18.

Gulf Crises and American Reassertion

54. Gary Sick, 'The evolution of U.S. strategy toward the Indian Ocean and Persian Gulf regions', in Alvin Z. Rubinstein (ed.), *The great game: rivalry in the Persian Gulf and South Asia* (New York: Praeger, 1983): 71.

55. Brzezinski, *Power and principle*, p. 447.

56. For details, see *New York Times*, June 28, 1979: A6; *Washington Post*, June 3, 1979: D2; *New York Times*, January 25, 1980: A6.

57. *New York Times*, March 1, 1979: A14; *New York Times*, March 9, 1979: A5.

58. Admiral Thomas H. Moorer and Alvin J. Cottrell, 'A permanent U.S. naval presence in the Indian Ocean', in Alvin J. Cottrell et al., *Sea power and strategy in the Indian Ocean* (Beverly Hills, CA: Sage 1981): 122; see also Norman L. Stone, 'An Indian Ocean fleet — the case and the cost', *U.S. Naval Institute Proceedings* (July 1981): 54–57.

59. L. Edgar Prina, 'The Fifth Fleet: a permanent U.S. Indian Ocean force?' *Sea Power* (April 1979): 28; U.S. Congress. House. Committee on Foreign Affairs. *U.S. interests in, and policies toward, the Persian Gulf* (1980): 413; James Canan, 'Brown advocates a new Mideast presence for the U.S.', *Business Week*, March 5, 1979:44.

60. U.S. Congress. House. Committee on Armed Services. *Hearings on military posture and H.R. 2970 (H.R. 3519), FY1982*, Part 3: 52.

61. Ibid.

62. Brzezinski, *Power and principle*, p. 177.

63. Ibid.

64. *A discussion of the Rapid Deployment Force with Lieutenant General P. X. Kelly* (Washington, D.C.: American Enterprise Institute for Public Policy Research, 1980): 3.

65. Quoted in the Joint Chiefs of Staff, *United States military posture for fiscal year 1982*, p. 55.

66. Jan Austin and Banning Garrett, 'Quick strike', *Inquiry*, July 24, 1978: 12–15; see also Louis Kraar, 'Yes, the Administration does have a defense policy (of sorts)', *Fortune*, June 19, 1978: 128–32.

67. Brzezinski, *Power and principle*, p. 177.

68. U.S. Congress. Senate. Committee on Armed Services. *Department of Defense authorization for appropriations for fiscal year 1981*, Part 1: 444.

69. Lt. General P. X. Kelly, 'Rapid deployment: a vital trump', *Parameters* (March 1981): 51.

70. Paul K. Davis, Director of Special Regional Studies and Acting Deputy Assistant Secretary of Defense (Regional Programs) between 1977 and 1981, reveals this in *Observations on the Rapid Deployment Joint Task Force: origins, direction, and mission*, P–6751 (Santa Monica, CA: Rand Corporation, 1982): 14.

71. Maxwell O. Johnson, *The military as an instrument of U.S. policy in Southwest Asia: the Rapid Deployment Joint Task Force, 1979–1982* (Boulder, CO: Westview Press, 1983): 61.

72. For details, see the *Washington Post*, June 22, 1979: A2; James B. Agnew, ' "Unilateral Corps": is the U.S. turning a new strategic corner?' *Army* (September 1979): 30–33.

73. Congressional Research Service, *Rapid Deployment Force (1985)*: 1.

74. *Los Angeles Times*, September 18, 1979: 9.

Gulf Crises and American Reassertion

75. *Washington Post*, December 6, 1979: A15.
76. *Public papers of the Presidents of the United States, Jimmy Carter, 1979*, Book II, p. 2235.
77. *Washington Post*, January 2, 1980: A14.
78. U.S. Congress. House. Committee on Appropriations. *Military construction appropriations for 1981*, Part 4, p. 526; see also *New York Times*, December 18, 1979: A10; *Washington Post*, January 4, 1980: A1; *New York Times*, January 5, 1980: A3; *New York Times*, January 10, 1980: A15; *New York Times*, January 11, 1980: 8.
79. *New York Times*, December 2, 1979: A1, A16.
80. Brzezinski, *Power and principle*, p. 446.
81. *Department of State Bulletin* (February 1980): B.
82. Cited in John M. Collins, *U.S. – Soviet military balance: concepts and capabilities, 1960 – 1980* (New York: McGraw-Hill, 1980): 374.
83. *Congressional Record*, January 30, 1980: S651 – S653.
84. *New York Times*, December 2, 1979: A16.
85. *Congressional Record*, February 1, 1980: S808 – S809.
86. U.S. Congress. Senate. Committee on Armed Services. *Department of Defense authorization for appropriations for fiscal year 1981*, Part 1: 38.
87. David D. Newsom, 'America engulfed', *Foreign Policy* (Summer 1981): 17.
88. U.S. Congress. House. Committee on Foreign Affairs. *U.S. interests in, and policies toward, the Persian Gulf* (1980): 166.
89. 'America's plans to meet Soviet challenges' (interview with Harold Brown), *U.S. News and World Report*, February 11, 1980: 33.
90. Jimmy Carter, *Keeping faith: memoirs of a President* (London: Collins, 1982): 483.
91. Brzezinski, *Power and principle*, p. 445.
92. Department of Defense, *Annual report to Congress, FY1982*: 191 – 2.
93. U.S. Congress. House. Committee on Foreign Affairs. *U.S. policy toward the Persian Gulf* (1982): 9 – 10; *The Age* (Melbourne), February 9, 1982: 8; *International Herald Tribune*, October 27, 1982: 3.

4

The Central Command

One of the most important characteristics of the U.S. military strategy in the Gulf developed under Carter and Reagan is its 'central reserve' approach to force projection. This approach is the alternative to 'forward deployment', which involves the peacetime stationing of large forces near potential trouble spots, prepared to intervene quickly in time of crisis. This approach, however, requires long-term access to foreign bases and commits forces to a single theatre, thereby reducing their flexibility. Since World War II, the 'forward deployment' approach had become steadily unattractive to the Pentagon due to increased U.S. security commitments worldwide and the growing uncertainties and political difficulties associated with foreign bases. In contrast, the 'central reserve' approach, which relies primarily upon a reservoir of forces stationed in the continental United States that could be deployed to an overseas theatre at the first hints of trouble, has appeared to be a more practical and flexible way of force projection.

One of the first major American strategists to recognize the merits of this approach was Robert McNamara. While serving as Defense Secretary under the Kennedy and Johnson administrations, McNamara observed:

A mobile 'fire brigade' reserve, centrally located in the United States and ready for deployment to a threatened spot anywhere in the world is basically a more economic and flexible use of military forces. Fewer men and less equipment can do the job and most of the problems involved in stationing large U.S. forces in foreign countries in peacetime could be avoided.[1]

The Central Command

During McNamara's term, the Pentagon developed a rapid deployment strategy based upon the 'central reserve' approach. It created the U.S. Strike Command, under which were assigned eight Army divisions and more than forty squadrons of reconnaissance, fighter, troop carrier, and tanker aircraft. The command's area of responsibility encompassed the Middle East, Africa south of the Sahara, and South Asia. It was headquartered at MacDill Air Force Base, Florida.[2] To facilitate the deployment of the Strike Command's forces in crisis time, the Kennedy administration increased U.S. airlift capability by 75 per cent, mainly by developing a new intercontinental transport plane, the C-5.[3] It also initiated a program to develop a fleet of 'fast deployment logistics' (FDL) ships. These ships were to have been stationed either at U.S. ports or near overseas bases with loads of combat equipment and supplies, which would have been used by troops flown in from the U.S. to intervene in a crisis anywhere in the globe. But the Vietnam War and the resultant anti-interventionist mood of the Congress killed the FDL project,[4] and the Strike Command was disbanded in 1971.

The Strike Command was a clear forerunner of the organizations created by the Carter and Reagan administrations for the planning and execution of contingency operations in the Persian Gulf/Southwest Asia region. Like its predecessor, the new organization, first a joint task force later upgraded to a unified Command, relies primarily on forces stationed in the continental United States. Its task

> is to provide a capability for deploying force packages, of varying size and structure. . . . This is neither a separate nor discrete category of forces of fixed size; i.e., 50,000 or 100,000 man force. Rather, the concept calls for a central 'reservoir', composed primarily of CONUS-based units from which forces can be drawn to cope with a specific contingency. Obviously, the size and composition of the force selected will depend on what is determined to be our mission. Forces could be developed capable of responding to situations ranging from minimum application of force to mid-intensity combat. One could draw a building block analogy. Phased deployments initiated with small show-the-flag forces could be built upon by other larger forces with significantly greater capabilities.[5]

The Central Command

From **RDJTF** to **CENTCOM**

In March 1980 the Carter administration activated the Rapid Deployment Joint Task Force (RDJTF) with overall responsibility to 'plan, jointly train, exercise and be prepared to deploy and employ designated forces in response to contingencies threatening U.S. vital interests'.[6] Although RDJTF theoretically had a worldwide mission, the Secretary of Defense soon clarified that it would 'focus exclusively on Southwest Asia contingencies'.[7]

A joint task force (JTF), according to its official definition, is a

> joint force composed of assigned or attached elements of the Army, the Navy (Marine Corps), and the Air Force, or any two of these Services, which is constituted and so designated by the Joint Chiefs of Staff, by the commanders of a unified command, or by the commander of an existing joint task force.

Unlike a unified command, which has a 'broad continuing mission', and 'which is composed of significant assigned components [component commands] of two or more services', a JTF is by definition a temporary arrangement. 'It is established when the mission to be accomplished has a specific limited objective.' Several JTFs have been established in the past with missions ranging from facilitating service participation in atomic testing to planning military operations in Africa and the Caribbean.[8]

The RDJTF was set up in an old Strategic Air Command alert bunker at MacDill Air Force Base, Florida (see Table 4.1). Also housed at MacDill was the U.S. Readiness Command, under whose operational command the RDJTF remained in all its peacetime planning, exercise, and predeployment phases in the continental United States. Upon deployment to a crisis theatre, however, the RDJTF commander had to report either directly to the National Command Authorities through the Joint Chiefs of Staff as designated by the Pentagon authorities.[9] The RDJTF headquarters functioned with a permanent staff of 261 military personnel. Like its force structure, this staff had a multi-service composition. Upon deployment and employment, the RDJTF headquarters staff could be augmented with personnel, including support elements, from the U.S. Readiness Command and other designated forces. An important feature of the RDJTF command organization was a four-service, nineteen-man Washington

The Central Command

Table 4.1: Evolution of the RDF Command Organization

1 March 1980	Activation of Headquarters, Rapid Deployment Joint Task Force, at MacDill Air Force Base, Tampa, Florida. Commander: Lt. Gen. P. X. Kelly, USMC. Mission: 'to plan, jointly train, exercise, and be prepared to deploy and employ designated forces in response to contingencies threatening U.S. vital interests'. Regional 'focus' — Southwest Asia.
24 April 1981	Secretary Weinberger announces that the RDJTF will transition into United Command status.
1 June 1981	Three component headquarters are designated and placed under the operational control of the Hq. RDJTF. These are:
	Rapid Deployment Army Forces (RDARFOR) Hq.: Headquarters XVIII Airborne Corps, Fort Bragg, N. Carolina. Under its operational control are the 82nd Airborne Division and the 101st Airborne Division (Air Assault).
	Rapid Deployment Air Forces (RDAFFOR) Hq.: Co-located with the 9th Air Force at Shaw Air Force Base, South Carolina.
	Rapid Deployment Naval Forces (RDNAVFOR) Hq.: Co-located with Hq. U.S. Pacific Command, Pearl Harbour, Hawaii.
17 July 1981	Lt. Gen. Robert C. Kingston U.S. Army, Commander-in-Chief, 2nd Infantry Division, South Korea, replaces Lt. Gen. P. X. Kelly as Commander RDJTF. Kelly is promoted to the rank of General and made Assistant Commander of the Marine Corps.
20 August 1981	Eleven tactical fighter squadrons are designated as RDF units and placed under the operational control of RDAFFOR.
1 October 1981	RDJTF moves out of its subordination to the Readiness Command and is made into a separate JTF reporting directly to the NCA through the JCS. It is asked to 'focus primarily' on Southwest Asia, though it had a capability to conduct operations worldwide.
1 January 1983	U.S. Central Command, 'the first geographic unified command created in over 35 years', replaces the RDJTF at MacDill AFB, with Gen. Kingston as its first CINC. The CENTCOM has geographic responsibility over nineteen countries in the SW Asia region and is responsible for all U.S. defence-related activities in its area of responsibility.
1 October 1983	CENTCOM assumes responsibility for administering U.S. security assistance to the countries in its area of responsibility.

The Central Command

Table 4.1 — *continued*

1 December 1983	A Forward Headquarters Element (FHE) is established by the CENTCOM aboard the USS LaSalle, the flagship of the U.S. Middle East Force stationed off Bahrain Island in the Persian Gulf.

Source: U.S. Congress. House. Committee on Appropriations. *Department of Defense appropriations for 1983*. Part 6: 14–15; Hq. Rapid Deployment Joint Task Force, *Fact Sheet* (1981); United States Central Command, *Fact Sheet* (1983); Department of Defense, *Annual Report to Congress, FY1984* (1983); Department of Defense, *Annual Report to Congress, FY1984)* (1983); Congressional Research Service, *Rapid Deployment Force* (1985).

Liaison Office, headed by an Army Brigadier General. Located in the Pentagon, the Liaison Office provided the RDJTF with the essential contact with the Joint Chiefs of Staff, the individual service headquarters, and other Washington bureaucratic agencies and the Congress.[10]

But despite assurances from its commander that the RDJTF was capable of providing the necessary command and control for U.S. forces deployed to the Persian Gulf, the organization attracted widespread criticism. The RDJTF had no peacetime operational control over its assigned forces. The latter remained under the day-to-day control of their original commands, subject to call-up by the RDJTF for exercise or deployment purposes. The overall lines of command were complicated, especially to critics who found that confused command lines were a major factor behind the disastrous failure of the Iranian hostage rescue mission in 1980. This problem was aggravated by an inter-service rivalry over the RDJTF.[11] Furthermore, the RDJTF was devoid of any specific geographic responsibility. The geographic responsibility for the Gulf/Southwest Asia region was awkwardly distributed between the U.S. European Command and the U.S. Pacific Command. While the former 'controlled' all land west of Afghanistan, plus the Red Sea and the Persian Gulf, the latter had responsibility for the Indian Ocean and the land east of the Iran–Afghanistan border, including Afghanistan and Pakistan. Pentagon officials acknowledged that the existing division was arbitrary.[12]

Responding to these criticisms, the Reagan administration in April 1983 announced that the RDJTF would be upgraded to a separate Unified Command. The new command, named the U.S. Central Command (CENTCOM), was activated at MacDill on

67

The Central Command

Map 4.1: CENTCOM Area of Responsibility

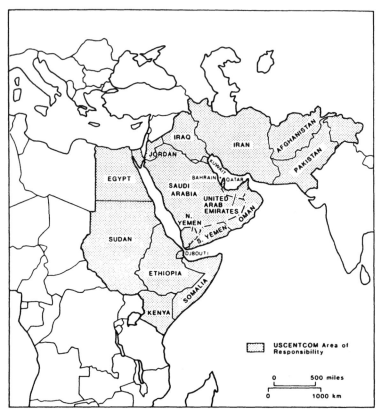

Source: Adapted from USCENTCOM Map in U.S. Congress. Senate. Committee on Armed Services. *Department of Defense authorization for appropriations for fiscal year 1985*, Part 2 (Washington, D.C.: U.S. Government Printing Office, 1984).

The Central Command

1 January 1983, with a staff of nearly 1,000 personnel, drawn from all the services.[13] The new command differed from its predecessor in several respects. As a Unified Command, the U.S. Central Command's mission encompassed a much broader range of activities and responsibilities than those of the RDJTF. Unlike the RDJTF, the CENTCOM was assigned 'its own geographic responsibilities, service components, forces, intelligence, communications, logistic facilities and other support elements'.[14] Nineteen countries were placed under the CENTCOM's area of responsibility (AOR). Notable omissions from the AOR were Israel (excluded perhaps on political grounds) and the Indian Ocean, which continued to be under the jurisdiction of the U.S. Pacific Command (see Map 4.1). Although CENTCOM officials saw no problem in coordinating their mission with PACOM, the new arrangement, which continues today, left some room for criticism that the complications in the RDJTF command structure were not fully remedied.

Unlike the RDJTF, the CENTCOM is responsible for the entire range of U.S. military activity within its assigned area. This includes contingency planning: assessment of threats and designing of 'force packages' tailored from its assigned 'reservoir' of Army, Navy, Air Force, and Marine components to meet a particular threat. Other activities consist of joint exercises involving U.S. and regional forces, administration of U.S. security assistance and operational command of U.S. forces in the theatre.[15] In 1985 the theatre forces under the CENTCOM's operational control included the U.S. MIDEASTFOR, the American element of the Sinai Multinational Force and Observers, and the AWACS deployed in Saudi Arabia.[16] As for those CENTCOM units not deployed in its AOR (i.e. the CONUS-based units), these remained under the peacetime operational control of their apparent services. The CENTCOM, however, could assume their crisis-time availability 'on a priority basis' for its planning, and it could exercise operational command of those units participating in its exercise program.[17]

While the Pentagon was in the process of deciding the final shape of the Persian Gulf command, some strategic analysts and members of Congress argued that the multi-service command structure for the rapid deployment forces should be abolished and a single service, the Marine Corps, should be designated to take over the primary responsibility for the rapid deployment mission. Such a move, they held, would be consistent with the Corps'

The Central Command

longstanding history as the nation's 'force in readiness', and its record of successful interventions in Third World regions. In addition, the Marines' unique amphibious capabilities could off-set, to some extent, the CENTCOM's lack of confirmed contingency access to regional ports and airfields. Furthermore, by assigning the Marines the primary responsibility for the rapid deployment mission, the Pentagon could remove much of the confusion and inter-service rivalry that was inevitable in a multi-service command organization.[18]

But these arguments were rejected by the Pentagon, on the ground that a single-service force would limit the flexibility in employing U.S. forces in the Persian Gulf. Since contingencies in the Gulf could be varied, multi-dimensional and complex, none of the services could be expected to possess the capability to accomplish the CENTCOM mission unilaterally. The Marines would not be very effective in fighting the enemy beyond the first 50 miles of any beach-head. A multi-service force and command structure, the CENTCOM authorities argued, was necessary to counter the 'worst-case' scenario — a massive and all-out Soviet invasion of Iran — which was the central basis of the CENTCOM's operational planning. The Marines, however important their role might be in such joint operations, could by themselves provide neither the force size nor the capabilities essential to conduct any credible defensive operations against the Soviet forces.[19]

Force structure

Apart from the issue of command organization, the major task facing the Pentagon in the Persian Gulf was deciding the size and composition of the RDJTF/CENTCOM's force structure and providing these forces with adequate logistics support and training. Table 4.2 gives the recent force structure list of the CENTCOM. The size of this force structure has grown steadily since the RDJTF was activated with a total of about 100,000 troops, with an approximately equal number of support personnel. In 1983, however, the number of military personnel assigned to the RDJTF/CENTCOM had reached more than 220,000. Later, the Pentagon announced a plan to double this force structure by 1989.[20] An important aspect of this expansion was that none of the units were newly created. Rather, they were earmarked for the

The Central Command

Table 4.2: U.S. Central Command Force Structure

U.S. Central Command Headquarters, MacDill Air Force Base, Tampa, Florida

Army Component (USARCENT), Hq.: Third U.S. Army, Ft McPherson, Georgia
1 Corps Headquarters; 1 Airborne Division; 1 Air Assault Division; 1 Mechanized Infantry Division; 1 Light Infantry Division; 1 Mechanized Brigade; 1 Cavalry Brigade (Air Combat)

Air Force Component (USCENTAF), Hq.: 9th Air Force, Shaw Air Force Base, South Carolina
7 Tactical Flight Wings; 2 Strategic Bomber Squadrons; Electronic Combat Squadrons; Tactical Reconnaissance Squadrons; Tactical Air Command and Control Squadrons; Tactical Airlift Squadrons

Navy Component (USNAVCENT), Hq.: Pearl Harbor, Hawaii
3 Carrier Battle Groups; 1 Surface Action Group; 3 Amphibious Groups; 5 Maritime Patrol Squadrons; U.S. Middle East Force

Marine Corps Component (USMARCENT), Hq.: Camp Pendleton, California
1 Marine Amphibious Force; 1 Marine Amphibious Brigade

Special Operations Component (SOCCENT), Hq.: MacDill Air Force Base, Tampa, Florida
1 Special Forces Group; 1 Air Force Special Operations Wing; 1 Navy Special Warfare Task Group

---

Source: *Fact Sheet* (Headquarters, U.S. Central Command, March 1983); *Statement of General George B. Crist, Commander-in-Chief, U.S. Central Command, before the Defense Policy Panel of the House Armed Services Committee*, March 17, 1987; U.S. Congress. Senate. Committee on Armed Services. *Department of Defense authorization for appropriations for FY1986*, Part 3, Hearings February 17 – March 1, 1985.

RDJTF/CENTCOM from the existing force structure of the services, in most cases without giving up their original missions.

Despite fears concerning the possibility of inter-service rivalry, the multi-service composition of the RDJTF/CENTCOM was hailed by the Pentagon officials as an impressive breakthrough. As General Kelly noted, 'it is the first time in the history of our country that we have amalgamated the combat capabilities of all four services under one headquarters in peacetime'.[21] A high degree of versatility and flexibility in the force's structure, he stated, would be necessary if the RDJTF was able to deal with threats across the spectrum of conflict, from domestic conflicts to a Soviet attack.

The Army units selected to the RDJTF/CENTCOM force structure featured both light and heavy divisions. There were initially three divisions, including the 24th Infantry (Mechanized),

71

The Central Command

the 82nd Airborne and the 101st Airborne (Air Assault). A light division was later added to the CENTCOM force structure. The 82nd Airborne, one of the U.S. Army's lightest divisions, has a brigade of about 4,000 troops, which can be sent to a contingency area within 24 hours of an alert.[22] The 101st Air Assault Division, also a light force with a large contingent of attack and utility helicopters, was selected because of its high tactical mobility. The division could be almost entirely transported within a combat theatre by helicopters — a fact which the Pentagon hoped could make it very effective in road-barren areas such as the Middle East/Persian Gulf region.[23]

The Marine Corps was assigned a leading role in the RDJTF/CENTCOM force structure. The Corps contributed two major units. The first was a Marine Amphibious Force (MAF), 'a roughly 50,000-man self-sustained, integrated air-ground team, which is fully capable of forcible entry over hostile shores'.[24] The second, the 7th Marine Amphibious Brigade (MAB), was activated in May 1980 from existing West coast-based units and headquarters at Twenty-Nine Palms, California. This brigade, which originally consisted of 11,000 marines, but later grew to 16,500, was unique in the sense that it would not go into combat by the traditional method of amphibious assault. Instead, it would be airlifted to a 'benign' port area (either in friendly territory or territory seized through airborne and amphibious assault) near the combat theatre, where its troops would 'marry up' with supplies and equipment brought in from Diego Garcia aboard the maritime pre-positioning ships. This method, while depriving the 7th MAB of forcible entry capabilities, none the less made it a more rapidly responsive unit than the normal amphibious forces.[25]

The critical role of airpower in contingency operations in the Gulf was recognized in the RDJTF/CENTCOM's force planning. Apart from being the most rapidly deployable element in the RDJTF/CENTCOM force structure, airpower and local air superiority would be crucial to the ability of early arriving U.S. forces to seize and defend key entry points to permit the later arrival of heavy forces and supplies. In addition, airpower would be necessary to disrupt enemy airborne insertions, and interdict an enemy ground offensive.[26] USAF contribution to the RDJTF/CENTCOM included aircraft for all essential missions, including F-15s and F-4Es for air superiority/defence, F-111Ds and B-52Hs for long-range conventional interdiction, A-10s and A-7s for ground attack and close air support, EC-130s and F-4Gs for

72

The Central Command

electronic warfare, RF-4Cs for reconnaissance, and E-3As for airborne command and control.[27] These would be complemented by carrier-based aircraft (A-6, A-7, F-4, F-14, FA-18, E-2), drawn from three carrier battle groups that were assigned for contingency missions in the Gulf.

An important element of the Air Force units assigned to the RDJTF/CENTCOM was the Strategic Projection Force (SPF), organized by the Strategic Air Command (SAC) at Minot Air Force Base, North Dakota (57th Air Division). Consisting of 28 B-52H bombers modified to carry conventional armament, as well as contingents of KC-135s, RC-135s, U-2s, EC-135s, and SR-71s, the SPF was designed to support the RDJTF/CENTCOM with a package of deep interdiction, intelligence, command, control, and communication and reconnaissance capabilities. With a low-altitude penetration capability and a long unrefuelled range which would enable it to stage further from the hostile fighter threat area, the B-52H bombers were slated to carry out interdiction missions 'within 48 hours' of mobilization against invading enemy forces.[28]

The versatility of the RDJTF/CENTCOM's 'reservoir' of combat units did not, however, fully compensate for some serious problems and deficiencies in their warfighting potential. To the Pentagon planners, the challenge of building a credible force projection capability for Persian Gulf contingencies was formidable. The problem, first and foremost, was a function of distance. The Gulf is 7,450 miles from the U.S. East coast and 8,150 miles from the West coast by the shortest air routes. By sea, the Strait of Hormuz is 8,250 miles from Charleston, Virginia, through the Suez Canal; 11,500 miles around Africa if the canal is closed (a reasonable assumption in the event of a U.S.–Soviet conflict); and 11,477 miles from San Diego on the West coast.

But long logistics lines were only part of the problem. Once in theatre, U.S. forces would have to operate in a natural and operational setting that is as unique as it is problematic. The region is noted for its harsh and extremely varied climatic conditions: from sub-zero temperatures in the Iranian mountains to very hot and dry conditions in the deserts. The difficulties with the operational environment could be best illustrated by comparing the theatre conditions in the Gulf with those in Europe. As General Kelly testified before the Senate Armed Services Committee:

There are sizeable U.S. forces in place in Western Europe —

The Central Command

with the exception of naval forces in the Indian Ocean we have none in Southwest Asia.

There are sizeable amounts of pre-positioned supplies and equipment in Western Europe for reinforcing units — we have none in Southwest Asia.

There is an in-place command and control system in Western Europe — we have none in Southwest Asia.

There is an extensive in-place logistics infrastructure in Western Europe — we have none in Southwest Asia.

There are extensive host-nation support agreements between the United States and Western Europe countries — we have none in Southwest Asia.

There is an alliance of military allies in Western Europe — there is no such alliance in Southwest Asia.[29]

The decision to build a rapid deployment force from existing service units, without creating any new forces, raised the possibility of a serious problem of resource allocation in the event of simultaneous crises in multiple theatres. Several constituent units of the RDJTF/CENTCOM, such as the Army's 82nd, 101st, and 24th divisions, several tactical air wings, and the naval and marine forces, had already been earmarked for use, either in a primary or reinforcing role, in NATO and other strategic theatres in time of crisis. In March 1983 the staff of the House Appropriations Committee, in a report on the readiness of the U.S. military, claimed that there was a 'general consensus within the Army' that it did not 'have the capability (resources) to support' operations in more than one theatre at a time.[30] America's NATO allies had already expressed their concern over the impact of the RDF on the U.S. ability to reinforce NATO during a simultaneous crisis in Europe and the Gulf. In 1982 the then West German Defence Minister, Hans Apel, noted that

the political and material implications of the Rapid Deployment Force as conceived by the United States . . . [are] closely meshed with the plans which the Alliance has adopted to assure its deterrence and defense capability within the NATO area. One need only think of the possible use of supply depots in Western Europe in support of missions of the Rapid Deployment Force. Such activities must not jeopardise

The Central Command

the balance of forces in Europe. . . . The global commitment of the United States and regional stability in Central Europe must be harmonized with each other.[31]

But harmonizing the U.S. commitment to NATO with its relatively new Persian Gulf commitment proved to be difficult. NATO's efforts to cope with the problem of a possible diversion of U.S. resources to the Gulf were undertaken within the framework of a 'division of labour'. According to this approach, those European NATO allies unwilling or incapable of contributing to military operations in the Gulf were required to 'increase their contribution to NATO in the European area to take up the slack caused by the potential diversion of U.S. forces to SWA [Southwest Asia]'.[32] Meeting in December 1980, NATO defence ministers worked out a package of measures (called Post-Afghanistan Measures, Phase II) to 'help fill the gap in European defense if U.S. NATO-allocated forces were diverted elsewhere . . .'. These included steps to enhance allied capabilities in areas such as readiness, reserve mobilization, airlift, maritime defence, and host nation support.[33]

Later NATO achieved some progress in implementing these measures. In the key area of strategic lift, the European allies agreed to provide 600 commercial ships and 49 long-range cargo aircraft to augment U.S. strategic mobility resources for wartime reinforcement of Europe. This would release additional U.S. lift assets for a Persian Gulf contingency. The United States also concluded new host nation support agreements with a number of NATO countries, including West Germany, Belgium, and the Netherlands. These agreements provided for additional wartime support to forward deployed or reinforcing U.S. forces by the European host nation in areas such as logistics, transport, security, material-handling, and casualty evacuation. NATO members such as West Germany and Italy agreed to make compensatory naval deployments in their adjacent seas to lessen the impact of diversions of U.S. naval units to the Indian Ocean.[34]

But there were continuing concerns that U.S. and allied response to a Persian Gulf contingency would leave dangerous gaps in the defence of Europe itself. In his 1982 *Report on Allied Contributions to the Common Defense*, U.S. Defense Secretary Caspar Weinberger noted that 'even when fully implemented, the [post-Afghanistan] measures will only partially compensate for potential weaknesses in Alliance defenses should forces currently committed

The Central Command

to NATO by the U.S. and possibly other allies be deployed to a contingency in SWA [Southwest Asia]'.[35] In addition, the post-Afghanistan measures did almost nothing to alleviate the problem of reduced availability of U.S. *combat manpower* to reinforce NATO in the event of a simultaneous crisis in the Gulf. The dimensions of this problem were highlighted in a report by the Congressional Budget Office in 1983. The report estimated that commitment of the existing CENTCOM forces (about 222,000 troops) to a Persian Gulf contingency would decrease by 20 per cent the number of combat divisions available for a simultaneous NATO reinforcement during the first 60 days of a conflict. This in turn would reduce the NATO–Warsaw Pact force ratio by 6 per cent against NATO, from 1:1.7 to 1:1.8. To offset such shortfalls, the report found, the United States would need to create two fully supported combat divisions at a 5-year cost of about \$18.9 billion. The shortfalls will increase when the current CENTCOM force structure is further expanded.[36]

Even if all the combat units earmarked for the RDJTF/ CENTCOM were made available for operations in the Persian Gulf, there was concern that the U.S. ability to outfight its opponents in high-intensity combat in the region would be questionable due to deficient armour, firepower, and battlefield mobility. The early arriving U.S. forces, such as the 82nd Airborne and the Marines, are light, footmobile infantry possessing very little firepower. In contrast, potential Middle Eastern opponents of the United States, such as Iran, the Soviet Union, or Syria, would field significant numbers of tanks and artillery units. While the utility of tanks and armoured vehicles might be restricted in mountainous terrain or in jungles and cities, the tactical mobility and firepower afforded by them would be indispensable assets in flat, open, and spacious environments such as deserts. And U.S. military planners were aware that the crucial final battles for the control of Middle Eastern oil fields would most likely be staged in such terrain.

These problems were to some extent addressed by the Carter and Reagan administrations. A program to modernize the firepower systems of the RDJTF/CENTCOM Army and Marine units was initiated. The ground mobility and firepower of the marine infantry forces were enhanced with the introduction of light armoured vehicles (LAV).[37] The Army's efforts to introduce a similar vehicle for its airborne and light forces was, however, plagued by delays and later abandoned. But the Army took a

The Central Command

major step to enhance the anti-armour capabilities of its rapidly deployable forces by fielding a high-technology motorized division (HTMD). The HTMD was 'oriented on mid-intensity conflict theatres, open terrain, and a heavily armoured threat',[38] which would make it suitable for a Middle East mission. The Army's 9th Infantry Division, based in Washington state, was transformed into a HTMD. The HTMD concept sought to combine the strategic mobility and sustainability of a light division with the tactical mobility, firepower, and survivability of a heavy division, by incorporating new technology, organization, equipment, and training. The 14,500-strong division would be transported by the C-141 aircraft rather than the C-5, and would require about 1,400 C-141B sorties as compared with the more than 1,500 sorties for a standard infantry division. It would fight under the Army's new firepower-intensive Air Land Battle doctrine.[39]

The logistics problems facing the RDJTF/CENTCOM planners lay in meeting the water, medical, communications, and intelligence support requirements of combat troops in the Gulf. In the arid environment that characterizes much of the Gulf region, water could be a decisive factor in the outcome of a combat situation. A Pentagon study found that 'a 50,000 man Marine Amphibious Force would require at least 750,000 gallons of fresh water daily'.[40] The requirement of medical facilities would be greater than normal due to harsh climatic conditions, extreme variations in temperature and a scarcity of fresh water supplies. Moreover, secret DOD studies established that the early arriving units could be expected to receive very high rates of combat casualties in encounters with Soviet forces.[41]

The Persian Gulf, unlike more 'mature' theatres such as Europe or Korea, has little established communications infrastructure that the RDJTF/CENTCOM could use. U.S. forces must carry their required communications equipment from the United States. This also meant that there would be little backup equipment. The distances over which U.S. forces in the Gulf would have to communicate are considerably larger than those in Europe; the varying climatic conditions would necessitate extra care with delicate electronic equipment.[42] In addition to communications, intelligence support to the CENTCOM was a problem.[43] An investigation into the problem by *New York Times* columnist Richard Halloran revealed that the RDJTF/CENTCOM had 'no network of listening posts to intercept radio and telephone transmissions', no 'places to put sensors that can find, through radar or

The Central Command

infrared detection, movements of tanks, missiles and aircraft', and no 'agents to gather information that satellite photos are unable to pick up'.[44]

U.S. forces' lack of experience of the natural environment in Southwest Asia presented another problem. Much of the equipment carried by U.S. forces, and the tactical doctrines for the employment of combat forces, were considered unsuitable for desert combat. Moreover, several of the Force's operational concepts such as the 'match up' process for the 7th MAB, and command and control systems, to cite a few examples, involved extremely complex procedures. In addition, despite the increased spending on readiness by the Reagan administration, congressional investigations revealed that the Army combat units assigned to the CENTCOM had 'all indicated serious readiness problems'.[45]

To test and enhance its forces' ability to operate in the natural and operational conditions in the Gulf, the RDFTF/CENTCOM devised a broad-based and intensive program of exercises (see Table 4.3). These exercises enabled the practice of joint operations of combat units, familiarization of U.S. forces with the environment in which they could be called upon to fight, testing and improvement of command and control procedures, and interface

Table 4.3: Selected CENTCOM exercises, 1980–85

Exercise	Frequency	Location	Description/Size[b]
Gallant Knight	Annual	Fort Bragg, NC	CPX/Corps
Bright Star or Gallant Eagle	Annual[a]	SWA Region or United States	FTX/Brigade or FTX/Division
Communications exercise	Annual[a]	Varies	COMMEX
Rapid deployment readiness exercise	Varies	United States	Alert exercise deploying headquarters for RDJTF/CENTCOM
Bold Eagle	Biennial	United States	CPX; FTX
Bold Star	Biennial	United States	CPX; FTX

Source: U.S. Department of Defense, *Annual Report to Congress*, FY1984: 205.

[a]The Pentagon planning called for conducting at least one exercise (either Bright Star or a communications exercise) in the SWA region each year. In years when Bright Star was not held, a division-sized Gallant Eagle exercise was held in the continental United States.

[b]CPX, Command post exercise; FTX, Field training exercise; COMMEX, Communications exercise.

The Central Command

between RDJTF/CENTCOM forces and the military personnel of the host nation.[46]

The most significant and visible U.S. exercises in the Middle East region were those of the Bright Star series. These exercises provided useful tests of U.S. airlift and sealift capabilities and gave RDJTF/CENTCOM units valuable experience of the regional environment. In addition to deployments by the army airborne and infantry units, the Bright Star exercises featured Marine amphibious landings, air defence manoeuvres, logistics training, and unconventional warfare operations by Army Green Berets and Rangers. The extensive range of experience gained from such regional exercises was complemented by those conducted in the continental United States. Among the most important in this category were the Command Post exercises of the Gallant Knight series, the first one of which, held in October 1980, simulated a successful RDJTF defence of Iran against a Soviet invasion; and the field training exercises of the Gallant Eagle series, which provided some of the largest and most comprehensive tests of the CENTCOM in desert conditions.[47]

Strategic mobility programs

Strategic mobility is the very essence of power projection. All three legs of the mobility triad — airlift, sealift, and pre-positioning — have special strengths and roles, and should be viewed as complementing rather than substituting for each other. Airlift offers the fastest and most flexible means of deploying forces over long distances. Typically, airlift would deliver over 90 per cent of U.S. combat forces during the first weeks of a conflict. On the other hand, airlift is expensive and limited in the tonnage it can carry. Sealift, while not rapid, is crucial to sustaining and reinforcing the initial forces. Sealift moves most of the heavy and bulky equipment; in an extended crisis sealift would carry more than 90 per cent of the total tonnage delivered to an overseas theatre. Pre-positioning satisfies the requirements of both timeliness and adequacy in the movement of combat equipment and supplies. It is a highly cost-effective means of delivering tonnage to a pre-identified, single theatre, although for the same reason it is less flexible.

Although U.S. strategic mobility resources were acknowledged to be the world's best in terms of both size and sophistication,

The Central Command

meeting the mobility burdens of the Carter Doctrine required a substantial enhancement of its existing capacity. The requirements were identified by a congressionally mandated mobility study (CMMS) in 1981. The CMMS evaluated requirements for four scenarios: (1) a Soviet-backed Persian Gulf State attacking Saudi oil fields; (2) a Soviet invasion of Iran; (3) a NATO/Warsaw Pact conflict; and (4) a simultaneous conflict in Europe and the Gulf. The study found significant gaps between requirements and existing capability in all the scenarios, especially in the area of airlift. It established the following requirements in each leg of the mobility triad: 66 million ton-miles per day (MTM/D) of strategic airlift capability; 100,000 tons of additional roll on/roll off (RO/RO) shipping; maritime pre-positioning ships for three Marine brigade-sized air-ground task forces; and pre-positioning of 130,000 tons of ammunition and resupply in Southwest Asia.[48]

Improving airlift support for RDJTF/CENTCOM in the Gulf posed a special challenge due to distance, demanding enroute support requirements, and the poor quality of regional airfields. Flying to the Gulf from the U.S. East Coast, strategic airlifters would need to be refuelled twice each time on the enroute and return legs of a round trip. Keeping in mind estimates that it took over 6 tons of fuel to deliver 1 ton of cargo to Israel during the 1973 October War airlift, enormous quantities of aviation fuel at enroute and theatre airfields would be essential to support large-scale airlift missions to the Gulf. If local states proved unwilling to cooperate, this fuel would have to be carried from the United States. And the bare conditions of most of the regional airfields would limit their use by most type of transport aircraft — especially the civilian cargo planes which could be requisitioned for military service during a major contingency.[49]

The Pentagon's efforts to improve airlift support for the RDJTF/CENTCOM took two forms. The first was an effort to enhance the capabilities of the existing inventory. Programs undertaken as part of this effort included the rewinging of the C-5 Galaxy strategic transport to give it an additional service life of 30,000 flying hours, which would keep the fleet operational into the twenty-first century.[50] Another program was to stretch the C-141 Starlifter to increase its payload capacity by one-third and to give it an air-refuelling capability.[51] In addition to these, the Pentagon contracted 21 wide-bodied passenger aircraft under its Civil Reserve Air Fleet (CRAF) enhancement program. Under this program, the aircraft would be modified, at U.S. government

The Central Command

expense, for possible military use by adding cargo-carrying features such as stronger floors and wider doors.[52] The second part of the Pentagon's efforts to increase airlift capability involved procurement of new transport aircraft. The major components of this program included acquisition of 50 C-5B aircraft (a modified and improved version of the C-5A) and 44 KC-10 advanced tanker/cargo aircraft. The KC-10 is a modified version of the DC-10 with both tanker and cargo capability. With its longer range and fuel-carrying capability, it would substantially facilitate airlift operations into the Gulf region by reducing the number of tankers needed and alleviating enroute support requirements.[53] But even with these additions, the total U.S. airlift capability fell well short of the CMMS goal of 66 MTM/D. And the 66 MTM/D target itself would not have met the requirements of any of the four scenarios examined in the CMMS; the least demanding one required an 83 MTM/D capability.[54] To meet the shortfall, the Pentagon proposed to build a new transport, the C-17. The C-17 was conceived as a dual-role transport (both inter-theatre and intra-theatre capable) which could carry heavy outsize cargo over intercontinental ranges to small, austere airfields. The C-17 program has been delayed due to initial congressional opposition, but was later approved as the next generation airlifter replacing some of the C-130s (in an intra-theatre role) and C-141s as they reach the end of their service lives in the 1990s. The Air Force's new airlifter master plan envisages the procurement of 180 C-17s by the year 2000 (see Table 4.4). This would meet the 66 MTM/D goal established by the CMMS.[55]

U.S. sealift capability went through a period of extensive decline since the Vietnam War. This could be attributed to two factors. First, much of the U.S. military planning since Vietnam focused on a short war in Europe, which in effect meant heavy reliance on airlift and land pre-positioning. Sealift requirements were further 'masked' by the availability of some 400 NATO pool vessels for ferrying U.S. reinforcements to Europe in a war. Another factor was the rapidly declining ability of the U.S. Merchant Marine to contribute to military sealift needs. In 1950 the U.S. Merchant Marine was the largest in the world and carried 42 per cent of the country's foreign trade. In the early 1980s, it ranked eighth in size and carried less than 4 per cent of U.S. foreign trade.[56] Additionally, the general shift from breakbulk to container ships undermined the U.S. Merchant Marine's ability to transport military cargo, much of which cannot be containerized.

81

The Central Command

Table 4.4: U.S. airlift and sealift forces improvements FY1980 – FY1989

	FY1980	FY1984	FY1986	FY1987	FY1988	FY1989
Inter-theatre airlift (PAA)[a]						
C-5A	70	70	66	66	66	66
C-5B	—	—	5	14	32	44
C-141	234	234	234	234	234	234
KC-10A	—	25	48	57	57	57
C-17	—	—	—	—	—	—
Intra-theatre airlift (PAA)[a]						
Air Force						
C-130	482	520	504	559	521	513
C-123	64	—	—	—	—	—
C-7A	48	—	—	—	—	—
Navy and Marine Corps						
Tactical support	97	85	88	88	92	92
Sealift ships, active						
Tankers	21	21	24	20	20	20
Cargo	23	30	40	41	41	41
Reserve[b]	26	106	122	135	144	151

Source: U.S. Department of Defense, *Annual Report for FY1988* (Washington, D.C., 1987).

[a]PAA, Primary aircraft authorized.

[b]Includes useful National Defense Reserve Fleet ships and the Ready Reserve Force.

The major initiative undertaken by the Pentagon to meet the rapid sealift requirement of the CENTCOM was the acquisition of eight SL-7 ships and their conversion into fast logistics ships (TAKR). The SL-7 ships, built in Europe in the early 1970s, were distinguished by their high maximum speed (33 knots) and fuel consumption. After conversion into a partial roll on/roll off configuration, the ships were maintained at a reduced operational status and berthed at continental U.S. loadout ports, ready to load and sail when a crisis situation required. Due to their large size and fast speed, the SL-7s could 'move a heavy division plus some of its support simultaneously to . . . the Persian Gulf within 14 to 16 days'.[57]

Due to the absence of secure land sites in the Gulf region to pre-position equipment, the Pentagon decided to rely on maritime pre-positioning, a mode that would also allow for greater flexibility than fixed, land-based pre-positioning. The maritime pre-positioning program was undertaken in two phases. The near-term program began in mid-1980 with the deployment of a near-term

The Central Command

pre-positioned force (NTPF) of seven ships to Diego Garcia in the Indian Ocean. Included in the NTPF were two tankers (one carrying fresh water, the other, fuel) and five dry cargo ships (three RO/RO and two breakbulk) carrying enough equipment and supplies to support a marine amphibious brigade of 11,200, along with ammunitions for 'several' Air Force tactical squadrons and some Army units.[58] But this package, which included 53 M-60 tanks, 95 armoured amphibians, and 36 howitzers, could support the CENTCOM units for only 15 days. So the DOD expanded the flotilla in two stages: first in 1981 by adding six ships (two tanker and four breakbulk), and again in 1982 by activating five NDRF ships loaded with munitions. This 18-ship enhanced NTPF (ENTPF) could support a brigade-sized Marine air-ground task force (MAGTF) of about 12,000 troops for about 30 days; it also carried selected sustaining supplies for some Air Force and Army units.[59]

But NTPF/ENTPF ships were mostly single-cargo vessels, and many of them could not unload at austere port facilities or over the beach. Recognizing these limitations, the Pentagon pursued a longer-term alternative, the maritime pre-positioning ship (MPS). The MPS design features would permit it to be 'spread-loaded', to unload over the beach or at poorly equipped ports, and have some onboard maintenance facilities. The program involved a total of 13 ships, each about 750 feet long with a speed of up to 18 knots. They would be divided into three groups, each carrying equipment for a 16,500-strong MAB along with support for 30 days. One TAKX group would be stationed in each of the three oceans — the Atlantic (eastern), the Pacific (western), and the Indian Ocean (Diego Garcia) — although all three would be 'capable of sequentially responding to a SWA contingency'. The Diego Garcia group replaced only those five NTPF ships that carried unit equipment and supplies for one MAB. The rest of the NTPF, carrying equipment and supplies for Army, Air Force, or joint service usage, continued to be stationed as before.[60]

The pre-positioning program held a key place in the U.S. military strategy for the Persian Gulf. It was highly cost-effective; the Pentagon estimated that the dry cargo aboard the NTPF at Diego Garcia alone would equal 125,000 short tons, representing about 6,400 C-141 sorties.[61] It served as a signal of the U.S. determination to protect its interests in the region, and provided the speediest means (5 days' steaming time from Diego Garcia to the Gulf) of introducing the necessary heavy combat equipment against a mechanized enemy force.

However, the maritime pre-positioning concept, which called for the Marines to be airlifted to a suitable regional location and 'marry up' with their equipment brought abroad the MPS flotilla, compromised the Corps' traditional doctrine of forcible entry. Moreover, critics charged that the match-up process between the troops and the equipment would be an enormously demanding exercise, requiring, above all, a 'benign' location near the zone of conflict. This requirement posed a major limitation, because it might invite hostile preemption of airfields and port facilities. Besides, the MPS ships, being unarmed, could be a tempting target for enemy submarines and aircraft, despite the DOD's plans to offer them protection from naval warships. Thus the decision to go for the MPS instead of spending the money in modernizing the Corps' amphibious lift was questioned by some critics.

U.S. amphibious lift resources received increased attention during the Reagan administration. Until then, the Corps possessed enough amphibious shipping to lift only one Marine division/wing team's assault echelon. Its inventory of amphibious ships had declined by 100 units from 1967 levels to some 63 ships in 1980, including those in overhaul.[62]

As part of the Reagan administration's general build-up of naval forces, the Navy revised its amphibious lift goals. The mid-term objective was to provide sufficient ships to simultaneously lift the assault echelons of one Marine amphibious force (division plus air wing) and one Marine amphibious brigade. The long-term goal (1994) was to simultaneously lift the assault echelon of one MAF and one full (assault and follow-on echelons) MAB.[63] A number of shipbuilding/service life extension programs were undertaken to support the objective, including construction of new amphibious assault ships (LHA), landing ship docks (LSD), and air-cushioned landing craft (LCAC).[64]

As a result of the initiatives undertaken by the Carter and Reagan administrations, the RDJTF/CENTCOM's capability for projecting military power into the Persian Gulf region improved substantially. The RDJTF/CENTCOM units substantially improved their training, equipment, and support systems to fight in a Southwest Asian environment. Command and control arrangements were improved, thereby eliminating a major source of confusion and inter-service bickering. Strategic mobility systems to support the RDJTF/CENTCOM were enhanced in every important respect. Many of these measures, especially in the field of strategic mobility, would have been needed and probably

The Central Command

undertaken irrespective of the establishment of the RDJTF/ CENTCOM. But the latter were a catalyst in producing a greater awareness of the limitations of U.S. ability to intervene in distant areas and in creating a sense of urgency in rectifying some of the limitations. As a consequence, while the RDJTF/CENTCOM programs not only led to a major improvement in the U.S. military position in the Gulf region, they also reversed the decline of the U.S. position as a superpower with global military capabilities.

Notes

1. U.S. Congress. House. Committee on Armed Services. *Hearings on military posture and H.R. 9751, FY1963*: 3269.

2. General Paul D. Adams (Commander-in-Chief, U.S. Strike Command), 'Strikecom's potentialities', *Army* (November 1962): 46; Joint Chiefs of Staff, *The rapid deployment mission* (1981): 5.

3. William P. Mako, *U.S. ground forces and the defense of Central Europe* (Washington, D.C.: Brookings Institution, 1983): 18–19.

4. 'Congress sinking McNamara's "Floating Arsenal" plan', *Congressional Quarterly Weekly Report*, April 21, 1967: 639.

5. U.S. Congress. Senate. Committee on Armed Services. *Department of Defense authorization for appropriations for fiscal year 1981*, Part 1: 440–1.

6. Hq., Rapid Deployment Joint Task Force, *Fact sheet* (1981): 1.

7. Joint Chiefs of Staff, *United States military posture for FY1982*: 55.

8. Department of Defense, *The rapid deployment mission*, pp. 3–4; John L. Frisbee, 'Command lines for combat forces', *Defense/81* (August 1981): 9.

9. Hq., Rapid Deployment Joint Task Force, *Fact sheet* (1981): 3.

10. U.S. Congress. Senate. Committee on Armed Services. *Department of Defense authorization for appropriations for fiscal year 1982*, Part 4: 1706.

11. *Washington Post*, February 3, 1981: A3; *Washington Star*, January 11, 1981: A8.

12. Jacob Goodwin, 'Persian Gulf command: "shambles"', *Defense Week*, January 5, 1981: 1.

13. *The RDJTF command decision*, news release (Office of Assistant Secretary of Defense, Public Affairs, April 24, 1981); *Air Force Times*, June 22, 1981: 1, 16.

14. *The RDJTF command decision.*

15. U.S. Congress. Senate. Committee on Armed Services. *Department of Defense authorization for appropriations for fiscal year 1985*, Part 2: 1216.

16. U.S. Congress. House. Committee on Appropriations, *Department of Defense appropriations for 1984*, Part 1: 602.

17. Department of Defense, *Annual report to Congress, FY1984*: 194.

18. The most articulate exponent of these views is Jeffrey Record, *The Rapid Deployment Force and U.S. military intervention in the Persian Gulf* (Cambridge, MA: Institute for Foreign Policy Analysis, 1981).

19. U.S. Congress. House. Committee on Appropriations. *Department*

The Central Command

of Defense appropriations for 1982, Part 1: 277; House. Committee on Armed Services, *Hearings on military posture and H.R. 2970 (H.R. 3519), FY1982*, Part 1: 1117–18.

20. Congressional Budget Office, *Rapid deployment forces: policy and budgetary implications* (1983): 1.

21. Testimony, U.S. Congress. House. Committee on the Budget. *Military readiness and the rapid deployment joint task force* (1980): 44.

22. William P. Schlitz, 'The Airborne/Air Force Team — spearhead for rapid deployment', *Air Force Magazine* (February 1980): 39.

23. U.S. Congress. Senate. Committee on Appropriations. *Department of Defense appropriations for fiscal year 1981*, Part 1: 951.

24. U.S. Congress. Senate. Committee on Armed Services. *Department of Defense authorization for appropriations for fiscal year 1982*, Part 4: 1709.

25. U.S. Congress. House. Committee on Armed Services. *Hearings on military posture and H.R. 2970 (H.R. 3519), FY1982*, Part 3: 268–71.

26. For an excellent discussion of the CENTCOM's airpower potential, see Cristopher J. Bowie, *Concepts of operations and USAF planning for Southwest Asia*, R-3125-AF (Santa Monica, CA: Rand Corporation, 1984).

27. U.S. Congress. House. Committee on Armed Services. *Hearings on H.R. 1816 (H.R. 2972), FY1984*: 961.

28. 'SAC's RDF: here now, and it works', *Armed Forces Journal International* (September 1981): 36; 'Modification program planned for B-52HS', *Aviation Week and Space Technology* (July 28, 1980): 72; William R. Liggett, 'Long-range combat aircraft and rapid deployment forces', *Air University Review* (July/August 1982): 78; House. Committee on Appropriations. *Department of Defense appropriations for 1982*, Part 4: 372–8.

29. U.S. Congress. Senate. Committee on Armed Services. *Department of Defense authorization for appropriations for fiscal year 1982*, Part 4: 1707.

30. This is taken from an unclassified version of the report in U.S. Congress. House. Committee on Appropriations. *Department of Defense appropriations for 1985*, Part 1: 665.

31. Text of address before the 19th Wehrkunde Conference, Munich, FRG, February 13, 1982, in U.S. Congress. Senate. Committee on Armed Services. *Europe and the Middle East: strains on key elements of America's vital interests (1982)*: 30.

32. U.S. Congress. House. Committee on Foreign Affairs. *United States – European relations in 1980*: 309.

33. Department of Defense, *Report on Allied contribution to common defense* (March 1982): 78.

34. Department of Defense, *Report on Allied contribution to common defense* (March 1983): 61; Department of Defense, *Annual report to Congress, FY1983*: III–93; Department of Defense, *Report on Allied contribution to common defense* (March 1984): 58–60; U.S. Congress. House. Committee on Foreign Affairs. *NATO after Afghanistan* (1980): 34.

35. Department of Defense, *Report on Allied contribution to common defense* (March 1982): 78.

36. Congressional Budget Office, *Rapid deployment forces: policy and budgetary implications* (1983): 26–27.

37. 'U.S. Marine Corps organizes LAV battalions', *International Defense Review* (February 1982): 191.

The Central Command

38. U.S. Congress. House. Committee on Appropriations. *Department of Defense appropriations for 1985*, Part 2: 473.

39. For these and other details regarding the HTMD, see Ramon Lopez, 'The US Army's future light infantry division: a key element of the RDT', *International Defense Review* 2 (1982): 185–92; F. Cliften Berry, 'The U.S. Army's 9th Infantry Division', *International Defense Review* 9 (1984): 1124–29.

40. U.S. Congress. House. Committee on Appropriations. *Department of Defense appropriations for 1982*, Part 4: 264. On DOD's management of this problem, see Lt. Gen. Richard H. Thompson (Army deputy chief of staff for logistics) and Capt. D. G. Mongeon, 'A logistics function — DOD water "works" ', *Army Logistician* (January–February 1982): 6–8.

41. *Washington Post*, August 7, 1981: C15.

42. Col. Thomas B. McDonald, 'RDJTC C^{4}Is support', *Signal* (November 1982): 35–42; John C. Cittadino and Frank McLeskey, 'C^{3}I for the rapid deployment joint task force (RDJTF)', *Signal* (September 1981): 31–36.

43. Rear Admiral Jerry O. Tuttle, 'Intelligence support to the rapid deployment force', *Signal* (August 1980): 75–78.

44. Richard Halloran, 'Poised for the Persian Gulf', *New York Times Magazine*, April 1, 1984: 61.

45. Unclassified text of the report, U.S. Congress. House. Committee on Appropriations. *Department of Defense appropriations for 1985*, Part 1: 665–6.

46. U.S. Congress. Senate. Committee on Armed Services. *Department of Defense authorization for appropriations for fiscal year 1985*, Part 2: 1219.

47. *Statement of General George B. Crist, Commander-in-Charge. U.S. Central Command, before the Defense Policy Panel of the House Armed Services Committee*, March 17, 1987: 83–85.

48. 'Strategic mobility: requirements and future trends' (speech by Lt. Gen. O. E. DeHaven, Director of Logistics, OJCS) *Airlift* (Fall 1982): 12; U.S. Congress. Senate. Committee on Armed Services. *Department of Defense authorization for appropriations for fiscal year 1983*, Part 6: 3964–5; Deborah M. Kyle and Benjamin F. Schemmer, 'New DOD mobility study asks $18–31 billion to beef up airlift, preposition more forces', *Armed Forces Journal International* (May 1981): 28–34.

49. U.S. Congress. House. Committee on Armed Services. *Hearings on military posture and H.R. 2970 (H.R. 3519), FY1982*, Part 3: 249.

50. U.S. Congress. Senate. Committee on Armed Services. *Department of Defense authorization for appropriations for fiscal year 1982*, Part 4: 1808.

51. Department of the Air Force, *C-141B Starlifter, fact sheet 83–11* (Office of Public Affairs, April 1983).

52. U.S. Congress. Senate. Committee on Armed Services. *Civil Reserve Air Fleet (CRAF) enhancement program* (1979); House. Committee on Appropriations. *Depart of Defense appropriations for 1985*, Part 1: 164; Debroah G. Meyer, 'You can't be there til you get there', *Armed Forces Journal International* (July 1984): 86.

53. Deborah G. Meyer, 'USAF will fund 50 C-5Ns, 44 KC-10s; C-17 on shelf', *Armed Forces Journal International* (March 1982): 20; Department

The Central Command

of the Air Force, *KC-10A extender, fact sheet* (Office of Public Affairs, September 1982).

54. U.S. Congress. Senate. Committee on Armed Services. *Department of Defense authorization for appropriations for fiscal year 1983.* Part 6: 3965.

55. U.S. Congress. Senate. Committee on Armed Services. *Department of Defense authorization for appropriations for fiscal year 1985,* Part 8: 3895.

56. U.S. Congress. House. Committee on Armed Services. *Hearings on military posture and H.R. 5968 (H.R. 6030), FY1983,* Part 4: 270; National Marine Engineers' Beneficial Association, 'Measures to rebuild the U.S. merchant marine', *Defense Transportation Journal* (June 1983): 20–21.

57. U.S. Congress. House. Committee on Armed Services. *Hearings on military posture and H.R. 2970 (H.R. 3519), FY1982,* Part 3: 253–4; House. Committee on Appropriations. *Department of Defense appropriations for 1984,* Part 6: 477–8.

58. Rear Admiral F. C. Collins USN (Director, Logistics Plans, CNO), 'Near-term prepositioned ship force', *U.S. Naval Institute Proceedings* (September 1980): 117–18.

59. U.S. Congress. House. Committee on Armed Services. *Hearings on military posture and H.R. 5968 (H.R. 6030), FY1983,* Part 4: 496; House. Committee on Appropriations. *Department of Defense appropriations for 1982,* Part 2: 613.

60. Eugene E. Shoults, 'Maritime prepositioning: long-term solution — MPS', *Marine Corps Gazette* (August 1980): 57–59; R. J. L. Dicker, 'RDF sealift programs', *International Defense Review* 7 (1983): 956–8; Deborah G. Meyer, 'New storage ships are "incalculable" USMC readiness asset, Kelly says', *Armed Forces Journal International* (April 1985): 16; House. Committee on Appropriations. *Department of Defense appropriations for 1985,* Part 1: 614–15.

61. U.S. Congress. Senate. Committee on Armed Services. *Department of Defense authorization for appropriations for fiscal year 1985,* Part 2: 1221; Meyer, 'New storage ships', p. 16.

62. James D. Hessman, 'The amphibious forces: coming up short', *Sea Power* (November 1979): 27–28; John M. Collins, *U.S. –Soviet military balance: concepts and capabilities, 1960–1980* (New York: McGraw-Hill, 1980): 284–5.

63. U.S. Congress. Senate. Committee on Armed Services. *Department of Defense authorization for appropriations for fiscal year 1984,* Part 6: 3026.

64. For details, see Deborah M. Kyle, 'New assets for amphibious lift', *Armed Forces Journal International* (July 1983): 78–80.

5

Bases, 'Facility Access', and Geopolitics

A key aspect of the U.S. response to the Iranian and Afghan crises of 1979 was an effort to seek closer strategic ties with the pro-Western countries in the Southwest Asia region. As Harold Brown emphasized in an address to the Council on Foreign Relations in March 1980, 'we cannot hope, nor do we plan, to defend peoples in the region who will not help defend themselves'.[1] The political support of important regional states was viewed by Washington as an indispensable adjunct to its military strategy, particularly in view of the need for access to regional military installations. While Carter's Presidential directive 18 envisaged a light, agile force capable of operating 'independent of overseas bases and logistical support',[2] the subsequent expansion of the size and mission of RDJTF/CENTCOM and a realization of the sheer logistical problems involved in projecting U.S. power to the Gulf soon convinced the Pentagon that the credibility of its military posture in the region depended critically on the collaboration of friendly regional countries in permitting the construction and use of logistics facilities on their territory.[3]

The Carter administration's efforts to secure the participation of regional states in its military strategy in the Gulf was publicized as a 'regional cooperative security framework'. The Reagan administration, during Alexander Haig's term as Secretary of State, sought to develop a 'strategic consensus' in the region against Soviet influence. The two concepts bore many similarities. First, the regional states whose cooperation was solicited included, in the case of both the doctrines, not only the conservative regimes of the Arabian Peninsula but also other key pro-Western countries in the broader Middle East and North African region, especially

89

Egypt, Pakistan, Turkey, and Jordan. The Reagan administration, however, started on a more ambitious note by seeking to include Israel within the 'strategic consensus' framework. Second, both linked the success of their efforts to their ability to exploit what they believed and publicized as a growing perception within the region of the threats to regional security posed by the Soviet Union. Haig was far more optimistic in pushing this view; the Arabs, he asserted, had come to feel 'equally — and perhaps as grievously — threatened' by Soviet and Soviet-sponsored activities as by the 'frustrations of the Arab-Israeli problem and the threat that has historically posed'.[4] He claimed that 'strategic consensus' was not something the United States was seeking to build anew, because such a consensus had *already* developed within the region as its leaders perceived Soviet interventions from Angola to Afghanistan as heralding 'a new phase of . . . Soviet imperialism'.[5]

Third, both the Carter and Reagan administrations understood that political constraints would prevent their regional allies from participating within a formal alliance framework similar to the CENTO. Rather, their cooperation could be best secured through bilateral and informal arrangements.[6] Finally, both stressed that while such arrangements would provide for several types of allied support, the 'principal focus' would be 'on the need for regional states to provide access to local facilities'.[7] Since several states in the periphery of the region, such as Kenya, Somalia, and Morocco, were found willing to help in this quest, they also became important targets for the United States in its quest for a 'regional cooperative security framework' and 'strategic consensus'.

Access to regional military installations was deemed essential for fulfilling requirements of the U.S. strategy in the Gulf: '(1) support for peacetime force presence; (2) enroute access for closure of reinforcements; (3) rearstaging and resupply; (4) forward operating bases; (5) support for sea control operations'.[8] Peacetime naval presence required access to ports and airfields in the Indian Ocean for refuelling, supply, and repair of ships and providing rest and recreation for the crew. Enroute access bases, consisting of ports and airfields along the air and sea lines of communications between the United States and the Gulf, were considered vital in view of the long distances involved in projecting U.S. power into the Gulf. Enroute support bases were needed especially to refuel strategic airlifters and tactical combat aircraft,

Bases, 'Facility Access', and Geopolitics

as well as to pre-position supplies and equipment in order to lighten the initial burden on strategic airlift.

The need for rear or intermediate staging bases was conceived in view of their role as points where airlifted troops with their early load of light equipment could link up with either sealifted or pre-positioned heavy equipment and supplies and transfer from strategic to tactical transports in proceeding to the combat theatre. Such operations required large and secure facilities near the area of operations with an airfield, a port, and the necessary infrastructure to store equipment, fuel, and supplies and accommodate large numbers of personnel.

Forward operating bases, while not needing to be very large, must be within close proximity to the area of combat from which tactical air and fleet operations could be conducted in direct support of combat. Finally, sea control missions — the employment of naval forces, supported by land-based tactical air forces, to destroy enemy naval forces and secure vital sea lanes for use by U.S. forces — required ports and airfields from which ships and aircraft could cover wide parts of the northwest Indian Ocean waters. For the RDJTF/CENTCOM, a sea control capability was considered especially important near the chokepoints of the Straits of Hormuz, the Bab-al-Mandeb, as well as the Mozambique Channel.[9]

In seeking to persuade regional countries to permit the use of their ports and airfields by American forces, U.S. officials were careful to use the term 'facility access', rather than 'base'. The Pentagon insisted that the distinction was not purely a matter of semantics. As Harold Brown stated in 1980, 'It is a difference in the way we would behave and the presence we would have.'[10] The term 'base', according to the former Under Secretary of Defense, Robert Komer, means 'formal bases of the sort we had in the fifties where we were flying the American flag with thousands of American troops present'.[11] 'Facility access', on the other hand, would preclude any visible and large-scale presence of U.S. troops in the host country. Moreover, while facility access arrangements would give the United States the right to use certain ports and airfields in the host country for certain agreed purposes, they would be subject to the proviso that: (1) 'host governments . . . retain sovereign rights over all facilities and ownership of all real property', and (2) that the United States 'must "consult" with host governments on major exercises and deployment'.[12] Thus, Pentagon officials stressed that while Diego Garcia in the Indian

Bases, 'Facility Access', and Geopolitics

Ocean or Subic Bay in the Philippines were U.S. 'bases', in Oman, Kenya, or Somalia, the United States would only have 'access to facilities'.

It should be noted here that although the distinction is valid in a legalistic sense, and politically important for the host regimes, it would be practically meaningless during contingency operations, in which, once American forces arrive in the theatre, facility access would be used for purposes similar to those involving the use of a base. Moreover, as noted earlier, the current U.S. strategy in the Gulf is based on the 'central reserve' approach, and does not require the presence of large-scale forces in regional bases in advance of need. Due to major qualitative and quantitative improvements to its long-range mobility assets, U.S. power projection into the Gulf could be made feasible by relying on facility access arrangements, rather than on bases.

The access network

As the result of an intensive effort, backed by generous amounts of military and economic aid to the host nation, the United States negotiated access arrangements with several countries in the Southwest Asia region, both on a formal and informal basis (Table 5.1). In northwest Africa, written agreements were concluded with Morocco in May 1982, permitting the use of at least two airfields — Sidi Slimane near Rabat and Mohammed V airport outside Casablanca. A similar agreement with Liberia, signed in February 1983, provided 'contingency' access to the international airport outside Monrovia. These airfields would be used primarily for providing enroute support for U.S. strategic airlift.[13] Enroute support to the RDJTF/CENTCOM was also obtained at Spanish airbases, and at the important Portuguese airbase, Lajes, in the Azores. A new agreement signed in December 1983 extended U.S. access to Lajes for another 8 years. Construction at the airfield was undertaken with the goal of almost tripling its aircraft throughput capability to some 200 sorties per day, 'more than enough to support any anticipated Southwest Asia contingency'.[14]

In East Africa, the United States signed formal agreements with Kenya and Somalia allowing for naval support and sea control activities. Djibouti, the tiny former French colony, agreed to the use of its port by U.S. Navy ships and airfield by U.S. maritime patrol aircraft, thereby becoming an important port of the U.S.

Bases, 'Facility Access', and Geopolitics

Table 5.1: RDJTF/CENTCOM military construction funding,
FY1981 – FY1985

Country	Project/Service	Amount (millions U.S.$)
Diego Garcia[a]	Facilities expansion (Navy)	400.2
	Facilities expansion (Air Force)	217.5
Egypt	CENTCOM Facility (Ras Banas) (Air Force)	49.0
Kenya	Facilities expansion (Navy)	57.9
Morocco	Facilities expansion (Air Force)	30.0
Oman	Facilities expansion (Air Force)[b]	255.2
Portugal	Lajes field facilities expansion (Air Force)	66.0
Somalia	Facilities expansion (Navy)	54.4
Total (FY1981 – FY1985)		1,130.2[c]

Source: U.S. Congress. House. Committee on Appropriations. *Military Construction appropriation bill, 1985.* House Report 98 – 850 (June 20, 1984): 12.

[a]Figure for Diego Garcia includes funding during the FY1970 – FY1985 period.

[b]Further construction requirements identified, including an intermediate staging facility.

[c]The total estimated cost of 'essential facilities' for the CENTCOM within its area of responsibility is approximately $1.4 billion.

Navy's operations in support of Southwest Asia contingencies.[15] An unwritten understanding with Egypt and a 'strategic cooperation' agreement with Israel linked these two most important Middle East powers into the RDJTF/CENTCOM 'access network' (Map 5.1).

A more ambiguous attitude was evident in the response of Turkey and Pakistan to the U.S. request. Turkey insisted that its base agreements with the United States were strictly for NATO purposes. This, however, left unclear whether the use of Turkish facilities by U.S. forces deployed to the Gulf might be allowed if NATO as a collective body were to lend its formal endorsement to U.S. military operations in the Gulf. Turkish bases are up to NATO standards and lie close to the Soviet force structure in Transcaucasus. U.S. officials were quick to recognize that access to Turkish bases would 'have a significant value in deterring possible Soviet expansion into the Middle East or the Persian Gulf'.[16]

In the case of Pakistan, the Zia regime rejected the idea of a

93

Map 5.1: The RDF 'access network'

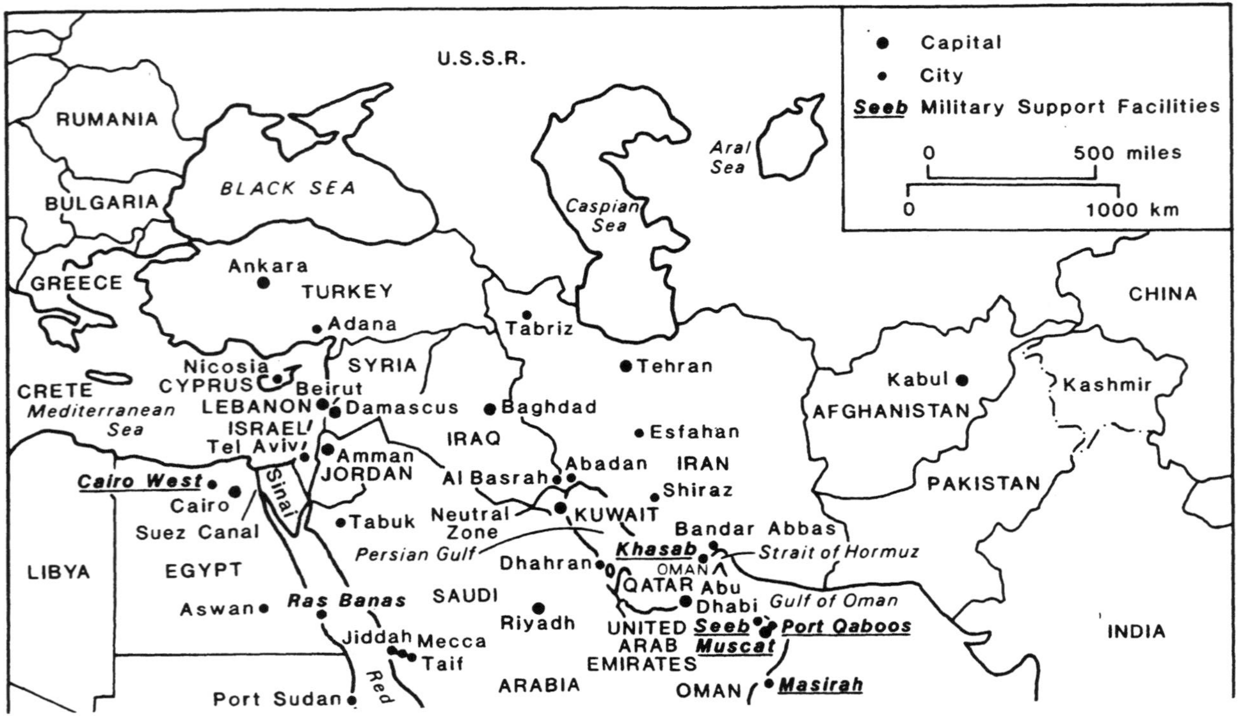

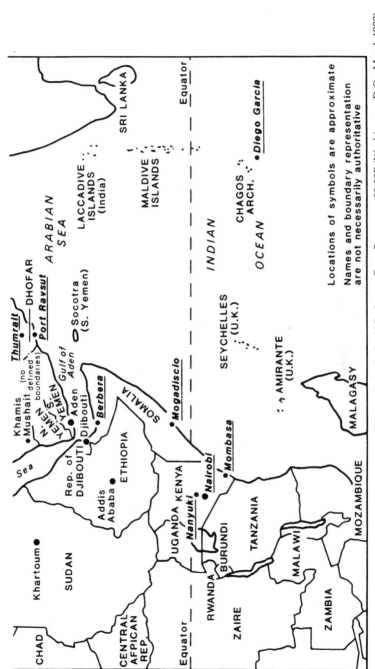

Source: Congressional Research Service, *Regional support facilities for the Rapid Deployment Force*, Report no. 82-53F (Washington, D.C., March 1982).

Bases, 'Facility Access', and Geopolitics

formal bilateral access agreement with the United States. But this did not prevent informal cooperation, which included 'Pakistani supply ships providing rations' to U.S. naval units operating in the region and the U.S. use of Pakistani airfields for maritime surveillance operations.[17] U.S. military and civilian officials surveyed the potential of Karachi and Gwadar (in Baluchistan) for providing contingency access to U.S. forces, a potential that had earlier been recognized and strongly advocated by such Americans as the former JCS Chairman Admiral Thomas H. Moorer. Given the massive U.S. military and economic aid to Pakistan following the Soviet invasion of Afghanistan, and Pakistan's own interest and military presence in the Gulf, it would be unrealistic to rule out the possibility of the CENTCOM using Pakistani bases for operations during a contingency.[18]

In the Arabian Peninsula, only Oman agreed to sign an agreement with the United States permitting use of several airfields and ports. A longstanding agreement with Bahrain allowing limited access to its port by the U.S. Middle East Force was also continued. Although Saudi Arabia and the other GCC states refused to enter into any agreement with the United States, there were indications that the Saudis could make their military installations available to U.S. forces in a contingency. Certainly, the availability of Saudi facilities was assumed in the RDJTF/CENTCOM's contingency planning, as will be discussed later in the chapter.

Diego Garcia

Before looking at the major U.S. facility access agreements in detail, it is necessary to examine the role of Diego Garcia, the only permanent U.S. base between Naples and the Philippines, in the U.S. strategy in the Gulf. Diego Garcia was originally intended to be an 'austere communications facility' for the U.S. Navy. But the post-Shah U.S. strategy in the Gulf saw its rapid transformation into a major multipurpose base, capable of supporting a wide range of operations: communications, naval support, maritime pre-positioning, Strategic Projection Force (B-52) operations, enroute support for strategic airlift, maritime reconnaissance, and anti-submarine warfare.[19] Diego Garcia became the hub of U.S. efforts to project power into the Gulf region.

Diego Garcia is the southernmost of a group of coral atolls forming the Chagos Archipelago, lying about 10,000 miles from

Bases, 'Facility Access', and Geopolitics

the southern tip of India. It is 3,400 miles from the Cape of Good Hope, 2,600 miles from the North West Cape, Australia, 1,900 miles from Masirah Island near the Strait of Hormuz and 2,200 miles from Berbera, Somalia. The island is shaped like a horseshoe (Map 5.2), and encloses a deep-water lagoon. The island is one-quarter to one-half mile wide, but is long and flat enough to permit the construction of an airfield and other infrastructure. The total land area is about 6,720 acres. The lagoon, the chief attraction of the island, is 9 miles across at its widest point, and about 15 miles long. The entrance to the lagoon, at the northwestern side of the island, is ridden with reefs, but navigable through channels. The climate is hot and wet for most of the year, though relatively free from cyclonic storms.[20]

U.S. access to the island dates back to an executive agreement signed with Britain in 1966, a year after the latter detached the island from its then colony, Mauritius, along with three other islands from the Seychelles, to form the British Indian Ocean Territory. This arrangement had the prior blessings of Washington, which secretly paid $14 million to London to cover the detachment costs. Under the agreement, the United States gained the lease of Diego Garcia for an initial period of 50 years (until 2016) with a provision for an automatic extension for another 20 years unless either side asked for its termination within 2 years of the initial 50 years.[21]

After 'depopulating' the island to turn it to an exclusively military facility, the United States and Britain signed a supplementary agreement in October 1974, which gave the former the 'right to construct, maintain and operate a limited naval communications facility on Diego Garcia', consisting of 'transmitting and receiving services, an anchorage, airfield, associated logistic support and supply and personnel accommodation'.[22] But even before the 'U.S. Naval Communication Station — Diego Garcia' became operational in 1973, the Pentagon was already talking of expanding it to a 'naval support facility'. The British withdrawal from east of Suez, the Soviet entry into the Indian Ocean, the failed U.S. gunboat diplomacy during the 1971 India–Pakistan war, and the 1973 Arab oil embargo contributed to this defeat.

After overcoming initial congressional resistance, new construction was undertaken by the Pentagon to improve facilities at Diego Garcia for naval support. This included projects to dredge the harbour to 45 feet, extend the runway to 12,000 feet, and build POL storage facilities, a fuel pier for loading/unloading fleet

97

Bases, 'Facility Access', and Geopolitics

Map 5.2: Diego Garcia: Island key map

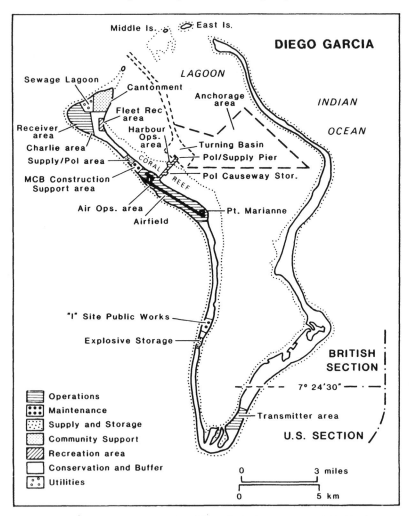

Source: U.S. General Accounting Office, *Further improvements needed in Navy's oversight and management of contracting for facilities construction on Diego Garcia*, GAO/NSIAD-84-62 (Washington, D.C., May 23, 1984).

Bases, 'Facility Access', and Geopolitics

oilers, ammunition storage facilities, and personnel accommodation. Upon completion of the projects funded up to 1980, Diego Garcia was able to 'support communications throughout the Indian Ocean region, plus periodic deployments of a carrier task force into the Indian Ocean'. The harbour could accommodate the largest of aircraft carriers, the fuel storage could supply a carrier task force for up to a month, and the airfield could take on the largest U.S. transport (C-5, C-141) and tanker aircraft, as well as P-3 maritime patrol planes and B-52 bombers.[23]

The advent of the RDJTF/CENTCOM helped Diego Garcia to complete its transition from 'a communications station to a logistic support facility, to . . . an operational support facility'.[24] As U.S. naval activities in the Indian Ocean increased dramatically in response to the developments in Iran and Afghanistan, Diego Garcia was well placed to become 'the single most important facility for logistics and communications support of the Naval Task Force . . . deployed in the Arabian Sea'.[25] But the facilities on the island were found to be inadequate for the requirements of the continuous presence of two carrier battle groups and a Marine amphibious group — which was U.S. policy between late 1979 and early 1981. Moreover, Diego Garcia needed more facilities to support the various types of contingency operations envisaged under the recently activated RDJTF. As the then Commander-in-Chief of the U.S. Pacific Command, Admiral Robert Long, revealed, the Pentagon wanted to develop Diego Garcia's 'ability to support *large-scale air, ground and sea forces* deploying through the Indian Ocean to the Middle East/Persian Gulf region' (emphasis added).[26] In addition, Diego Garcia provided the anchorage for the Near-Term Pre-positional Ship Force, and plans to deploy the B-52 bombers of the Strategic Projection Force to the Gulf on conventional interdiction missions necessitated regional staging and support facilities at a relatively remote location so that the forward bases could be freed for tactical air operations. Diego Garcia was well suited for such a role. Also Diego Garcia was seen as a vital link for strategic airlift operations into the Gulf from the Pacific side: as an air-refuelling, staging, or transfer point.[27]

In the light of these developments the Joint Chiefs of Staff, in January 1980, completed a study examining possible future uses of Diego Garcia. The study recommended that additional capabilities be developed involving the use of the 'entire island' area. In early 1980 the Pentagon stated that facilities on Diego Garcia would be expanded not only 'to support an increased U.S. presence in the

Bases, 'Facility Access', and Geopolitics

Table 5.2: Diego Garcia facilities expansion program, FY1981 – FY1985 (estimated project costs in millions U.S. dollars in parentheses)

Major* Navy Projects

*FY1981 projects (total appropriation** — 108.1)*
Dredging (13.0); air cargo/passenger terminal (3.1); wharf (19.0); small-craft berth (29.8); power plant (7.0); electrical distribution (4.7); potable water (8.1); dining facility (5.6); runway approach lighting (2.9); ocean surveillance (2.9); utilities upgrade (2.0)

FY1982 projects (total appropriation — 122.7)
Taxiway[a] (14.3); parking apron[a] (4.9); wharf[b] (18.7); waterfront transit (2.8); cold storage (2.8); high-explosive magazines (3.3); roads and parking (2.5); enlisted housing[c] (19.4); officer housing[d] (13.0); tracked vehicle maintenance shop[e] (2.0); utilities (7.6); vertical replenishment pad (2.1); airfield utilities (6.0); enlisted housing[f] (12.9)

FY1983 projects (total appropriation — 3.3)
Control tower (4.3); electrical power distribution (8.2); utilities (2.0); photo laboratory (2.3); gymnasium (3.4); enlisted housing[g] (7.9); anti-submarine warfare operations centre (6.3); communications facility (3.3); command centre (4.4); officer housing (8.4)

FY1984 projects (total appropriation — 31.8)
Public works/transport facility (6.3); enlisted personnel housing (6.8); administration facility (4.1); transmitter building addition (8.2); warehouse (3.5); waterfront operations/POL operations/weapons complex (2.4)

FY1985 projects (total appropriation — 6.3)
Water system improvements (5.9)

Air Force Projects

*FY1981 projects (total appropriation*** — 23.7)*
Petroleum, oils, and lubricants storage (23.7)

FY1982 projects (total appropriation — 114.9)
Hydrant refuelling (3.5); airfield pavement apron[h] (83.2); hazardous cargo pad (3.7); dredging (8.0); airfield lighting (3.4); demineralized water plant (1.2); operations/administration facility (4.1); cargo storage (1.6)

FY1983 projects (total appropriation — 4.5)
Avionics shop (3.4); avionics warehouse (2.0)

FY1984 projects (total appropriation — 58.2)
Runway upgrade (41.3); Space Track observation facilities (14.1); tracking/monitoring station — NAVSTAR GPS (2.8)

FY1985 projects (total appropriation — 16.1)
Space surveillance facility officer housing (7.6); ammunitions storage/maintenance (8.5)

Sources: FY1981–FY1983 projects are taken from: U.S. General Accounting Office, *Further improvements needed in Navy's oversight and management of contracting for facilities construction on Diego Garcia. A report to the Secretary of Defense*, GAO/NSIAD-

100

Bases, 'Facility Access', and Geopolitics

84-62 (Washington, D.C.: May 23, 1984): Appendix I, II; FY1984 projects are taken from: U.S. Congress. House. Committee on Appropriations. *Making appropriations for military construction for the Department of Defense for the fiscal year ending September 30, 1984, and for other purposes*, Conference Report. House Report no. 98-378 (September 22, 1983): 59; FY1985 projects are taken from U.S. Congress. House. Committee on Appropriations. *Military construction appropriation bill, FY1985*, House Report 98-850 (June 20, 1984): 95.

Notes

*Only projects costing $2 million or more are cited.

**Total congressional appropriation for Navy construction at Diego Garcia as reported in the House–Senate Appropriations Conference Committee report for the relevant fiscal year.

***Total congressional appropriation for Air Force construction at Diego Garcia as reported in the House–Senate Appropriations Conference Committee report for the relevant fiscal year.

[a]Jointly funded with the Air Force; [b]second increment; [c]buildings/94 rooms each; [d]2 buildings/58 rooms each; [e]cancellation costs; [f]2 buildings/94 rooms each; [g]1 building/94 rooms; [h] jointly funded with Navy.

Indian Ocean region in both peacetime and in a regional contingency situation', but also 'to increase logistic surge support for the Rapid Deployment Joint Task Force in a contingency role'.[28] Details of the construction programme in support of Diego Garcia's new role are given in Table 5.2.

Despite its pivotal role, Diego Garcia by itself was not considered by the Pentagon to be adequate to support the range of operations envisaged under the new U.S. strategy in the Gulf. Diego Garcia's remoteness from the Strait of Hormuz posed a major problem. Maritime pre-positioned ships anchored in its lagoon would take 5–6 days to reach the Gulf littoral. P-3 reconnaissance aircraft flying out of the island would have used up much of their endurance by the time they reached the Strait of Hormuz. Thus, the United States had to look for better located facilities. Diego Garcia, the Pentagon stated, could not be a substitute for facilities in Oman or Somalia, but complementary to them as an 'integral part of the overall Middle East base network'.[29]

An important factor affecting U.S. access to Diego Garcia was the controversy relating to the claim by the government of Mauritius to sovereignty over the island and the related issues of the demands by the island's former inhabitants for adequate compensation for their eviction.[30] The United States tried to keep out of the controversy by claiming that the issues were a political matter between Britain and Mauritius to be settled between those

Bases, 'Facility Access', and Geopolitics

two countries. After several rounds of negotiations, Britain and Mauritius reached an agreement in March 1982 in which the former agreed to pay £4 million (in addition to U.S.$1.43 million paid in 1968) to subsidize the resettlement costs of Diego Garcia's former inhabitants.[31] However, the compensation agreement did not settle the dispute over sovereignty, and it is still possible that a future government in Mauritius will revive its claim on Diego Garcia. But for the moment, they have not prevented the United States from going ahead with its ambitious construction program in Diego Garcia.

Somalia

The U.S. – Somali agreement, signed on August 22, 1980, granted the United States the right to upgrade and use airfield and port facilities in Berbera and Mogadishu.[32] To the United States, the chief attraction of Somali facilities, especially Berbera, lay in their relative proximity to the Gulf as well as their dominating access to the checkpoint at Bab el Mandeb. Also, U.S. military presence in Berbera was seen by the Pentagon as a counter to the Soviet access to Aden and Ethiopia. The United States sought to develop facilities in Berbera for three major purposes: (1) to 'support sea control and maritime air [P-3] operations in proximity to . . . Bab el Mandeb'; (2) 'to support urgent resupply (and refuelling) efforts, as a transshipment point, to [naval] task forces operating in the vicinty'; and (3) 'to make emergency [fleet] repairs by deploying a repair ship whenever it is necessary'.[33] At Mogadishu, the Somali capital, airfield and port facilities were obtained to support 'naval air operations', and to serve as a transit point for the U.S. Air Force. In a contingency, Mogadishu could be used to support sea control operations in the nearby ocean area.[34]

Contrary to the alarming claims made by the Pentagon in the 1970s, the Soviets had built the airfield and port at Berbera 'to a very low degree of quality'. The most useful facilities were a 13,500-foot runway, long enough to accommodate B-52 bombers and C-5 strategic airlifters, and some fuel storage tanks, bunkers for a dozen fighter aircraft, and a limited number of general operations and support buildings.[35] The U.S. Navy's construction program to improve Somali facilities included improvements to the runway and the parking area at the Berbera airfield and storage and a pipeline for fuel. The Berbera port was upgraded with an

Bases, 'Facility Access', and Geopolitics

extension of the wharf, construction of fuel storage facilities and pumping stations, and dredging of the harbour and the turning basin. Construction at Mogadishu airport was undertaken for runway and taxiway improvements, maintenance, and storage buildings and utilities.[36]

The U.S. – Somalia access agreement turned out to be the 'most flexible' offered by any state in the vicinity of the region. It required the United States to notify Somalia only 24 hours prior to a deployment (which can be waived in urgent circumstances). There were apparently 'no Somali restrictions on U.S. presence or construction projects in Somalia'. Somalia seemed more receptive than Kenya or Oman to 'large numbers of American Armed Forces and would allow extensive, high-visibility (CENTCOM) use of Somali facilities'.[37]

But the agreement initially aroused a great deal of controversy. The issue of Somali irredentism, and its conflict with Soviet-backed Ethiopia,[38] prompted fears in Congress that U.S. aid to Somalia under the facility access agreement might encourage Somalia to mount a fresh offensive in Ogaden, strain U.S. relations with other African states, and involve the United States in a potential conflict in the Horn.[39] To make matters worse, Ethiopia warned that the U.S. – Somali agreement was an 'act of provocation' that could 'draw the United States into a war situation'. Critics of the agreement feared that in a future Ethiopia – Somalia war, the United States might have to take military steps to protect its personnel and intallations at Berbera, located only 120 miles from the Ethiopian border.[40]

The administration reassured Congress by stating that military aid to Somalia would be given on the condition that U.S. weapons would not be used for attacks against Ethiopia. In early 1981 Congress lifted restrictions on arms sales to Somalia after receiving 'verified assurances' that Somalia no longer had troops within the Ogaden province of Ethiopia. A combined offensive into Somali territory by Ethiopia and an allied Somali opposition group, the Somali Democratic Salvation Front (SDSF), in July 1981 finally prompted Washington to make the first delivery of the promised arms package to Mogadishu, although heavier equipment, such as tanks or fighter aircraft, was still refused. This caused some dismay and disillusionment in Mogadishu, which may still affect the U.S. – Somali access agreement. In addition, the shaky domestic position of the Siad Barre regime, which has been actively opposed by several groups such as the Somali National

Bases, 'Facility Access', and Geopolitics

Movement, could well doom Somalia's access agreement with the United States. The leadership of the opposition groups have already said as much.[41]

Kenya

The U.S.–Kenya access agreement of June 26, 1980, was the culmination of a longstanding Kenyan policy of allowing overflight and landing rights to U.S. military aircraft and port call rights to U.S. Navy ships. The agreement formalized U.S. access to port (Kilindi harbour) and airfield (Moi international airport) facilities in Mombasa, and airfields at Nairobi and Nanyuki.[42] Distance limits the role of Kenyan bases in supporting U.S. military deployments to the Persian Gulf.[43] The Nanyuki airbase is about 1,900 miles from the nearest Gulf shore, while ships sailing from Mombasa will take about 4 to 6 days to cover the 2,700-mile journey to the Persian Gulf. None the less, Kenyan facilities, especially Mombasa, were considered by the Pentagon to be useful for a number of reasons.

First, Mombasa could be an ideal staging point for sea control operations near the Mozambique Channel, whose strategic importance would increase enormously in the event of a closure of the Suez canal during a major contingency. Second, Mombasa, eastern Africa's largest and best-equipped port, could provide logistics support to deployed U.S. naval units in the region. Facilities in Mombasa could support resupply, refuelling, maintenance, and small-scale repair of U.S. naval vessels.[44] Third, Kenya, unlike many other countries in the region, was willing to allow the use of Mombasa as a liberty port for U.S. sailors.[45] Finally, Nairobi airport was regarded by the U.S. Air Force as an ideal transit point for airlift supply operations to Diego Garcia.[46]

Construction work undertaken by the United States (Navy) to upgrade Kenyan facilities included a new air cargo terminal and extension of the existing partial taxiway to the full length at Moi airport. At the nearby Kenya Navy Base, a communications centre was built, along with an ammunition magazine and a general purpose warehouse for storage purposes. But the major construction work was done at the Kilindini harbour, which previously could not take aircraft carriers. Such vessels had to anchor 3 to 5 miles off the harbour, often in wind and wave conditions too severe to permit safe boat operations. A dredging project provided a 45-foot deep entrance channel along with a

104

Bases, 'Facility Access', and Geopolitics

1,500-foot radius turning basin in the harbour, permitting ships of the largest size to enter.[47]

Kenyan leaders shrugged off criticisms that by granting facilities to the United States, they effectively compromised the stand of the OAU and the Non-Aligned Movement against superpower presence in the region. As the Kenyan *Weekly Review* pointed out in October 1981, the agreement 'could make Kenya suspect in the eyes of certain African countries, but the minimal troop presence involved makes the offer pale in a continent replete with foreign troops of all shades and intentions'.[48] Kenya, however, was concerned about possible effects of a large-scale U.S. military presence on its soil. Although U.S. officials claimed that Kenya 'would allow almost any level of U.S. military presence as long as it is temporary',[49] the Moi government urged the United States to keep a minimum number of U.S. staff stationed on a regular, 'permanent' basis. Kenya was also initially opposed to the U.S. decision to sell, as part of the access deal, arms to Somalia, whose irredentist designs on its northern province had led Kenya to cooperate with Ethiopia.[50] But this opposition was later abandoned.

Egypt

Egypt's role in the U.S. strategy came into the limelight when, the day after U.S. forces used an Egyptian airbase (Qena) to mount the ill-fated Iranian hostage rescue attempt, President Sadat declared: 'I have promised the American people that I shall give facilities for the rescue of the hostages and for the rescue of any Arab state on the Gulf.'[51] This policy, subsequently reaffirmed by his successor Hosni Mubarak, was, however, not unconditional. First, it ruled out the establishment of 'permanent American bases' on Egyptian soil, allowing instead 'temporary' access for the duration of a crisis. This, however, did not prejudice U.S. rights to pre-position equipment at selected sites. Second, Egypt refused to formalize the offer by entering into a signed agreement with the United States. Third, Egyptian officials made a point of stressing that the use of the facilities would be 'conditional upon a request by any Arab or Islamic country for help in the event it is subjected to a threat of invasion', thereby leaving in doubt whether access would be permitted for 'uninvited' or coercive intervention or against domestic threats. Finally, the Egyptian

Bases, 'Facility Access', and Geopolitics

offer specifically excluded the Israeli-built airfields in Sinai, which the latter was to evacuate in accordance with the Camp David accords. This move disappointed some U.S. officials who envisaged important roles for these two ready-made, excellently built bases in the access network.[52]

The conditional Egyptian offer of access did not, however, deter the Pentagon from welcoming it with considerable enthusiasm. Of all the sites on offer, most interest was focused on Ras Banas on the Red Sea coast. A U.S. base there, given its proximity across the Red Sea to the Saudi cities of Jiddah and Yanbu, could be a symbol of U.S. support for the Saudi regime without provoking resentment from the Saudi populace.[53] The Pentagon's initial proposal to develop Ras Banas was highly ambitious. The idea was to make Ras Banas a 'primary rear staging facility' for CENTCOM army troops deploying to the Gulf and to stage B-52 bombers.[54] The plan fell through, however, as the result of congressional unwillingness to approve funding in the absence of a written agreement between the United States and the Egyptian government. The Mubarak regime refused to sign such an agreement, and negotiations between the United States failed to resolve the issue.[55] The Pentagon subsequently came up with a proposal to build a drastically scaled-down version of the original plan. This would make Ras Banas an 'austere rear staging area' for the CENTOM by building POL support facilities, water desalination/distribution systems, airfield improvements, and warehouses.[56] (Later Egypt reportedly turned down U.S. requests to build facilities for CENTCOM in two other locations: one near Alexandria and the other at Qena.[57]

Egyptian reservations against a formal base agreement with the United States and extensive CENTCOM facilities on its soil stemmed largely from a desire not to give the radical Arab regimes an additional excuse to frustrate its efforts to rejoin the Arab mainstream. Moreover, in the aftermath of Sadat's assassination, Mubarak could not afford to ignore the increasingly restive nationalistic, anti-Western, and Islamic fundamentalist forces within the country which had collectively denounced their government's separate peace with Israel and demanded Egypt's return to the Arab fold. Anti-American sentiments within the Egyptian population had been fueled by the government's decision to grant facilities to the United States. In May 1981 for example, the Cairo paper *Ash-Sha'b* denounced the proposed U.S. facility at Ras Banas as a 'threat to our independence and sovereignty'.[58] The former

Bases, 'Facility Access', and Geopolitics

Egyptian foreign minister, Mohammed Riad, also argued that the U.S. rapid deployment strategy in the Gulf was 'contrary to the aspirations and inspirations of the Arab people'.[59]

Despite Mubarak's reservations, the massive U.S. military and economic aid to Egypt that followed the Camp David accords has served as a key binding force in the U.S.–Egyptian access arrangement. Egypt continued to cooperate with the United States by playing host to Bright Star exercises in 1980, 1981, 1983, and 1985. Its offer of contingency access to Ras Banas, Cairo West, and other locations still stands, although the facilities would be made available only when specific requests are made by the United States. Egypt reserves the right to refuse such requests, as it did when the Reagan administration solicited its cooperation in 1985–86 for a joint operation against Libya.[60]

Israel

While Egypt's involvement in the U.S. Persian Gulf strategy was hindered by certain political reservations on its own part, the problems relating to Israel's role were quite the reverse. It was the United States which, in the interest of its ties with the Arab world, sought to make the Israeli involvement as discreet and low-key as possible, despite Israel's strong interest in a more concrete role. The Carter administration was particularly reluctant to allow for any Israeli participation in its rapid deployment strategy.[61] Under the Reagan administration, Israel fared better, although this cooperation did not fully accord with the concept of 'strategic consensus' that Haig hoped might bring the pro-Western Arabs and the Jewish state together in forming a common, though informal front against the Soviet Union.

Nothing illustrated the contradictions in the Haig policy more clearly than the AWACS controversy of 1981. Washington's decision to supply a $5 billion early warning and air defence package to Saudi Arabia provoked a bitter debate between the advocates of Saudi and Israel strategic interests in which the governments of the two countries fully participated. The Reagan administration sought to project the AWACS sale as a major breakthrough in its effort to prove U.S. credibility to the Arabs, and enhance their mind and its own capability to repel Soviet or Iranian threat to Gulf oil producers, while leaving Israeli security interests unharmed (thanks to the conditions attached to the sale

Bases, 'Facility Access', and Geopolitics

regarding the basing and surveillance zones of the AWACS). But the Israeli government and the pro-Israeli lobby in the United States were not only unimpressed by such strategic reasoning, but launched one of the most powerful lobbying efforts in Capitol Hill's recent history to defeat the sale. Prime Minister Begin actively contributed to this campaign by characterizing the AWACS sale as 'one of the most serious dangers to the Israeli population'.[62] Washington's dilemmas concerning the sale were aggravated as the Saudi leadership, indeed the entire official opinion in the conservative Gulf States, informed the Reagan administration that they viewed the passage of the sale as the key test of its sincerity in improving ties with Arab friends, and that failure to deliver the package could gravely jeopardize its Persian Gulf strategy.[63] Although the sale was finally approved after some strong lobbying by the President himself, the contradictions between Israeli and Saudi security interests were too evident to permit any further mention of the term 'strategic consensus'.

The problems with U.S. – Israeli cooperation on Persian Gulf strategy also surfaced during negotiations for a 'strategic cooperation' agreement which was signed by the Israeli Defence Minister and the U.S. Defense Secretary on November 30, 1981. Such an accord had been sought by Israel since the Reagan administration took office. But the latter resisted the idea until the sale of the AWACS aircraft to Saudi Arabia was completed. After overcoming Israeli objections to the sale, the administration offered to sign a strategic cooperation agreement as compensation. But negotiations leading to its conclusion revealed substantial differences between the two sides. The Israeli proposals were ambitious, calling for such provisions as Israeli air cover for U.S. aircraft, bringing equipment and supplies to the Gulf in a crisis, and pre-positioning of U.S. combat aircraft and heavy army equipment on Israeli soil for use by U.S. forces operating in the Gulf. But the United States chose to delete these items from the agreement, which in the end contained no specific agenda on which bilateral cooperation could be developed. The United States also rejected Israeli requests to sign the treaty at the highest levels of government and to have the document carry an explicit American promise to reciprocate Israel's cooperation by supporting it against all types of threats, Soviet or non-Soviet, including that posed by the 'front-line' Arab states.[64]

Therefore, U.S. – Israeli relations suffered a period of chill as Washington felt obliged to mollify moderate Arab opinion by criticizing Israel for such actions as the bombing of the Iraqi nuclear reactor in June 1981, the annexation of the Golan Heights in December 1981, as well as a refusal to cooperate with the administration's own Middle East peace plan announced by President Reagan in September 1981 in the aftermath of the PLO's evacuation from Beirut. Israel's isolation from U.S. Persian Gulf strategy was deemed imperative in the interests of the Reagan administration's efforts to seduce Arab support. Thus, when Israel annexed the Golan Heights, the 'strategic cooperation' agreement was 'suspended' by Washington.

But the crisis in U.S. – Israeli relations proved to be short-lived. The Reagan administration did not actually seek to develop its ties with the moderate Arab regimes at the expense of its bilateral relations with Israel in any real, long-term sense. The concession to the Saudi quest for sophisticated arms was not extended to Kuwait or Jordan. With the failure of the Reagan Middle East Peace Plan and a vociferous campaign by pro-Israeli groups in the United States projecting Israel as a 'strategic asset',[65] it was not long before the suspended 'strategic cooperation' agreement was revived. In December 1983 the first visit to Washington as Prime Minister by Yitzhak Shamir secured for Israel exactly what it had sought in 1981: an agreement with the United States that carried strictly bilateral obligations did not entangle Israeli interests in a broad set of relationships involving the moderate Arab regimes or require Israel to make concessions on the issue of arms sales to the Arab states. This time Israel was asked for 'nothing'.[66]

The scope of the new agreement went beyond that of the original. It envisaged joint contingency planning, pre-positioning of U.S. equipment in Israel, provision of Israeli medical facilities for U.S. soldiers, and regular joint exercises.[67] While satisfying Israeli concerns, the new agreement, however, served to highlight the failure of the original U.S. quest for a strategic consensus binding Israel and the moderate Arab states. In fact, the problems and obstacles encountered during the diplomatic process leading to the agreement and continuing Israeli intransigence over arms sales to the moderate Arabs strengthened a growing perception within the U.S. policymaking hierarchy that the security interests of the two sides in the Middle East were not always identical.[68]

Bases, 'Facility Access', and Geopolitics

The Gulf Cooperation Council States

The response of the Gulf Cooperation Council (GCC) states to U.S. military strategy in the region was shaped by conflicting demands. On the one hand, they shared a number of common objectives with the United States, the most important of which was their own survival as independent entities. To this end, the GCC states recognized the need for a strong U.S. rapid intervention capability in the region. On the other hand, their desire for strategic cooperation with the U.S. view of the United States as a strategic partner was tempered by their opposition to U.S. backing for Israel, their doubts and suspicions regarding U.S. objectives, and perhaps most importantly, their fear of provoking the radical, anti-Western, nationalist, and religious fundamentalist forces in the region.

The new U.S. strategy in the Gulf was greeted by the GCC states with considerable ambivalence. While U.S. officials on several occasions claimed that the Gulf monarchies 'would have *privately* welcomed the demonstration of American determination to resist Soviet aggression in the region, including the development of a U.S. rapid deployment force and an over-the-horizon presence' (emphasis added),[69] a survey of the public statements issued by the GCC revealed a completely different picture. A representative example of such public pronouncements was contained in the Final Statement of the first summit meeting of the Gulf Cooperation Council states held on February 25–26, 1981. In it, the leaders

> reaffirm that the region's security and stability are the responsibility of its peoples and countries. . . . They call for keeping the entire region free of international conflicts, particularly the presence of military fleets and foreign bases. . . . They declare that guaranteeing stability in the Gulf is linked to the achievement of peace in the Middle East, and this underlies the need to achieve a just solution for the Palestinian question — a solution that safeguards the Palestinian people's legitimate rights, including their rights to repatriation and the establishment of an independent state, and ensures Israeli withdrawal from all the occupied Arab territories, the foremost of which is Jerusalem.[70]

Such declarations, however, did not prevent the United States

Bases, 'Facility Access', and Geopolitics

from acquiring some form of access in three GCC countries, Oman, Bahrain, and Saudi Arabia, although only Oman agreed to conclude a written agreement. Signed on June 4, 1980, the U.S. – Omani access agreement gave the United States the right to improve and use facilities in at least six locations: airfields at the Masirah Island, Muscat (Seeb international airport), Thumrait, and Khasab and port facilities at Salalah (Port Rasyut) and Muscat (Port Qaboos).[71] Important because of their proximity to the most probable area of conflict, these Omani facilities were seen by the Pentagon as useful for four major purposes: 'extending sea control, basing tactical aircraft, and staging ground forces during contingencies, as well as for supporting U.S. naval forces'.[72]

The United States paid particular attention to the barren and rocky Masirah Island, an ideal staging point for sea control and tactical air operations near the entrance to the Gulf. Masirah could also be used as a stopover point for long-range maritime patrol aircraft and as a point of transfer from strategic airlift to small cargo planes, which made onboard deliveries of supplies to the U.S. fleet. Masirah's remoteness from Omani population centres would make it safe against sabotage or seizure, and politically suitable for use by the United States, especially for peacetime presence and exercise purposes.[73] On the other hand, the major and more modern airfields on the Omani mainland, Seeb and Thumrait, were intended to serve, most importantly, as forward bases for tactical air operations. Following the scaling-down of the proposed rear staging base at Ras Banas, the United States also proposed to build an Army 'brigade staging facitity' at Thumrait. The Seeb international airport was used to support P-3 and naval resupply operations. Khasab, a small airfield at the far end of the Musandam Peninsula, was considered suitable for supporting mine clearing operations in the Strait of Hormuz. Construction was undertaken to improve all three Omani locations. These included improvements to airfields at Masirah and Khasab, and new facilities at Seeb, Thumrait, and Masirah to stockpile POL, ammunition, and war readiness material.[74]

Bahrain used to be the official homeport for the U.S. Middle East Force (USMIDEASTFOR)[75] until U.S. support for Israel during the 1973 War provoked the Bahraini regime into serving notice on the agreement. Although the threat was not carried out, the status of homeporting was terminated under the terms of a new agreement reached in June 1977. The new agreement provided for a DOD 'Administrative Support Unit (ASU) . . . to carry out

111

Bases, 'Facility Access', and Geopolitics

administrative functions, including support of ship and aircraft visits', and extended the Status of Forces Agreement covering the U.S. personnel resident in Bahrain for purposes related to the ASU. U.S. fleet access to Bahrain was limited to 'non-exclusive use of berthing space for not more than three vessels per visit for periods totalling 120 days in each 12-month period'. It also provided for landing rights for the aircraft of the ASU, 'aircraft attached to ships visiting the port of Bahrain', and aircraft of the U.S. Military Airlift Command (MAC landings not to exceed 36 flights per quarter).[76]

The arrangements continued after the creation of the RDJTF, with the ASU still employing 65 'military station-keepers' and an undisclosed number of officers to manage communications links as well as the affairs of the MIDEASTFOR. The importance of the MIDEASTFOR increased after the fall of the Shah, when its strength was raised from three to five ships, and the outbreak of the Iran-Iraq War, when its four frigate/destroyers became the most regular and forward deployed (apart from the AWACS) forces belonging to the RDJTF/CENTCOM. The CENTCOM also set up its Forward Headquarter Element aboard the flagship *La Salle*, thereby enhancing the MIDEASTFOR's importance further. (Following the Iraqi attack on the U.S. frigate *Stark* in May 1987, the size of the MIDEASTFOR was increased to nine ships.)[77]

For any major U.S. military operation in the Gulf, access to Saudi military installations would be a critical requirement. Despite considerable U.S. pressure, the Saudi government refused to join the access network, even if it only meant granting 'facilities access' and not bases. None the less, there were strong indications that the Saudis would allow use of these facilities by U.S. forces on a contingency, case-by-case basis. In this respect, the U.S. quest was helped by the fact that several important Saudi military bases and other support installations had been built by the United States to NATO specifications. This, plus the large contingent (more than 500, although the exact number was not revealed) of U.S. military officials 'permanently stationed' in Saudi Arabia in connection with arms sales and training, ensured that the United States would have full knowledge of the types of facilities available at various Saudi air and naval bases.[78] In addition, U.S. arms sales to Saudi Arabia helped overcome problems of pre-positioning of combat equipment. This was especially true in the case of air defence systems, critical to operations during the early phases of a

U.S. intervention. U.S. equipment transferred to Saudi Arabia in the late 1970s and early 1980s, such as F-15 fighter/intercepters, AWACS early warning planes, Sidewinder air-to-air missiles, or Stinger surface-to-air missiles, were all front-line systems used by the U.S. military and therefore were fully interchangeable with RDJTF/CENTCOM equipment. In some cases the equipment had been 'oversold' just as bases had been 'overbuilt'. Visiting Saudi Arabia in July 1984, a Senate Foreign Relations Committee staff delegation reported that 'the Saudi airbase in Dhahran could *supply, support, and shelter* several squadrons of USAF F-15s *in addition* to Saudi aircraft now stationed there' (emphasis added).[79] In 1981 the Pentagon revealed that 'three years of spares for F-15s and AWACS, which would be compatible with U.S. equipment, would be stockpiled in Saudi Arabia'. Taking these into consideration, RDJTF Commander General P. X. Kelly testified before the Senate Armed Services Committee:

> It is our view that if the Government of Saudi Arabia perceived a serious threat to the Kingdom, the Government of the United States would be invited into Saudi Arabia. . . . In this scenario, the Saudis would make available for our use any *spare parts, bases, munitions, facilities . . . and support equipment, quite possibly even to the detriment of their own fighting capability.* (emphasis added)[80]

Although some GCC member states were less than faithful in adhering to the spirit of their collective protestations against superpower presence and access in the region, the extent of this breach should not be overstated. In the case of these arrangements, host country intentions in granting access could not be confirmed until actual clearance was received at the onset of a particular crisis. Even in the case of Oman, the GCC member most sympathetic to the U.S. strategy in the region and the only one in need and receipt of American military and economic aid, U.S. discretion in using the facilities was limited and uncertain. For example, there was some doubt as to whether Oman would approve the use of its bases by the RDJTF/CENTCOM in the event of the latter's intervention in a domestic crisis in the Gulf. A Senate Foreign Relations Committee staff report in 1984 concluded that the U.S.–Omani 'agreement was predicated on assisting the United States in meeting a potential Soviet threat to the region. Oman did not commit itself to United States use of these facilities to meet

Bases, 'Facility Access', and Geopolitics

threats originating from within the region'.[81]

The GCC states accommodated the U.S. strategy by seeking an 'over-the-horizon' role by the RDJTF/CENTCOM. While such a role was politically ideal, it was a poor way to send any signal to the regional adversaries the U.S. interventionist posture was designed to deter and counter. The uncertainties and limitations associated with the access relationships with Oman or Saudi Arabia undermined the credibility of the U.S. strategic posture in the Gulf.

Washington's efforts to elicit greater cooperation from the Gulf monarchies were not successful. Several factors were responsible for this failure, including U.S. policy toward the Arab–Israeli conflict. The U.S. friendship with Israel made open strategic cooperation with Washington politically risky for the conservative regimes. Although the Iranian threat increasingly came to dominate the security perceptions of the GCC, the historical importance of the Palestinian issue as a major 'legitimating and delegitimating factor'[82] in Arab politics had an important bearing on their desire to cooperate with the U.S. strategy. No regime could afford to collaborate with Israel's main ally without risking a major political fallout that could threaten its survival.

Contrary to the claims made by some pro-Israeli writers,[83] the GCC countries saw the continuing stalemate over the Palestinian question as a threat to stability in the Gulf. As Saudi Arabia's Crown Prince (later King) Fahd put it in the context of the Carter Doctrine, 'if we want to contain communism and alien influences, we should solve the Palestinian question justly and comprehensively, so that no one will find himself compelled to seek assistance from those [the Soviet Union] whom we fear may influence our principles'.[84] The continuation of the Arab–Israeli conflict was viewed by the GCC countries as a source of radicalism within the native population. The presence of expatriate Palestinians in the Gulf was also a potential source of instability. Finally, the GCC states, particularly Saudi Arabia, had to bear in mind that in a future Arab–Israeli war, they might come under considerable pressure to be directly involved or become victims of an Israeli preemptive attack.[85] Thus, to the GCC states, the issue of Gulf security could not be separated from the larger Middle Eastern conflict.

It was from this perspective that Haig's attempts to project a 'strategic consensus' were rejected by the GCC states as an effort to bypass the Palestinian issue. On the eve of Haig's trip to the

Bases, 'Facility Access', and Geopolitics

Middle East to sell the strategic consensus in 1981, a Manama newspaper commented that Haig's efforts to 'concentrate on the Soviet threat to the region and the need for a joint action by the United States, Arab countries and Israel to stave off this threat' was 'bound to fail' because what the Arab governments really wanted was for 'Haig to tell them what his government intends to do to resolve the Middle East crisis, which is the principal source of instability in the region and which — if we want to refer to the Soviet threat — opens the way for foreign threats and intervention'.[86]

But the Arab–Israeli problem was certainly not the only factor inhibiting the GCC states from cooperating closely with the U.S. strategy. Even a satisfactory solution to the Arab–Israeli conflict could still leave some gap in the strategic understanding between Washington and the GCC capitals. The states, much like other non-aligned nations, were fearful that a U.S. military build-up in the Gulf would provoke a countermove on the part of the Soviet Union, and that by openly cooperating with the United States, they would bring the Cold War to their doorsteps — and even become special targets for Soviet propaganda campaigns and subversion.[87] In addition, the GCC states harboured doubts whether the United States would faithfully and efficiently come to their rescue at the time of crisis. The question of U.S. credibility was a major legacy of the U.S. treatment of the Shah during his last months in power. But it was also fed from doubts as to whether the United States would be able to provide the kind of help that would be effective against a particular threat. In case of a domestic threat the presence of U.S. troops might further destabilize the situation. In the case of an all-out Soviet attack, which few in the Gulf viewed as likely, the ability of U.S. forces to defeat such a threat was all the more suspect.[88]

Last but not least, the ambivalent attitude of the GCC states towards U.S. strategy was partly explained by their memories of the threats of possible seizure of Arab oil fields issued by the Ford administration. The RDJTF/CENTCOM was seen in the Gulf, both at a popular and to a lesser extent official level, as the latest and most sophisticated instrument designed to carry out the threat if the need arose.[89] Such fears were regularly reflected in the controlled media in the Gulf. For example, commenting on the reports about the formation of the RDJTF and its first field exercises in the Californian deserts, Kuwaiti paper *As-Siyasah* noted: 'the Pentagon has begun to implement part of a plan

Bases, 'Facility Access', and Geopolitics

prepared by military experts for invading the Arab oil fields'.[90]
Realization of the political risks and uncertainties involved in dependence on outside help was an important factor in the Gulf monarchies' move toward closer mutual security cooperation under the auspices of the Gulf Cooperation Council, whose inaugural summit was held in Abu Dhabi in May 1981. Although in its early stages the GCC emphasized cooperation in economic and political matters, it was not long before security became its primary focus. As part of this effort several initiatives, including an integrated air defence network and a GCC 'rapid deployment force', were undertaken.[91] These attempts at security cooperation were particularly impressive for a region historically noted more for its myriad inter-dynastic and inter-state rivalries.

The GCC states, of course, realized that they could not become completely self-reliant in providing for their own defence. Against major threats, help from Western or Western-oriented regional sources (e.g. Jordan, Pakistan) could be necessary. Thus, to protect the GCC states from threats beyond their ability to counter, U.S. forces would have to be given access to local facilities. U.S. officials, as General Kelly's statement with respect to Saudi bases revealed, undoubtedly counted on such access and invitation. But the main thrust of the GCC's approach to security and its response to the U.S. strategy in the Gulf during the period under investigation was to minimize, wherever possible, dependence on outside help, especially from the United States. It is in this sense that U.S. efforts to seek a 'regional cooperative security framework' or a 'strategic consensus' remained essentially unfulfilled.

Notes

1. *Department of State Bulletin* (May 1980): 65.
2. Joint Chiefs of Staff, *United States military posture for FY1982*: 55.
3. U.S. Congress. House. Committee on Foreign Affairs. *U.S. interests in, and policies toward, the Persian Gulf* (1980): 65.
4. Department of State, *Secretary Haig: news conference*, Current Policy no. 304 (Washington, D.C., August 6, 1981): 3–4.
5. Department of State, *Secretary Haig: news conference*, Current Policy no. 325 (Washington, D.C., October 7, 1981): 3.
6. See testimony by Harold Brown, U.S. Congress. House. Committee on Foreign Affairs. *Foreign assistance legislation for FY1981*, Part 1: 234; Department of State, *U.S. strategy in the Middle East* (testimony by Secretary Haig before the Senate Foreign Relations Committee), Current

116

Bases, 'Facility Access', and Geopolitics

Policy no. 312 (Washington, D.C., September 17, 1981): 2.

7. U.S. Congress. House. Committee on Appropriations. *Department of Defense appropriations for 1982*, Part 1: 276.

8. Ibid., p. 368.

9. Congressional Research Service, *Regional support facilities for the rapid deployment force* (1982): 8; U.S. Congress. House. Committee on Appropriations. *Military construction appropriations for 1982*. Part 5: 104–5, 154, 171.

10. U.S. Congress. House. Committee on Foreign Affairs. *Foreign assistance legislation for FY1981*, Part 1: 245.

11. U.S. Congress. House. Committee on Foreign Affair. *U.S. interests in, and policies toward, the Persian Gulf* (1980): 76.

12. Congressional Research Service, *Regional support facilities*: 11.

13. For detailed information, see Congressional Budget Office, 'U.S.–Moroccan agreement and its implications for U.S. rapid deployment forces', appended to U.S. Congress. House. Committee on Foreign Affairs. *Review of U.S. Policy toward the conflict in the Western Sahara* (1983): 28–33; U.S. Congress. House. Committee on Appropriations. *Military construction appropriations for 1984*, Part 5: 51, 139–40; Claudia Wright, 'Journey to Marrakesh: U.S.–Moroccan security relations', *International Security* (Spring 1983): 163–79.

14. Congressional Budget Office, 'U.S.–Moroccan agreement': 31–32; U.S. Congress. House. Committee on Appropriations. *Military construction appropriations for 1983*, Part 5: 296.

15. U.S. Congress. House. Committee on Appropriations. *Military construction appropriations for 1984*, Part 5: 51.

16. U.S. Congress. House. Committee on Appropriations. *Military construction appropriations for fiscal year 1984*: 217. For a discussion of the straegic value of Turkish bases to the RDF, see Albert Wohlstetter, 'Meeting the threat in the Persian Gulf', *Survey* (Spring 1980): 183–7.

17. 'More U.S. aid for Zia', *The Middle East* (July 1984): 8.

18. The strategic value of Pakistani bases for U.S. deployment purposes is discussed in Francis Fukuyama, *The security of Pakistan: a trip report*, N-1584-RC (Santa Monica, CA: Rand Corporation, September 1980); Thomas H. Moorer and Alvin J. Cottrell, 'A permanent U.S. naval presence in the Indian Ocean', in Alvin J. Cottrell et al., *Sea power and strategy in the Indian Ocean* (Beverly Hills, CA: Sage Publications, 1981): 129–32. The possibility of Pakistani bases being offered to the United States is surveyed in 'A ring around the Gulf', *Far Eastern Economic Review*, December 11, 1981: 17–18; 'Zia's new role in the Gulf', *The Middle East* (April 1983): 33–34; Lawrence Lifschultz, 'From the U-2 to the P-3; the U.S.–Pakistan relationship', *New Left Review* (September–October 1986): 71–80; Jamal Rashid, 'Pakistan and the Central Command', *Middle East Report* (July–August 1986): 28–34.

19. U.S. Congress. House. Committee on Foreign Affairs. *U.S. interests in, and policies toward, the Persian Gulf* (1980): 413–14; J. Clementson, 'Diego Garcia', *RUSI* (June 1981): 33–39.

20. U.S. Congress. Senate. Committee on Armed Services. *Military construction authorization fiscal year 1981*: 221–2; Joel Larus, 'Diego Garcia: political clouds over a vital U.S. base', *Strategic Review* (Winter 1982): 46.

117

Bases, 'Facility Access', and Geopolitics

21. U.S. Congress. House. Committee on Appropriations. *Military construction appropriations for 1981*, Part 4: 564.

22. Cited in Monoranjan Bezboruah, *U.S. strategy in the Indian Ocean: the international response* (New York: Praeger, 1977): 67.

23. U.S. Congress. House. Committee on Appropriations. *Military construction appropriations for 1981*, Part 4: 563–4; Senate. Committee on Armed Services. *Department of Defense authorization for appropriations for fiscal year 1981*, Part 1: 318; 'Diego Garcia assumes new strategic role', *Aviation Week and Space Technology*, February 25, 1980: 19; Joe Stork, 'The Carter Doctrine and U.S. bases in the Middle East', *Merip Reports* (September 1980): 12–13.

24. U.S. Congress. House. Committee on Appropriations. *Military construction appropriations for 1981*, Part 4: 560–1.

25. U.S. Congress. House. Committee on Foreign Affairs. *U.S. interests in, and policies toward, the Persian Gulf* (1980): 413.

26. U.S. Congress. Senate. Committee on Armed Services. *Department of Defense authorization for appropriations for fiscal year 1981*, Part 1: 318.

27. U.S. Congress. House. Committee on Armed Services. *Hearings on H.R. 1816 (H.R. 2972)*, *FY1984*: 554, 982.

28. U.S. Congress. Senate. Committee on Armed Services. *Military construction authorization fiscal year 1981*: 223–5.

29. U.S. Congress. Senate. Committee on Armed Services. *Military construction authorization fiscal year 1981*: 226; House. Committee on Appropriations. *Military construction appropriations for 1982*, Part 5: 213.

30. For details, see Larus, 'Diego Garcia', pp. 44–55.

31. Colin Legum (ed.), *Africa contemporary record: annual survey and documents, 1982–1983* (London: Africana Publishers, 1984): B235–B236.

32. *Washington Post*, August 22, 1980: A1, A20; 'Somalia: a new home for the deployment force', *Newsweek*, September 1, 1980: 35.

33. U.S. Congress. Senate. Committee on Armed Services. *Military construction authorization fiscal year 1982*: 191, 324; House. Committee on Appropriations, *Military construction appropriations for 1983*, Part 5: 266, 314.

34. Congressional Research Service, *Regional support facilities*, p. 21.

35. U.S. Congress. House. Committee on Foreign Affairs. *U.S. security interests in the Persian Gulf. Report of a staff study missions* (1981): 51; *New York Times*, September 14, 1980: iv, 6E.

36. U.S. Congress. House. Committee on Appropriations. *Military construction appropriations fiscal year 1982*: 311–15; House. Committee on Appropriations. *Military construction appropriations for 1983*, Part 5: 314–19.

37. U.S. Congress. House. Committee on Foreign Affairs. *U.S. security interests in the Persian Gulf. Report of a staff study mission* (1981): 51; Senate. Committee on Armed Services. *Military construction authorization fiscal year 1982*: 191; House. Committee on Appropriations. *Military construction appropriations for 1982*, Part 5: 181.

38. For a detailed historical overview of the Horn of Africa conflict, see Mohammed Ayoob, 'Horn of Africa', in Mohammed Ayoob (ed.), *Conflict and intervention in the Third World* (Canberra: Australian National University Press, 1980): 136–70. For a history of U.S. policy toward the Horn of Africa, see B. H. Selassie, 'The American dilemma on the Horn', *Journal of Modern African Studies* (June 1984): 249–72.

Bases, 'Facility Access', and Geopolitics

39. U.S. Congress. House. Committee on Foreign Affairs. *U.S. security interests in the Persian Gulf. Report of a staff study mission* (1981): 49; House. Committee on Foreign Affairs. *Reprogramming of military aid to Somalia* (1980).

40. *Washington Post*, September 25, 1980: A22; *Washington Post*, September 3, 1980: A15.

41. U.S. Congress. House. Committee on Foreign Affairs. *U.S. security interests in the Persian Gulf. Report of a staff study mission* (1981): 51; *Washington Post*, September 18, 1980: A39; *Washington Post*, September 6, 1980: A18; *Washington Post*, August 28, 1980: A10; *New York Times*, May 21, 1980: A7; Legum (ed.), *Africa contemporary record, 1982–1983*, p. B273; Larry W. Bowman and Jeffrey A. Lefebvre, 'U.S. strategic policy in Northeast Africa and the Indian Ocean', *Africa Report* (November–December 1983): 6.

42. *Washington Post*, February 22, 1980: A23; 'In Mideast turmoil, Kenya stands up to be counted', *U.S. News and World Report*, March 31, 1980: 51–52.

43. U.S. Congress. House. Committee on Foreign Affairs. *U.S. security interests in the Persian Gulf. Report of a staff study mission* (1981): 44; House Committee on appropriations. *Military construction appropriations for 1982*, Part 5: 104, 158; House. Committee on Appropriations. *Military construction appropriations for 1983*, Part 5: 266, 315.

44. U.S. Congress. Senate. Committee on Armed Services. *Military construction authorization fiscal year 1982*: 188, 322–3.

45. U.S. Congress. House. Committee on Armed Services. *Report on the delegation to the Middle East and Africa* (1982): 18.

46. U.S. Congress. Senate. Committee on Armed Services. *Military construction authorization fiscal year 1982*: 188.

47. U.S. Congress. Senate. Committee on Appropriations. *Military construction appropriations for fiscal year 1982*: 307–10; House. Committee on Appropriations. *Military construction appropriations for 1982*, Part 6: 3–10.

48. Cited in Colin Legum (ed.), *Africa contemporary record: annual survey and documents, 1981–82* (London: Africana Publishing Company, 1981): B202.

49. U.S. Congress. Senate. Committee on Armed Services. *Military construction authorization fiscal year 1982*: 188.

50. Samuel M. Makinda, 'Conflict and the superpowers in the Horn of Africa', *Third World Quarterly* (January 1982): 98; *Washington Post*, October 20, 1980: A19; Legum (ed.), *Africa contemporary record, 1980–81*, pp. B222–3, B268.

51. Cited in 'Egypt's growing importance for U.S.', *U.S. News and World Report*, May 12, 1980: 39.

52. Egyptian Defence Minister Ahmed Badawi interviewed in Cairo *Domestic Service* (in Arabic), 2004 GMT, 5 October 1980, *FBIS-MEA-80-195*, 6 October 1980; Egyptian Foreign Minister Kamal Hassan Ali quoted by Cairo *MENA* (in Arabic), 1900 GMT, 16 May 1981, *FBIS-MEA-81-095*, 18 May 1981; Cairo *MENA* (in Arabic), 2157 GMT, 23 August 1981, *FBIS-MEA-81-163*, 24 August 1981; U.S. Congress. House. Committee on Armed Services. *Report on the delegation to the Indian Ocean area* (1980): 13; House. Committee on Appropriations. *Military*

Bases, 'Facility Access', and Geopolitics

construction appropriations for 1981, Part 4: 534 – 5.

53. Congressional Research Service, *Regional support facilities*, pp. 27 – 29; U.S. Congress. House. Committee on Armed Services. *Report of the delegation to the Middle East and Africa* (1982): 9 – 10.

54. U.S. Congress. House. Committee on Armed Services. *Hearings on H.R. 1816 (H.R. 2972), fiscal year 1984*: 975, 987 – 8; Senate. Committee on Armed Services. *Military construction authorization fiscal year 1982*: 225 – 31; *Washington Post*, August 26, 1980: A1; *Washington Post*, October 8, 1981: A20.

55. *Washington Post*, May 20, 1983: A8.

56. U.S. Congress. House. Committee on Appropriations. *Military construction appropriations for 1985*, Part 4: 552; 'House panel OKs funding for base in Egypt', *Congressional Quarterly Weekly Report*, December 3, 1983: 2541.

57. *The Economist Foreign Report*, October 30, 1986: 1.

58. Cairo *Ash-Sha'b* (in Arabic), May 5, 1981, *FBIS-MEA-81-096*, May 19, 1981.

59. Interview with Mohammed Riad, 'Plugging the gap', *South* (March 1983): 17. Former Foreign Minister Ismail Fahmi's criticism can be found in Cairo *Ash-Sha'b* (in Arabic), December 31, 1980, *FBIS-MEA-81-004*, January 7, 1981.

60. *The Economist Foreign Report*, October 30, 1986: 1.

61. U.S. Congress. House. Committee on Foreign Affairs. *U.S. security interests in the Persian Gulf. Report of a staff study mission* (1981): 75.

62. Begin's speech to Knesset, *Jerusalem domestic service* (in Hebrew), 0815 GMT, August 5, 1981, *FBIS-MEA-81-151*, August 6, 1981.

63. Manama, *Gulf News Agency* (in Arabic), 0835 GMT, October 17, 1981, *FBIS-MEA-81-201*, October 19, 1981.

64. For details of these differences, see Tel Aviv, *Davar* (in Hebrew), October 18, 1981, *FBIS-MEA-81-201*, October 19, 1981; Jerusalem *Domestic Service* (in Hebrew), 0505 GMT, November 29, 1981, *FBIS-MEA-81-229*, November 30, 1981; Joe Stork, 'Israel as a strategic asset', *Merip Reports* (May 1982): 11 – 12.

65. Articles espousing this view appeared regularly in the U.S. press. Examples: Jay Adams, 'Assessing Israel as a "strategic asset"', *Middle East Review* (Fall – Winter, 1981 – 82): 43 – 54; Steven L. Spiegel, 'Israel as a strategic asset', *Commentary* (June 1983): 51 – 55.

66. Prime Minister Shamir, cited in 'A new deal for Israel', *Time*, December 12, 1983: 40.

67. Ibid., *Middle East International*, December 9, 1983: 4.

68. This was one of the major conclusions of the Tower Commission, which investigated the 'Iran – Contra Affair' in 1987.

69. U.S. Congress. House. Committee on Foreign Affairs. *U.S. interests in, and policies toward, the Persian Gulf* (1980): 32.

70. Abu Dhabi *Domestic Service* (in Arabic), 1342 GMT, May 26, 1981, *FBIS-MEA-81-101*, May 27, 1981.

71. *Washington Post*, February 12, 1980: A1; *Washington Post*, April 22, 1980: A3; *Washington Post*, June 5, 1980: A1 – A10; U.S. Congress. House. Committee on Armed Services. *Hearings on military posture and H.R. 2970 (H.R. 3519), FY1982*, Part 1: 1137.

120

Bases, 'Facility Access', and Geopolitics

72. Department of Defence, *Annual report to Congress, FY1986*: 234.
73. Congressional Research Service, *Regional support facilities*, pp. 14–15; U.S. Congress. House. Committee on Foreign Affairs. *U.S. security interests in the Persian Gulf. Report of a staff study mission* (1981): 16–17; *Washington Post*, October 11, 1980: A21.
74. U.S. Congress. Senate. Committee on Armed Services. *Department of Defense authorization for appropriations for fiscal year 1983*, Part 6: 3764; 'Masirah likes company', *The Economist*, July 2, 1983: 50; Congressional Research Service, *Rapid deployment force* (1985): 5; Congressional Research Service, *Regional support facilities*: 15; U.S. Congress. Senate. Committee on Armed Services. *Department of Defense authorization for appropriations for fiscal year 1983*, Part 6: 3764; House. Committee on Appropriations. *Military construction appropriations for 1985*, Part 6: 579; J. E. Peterson, 'American policy in the Gulf and the Sultanate of Oman', *American – Arab Affairs* (Spring 1984): 126–7.
75. Peter W. DeForth, 'U.S. naval presence in the Persian Gulf: the MIDEAST Force since World War II', *Naval War College Review* (Summer 1975): 28–38.
76. U.S. Congress. Senate. Committee on Foreign Relations. *United States foreign policy objectives and overseas military installations* (1979): 112–14; House. Committee on Appropriations. *Military construction appropriations for 1981*, Part 4: 524.
77. *International Herald Tribune*, June 1, 1987: 1.
78. U.S. Congress. House. Committee on International Relations. *United States arms policies in the Persian Gulf and Red Sea areas* (1977): 28; 'Defending the Gulf: a survey', *The Economist*, June 6, 1981: 18.
79. U.S. Congress. Senate. Committee on Foreign Relations. *War in the Gulf* (1984): 21.
80. U.S. Congress. Senate. Committee on Armed Services. *Military and technical implications of the proposed sale to Saudi Arabia of airborne warning and control system (AWACS) and F-15 enhancements* (1981): 84.
81. U.S. Congress. Senate. Committee on Foreign Relations. *War in the Gulf* (1984): 32–33.
82. Michael C. Hudson, 'The U.S. decline in the Middle East: can it be stopped?' *Orbis* (Spring 1982): 22.
83. See especially, Irving Kristol, 'What a Palestinian solution won't solve', *Washington Post*, October 25, 1979: A21. The British historian, J. B. Kelly, espouses this view and is rebutted by Herman Eilts in 'Point/ Counterpoint', *International Security* (Spring 1981): 191–2, 200–1.
84. Riyadh, *Saudi Press Agency* (in Arabic), 0740 GMT, February 23, 1980, *FBIS-MEA-80-038*, February 25, 1980.
85. R. K. Ramazani, 'Security in the Persian Gulf', *Foreign Affairs* (Spring 1979): 826–7.
86. Manama, *Akharbar Al-Khalij* (in Arabic), March 4, 1981, *FBIS-MEA-81-044*, March 6, 1981.
87. Kuwait, *KUNA* (in Arabic), 1233 GMT, March 22, 1981, *FBIS-MEA-81-055*, March 23, 1981; Beirut, *Monday Morning* (in English), July 20–26, 1981, *FBIS-MEA-81-151*, August 6, 1981.
88. Abdul Kasim Mansur, 'The American threat to Saudi Arabia', *Survival* (January – February 1981): 37–38.

Bases, 'Facility Access', and Geopolitics

89. Christopher van Hollen, 'Don't engulf the Gulf', *Foreign Affairs* (Summer 1981): 1066; Anthony H. Cordesman, *The Gulf and the search for strategic stability* (Boulder, CO: Westview, 1984): 259.

90. Kuwait, *As-Siyasah* (in Arabic), November 13, 1979, *FBIS-MEA-79-226*, November 21, 1979.

91. For the evolution of the GCC, see Valerie Yorke, 'Bid for Gulf unity', *World Today* (July–August 1981): 246–9; see John Duke Anthony, 'The Gulf Cooperation Council', *Journal of South Asian and Middle East Studies* (Summer 1982): 3–18; Joseph A. Kechichian, 'The Gulf Cooperation Council: search for security', *Third World Quarterly* (October 1985): 853–81; Amitav Acharya, 'Gulf States' efforts to ensure collective security', *Pacific Defence Reporter* (April 1986): 11–13.

6
Threats, Contingency Planning, and Response

U.S. military planners designing a new strategic framework for the Gulf in the wake of the Iranian revolution recognized the need to plan for a wide variety of threats and contingencies. As the principal events of 1979–80, the Iranian turmoil, the Soviet invasion of Afghanistan, and the outbreak of the Iran–Iraq War proved, the sources of threats to Gulf security could be either internal, intra-regional, or external. Thus, any credible interventionist posture in the region must be flexible enough to deal with situations across the spectrum of conflict. This belief was clearly stated by General P. X. Kelly in 1980 when he described the task of the RDJTF as being to develop 'a number of force packages . . . each with its own political signals and each with its own combat capabilities'.[1] These packages, according to Kelly, could range from deployment of early warning aircraft to that of heavy ground forces, with the exact size and composition of the forces tailored to the needs of specific conflict situations. Pentagon officials left no doubt that the contingency planning for the Gulf would take into account 'threats of any magnitude, from internal subversion to a large-scale Soviet aggression'.[2]

'Non-Soviet' threats

As underscored in the President's 1980 State of the Union address, the Carter administration's declared military objective in the Gulf was a capability to counter a Soviet invasion. None the less, the RDJTF's contingency planning took into account other, 'non-Soviet' threats. The Under Secretary of Defense, Robert Komer,

123

Contingency Planning and Response

expressed concern regarding the possibility of 'outside-influenced coups, subversion, in the area' and declared that the United States would work 'to prevent adverse developments of that sort'. Komer also did not rule out U.S. involvement 'if Iraq invade[d] Saudi Arabia, or if South Yemen invade[d] Saudi Arabia'.[3]

As Western fears, raised in the wake of the Afghanistan crisis, of a Soviet military threat to the Gulf proved to be unfounded, non-Soviet contingencies came to figure more prominently in the U.S. strategy. The shadow cast by the Iran–Iraq War over regime stability in the GCC states contributed to this shift. As will be discussed later in the chapter, President Reagan added a corollary to the Carter Doctrine by announcing a commitment to the survival of the Saudi regime. Francis West, then an Assistant Secretary of Defense under the Reagan administration, told a congressional subcommittee that it would be the U.S. policy to

Support moderate states (e.g. Saudi Arabia, Oman, Jordan, Egypt) against overt attack by radical states;

Support moderate states against the spillover of regional conflicts and subversion aided and directed by outside powers.[4]

But while stressing the need for a capability to intervene in domestic and intra-regional conflicts in the Gulf, U.S. planners left it unclear exactly what form of intervention would be undertaken. In purely military terms, of course, U.S. forces could be used in situations of domestic instability in a variety of ways. An intervention could separate factions in an internal power struggle, or protect the personages of a threatened regime, as was the case with past U.S. intervention in Lebanon and the Dominican Republic. Light and mobile U.S. forces, such as the 82nd Airborne Division, could help secure at least some oil installations from organized saboteurs likely to operate in a case of domestic strife.[5] And aggression against a pro-Western regional state could possibly be deterred by prompt action in landing U.S. forces in the threatened country or conducting military exercises in the vicinity.

On the other hand, a direct U.S. intervention in crises such as coups, subversion, and other forms of domestic strife would be constrained by many factors. To begin with, a rapid response might not be possible due to lack of adequate warning time. Warning could be completely absent in some instances, such as the

Contingency Planning and Response

takeover of the Grand Mosque by religious fundamentalists in 1979. In other cases, warning indicators might be too ambiguous or uncertain to provide sufficient basis for action. The Iranian revolution was a case in point. Even as late as in August 1978, when many Iran watchers were pointing to the alarming trends of strife and unrest within a growing body of the Iranian population, the CIA was advising the U.S. President that Iran was 'not in a revolutionary or even a pre-revolutionary situation'.[6]

Even if adequate warning were available, political constraints on both the United States and the threatened regimes could prevent prompt, if any, action. Local regimes would be unlikely to ask for help unless and until the situation was well beyond their ability to control. That could be too late. In addition, adverse domestic reaction could interfere with the President's ability to take effective action. The U.S. public and Congress would be far less tolerant of intervention in domestic or intra-regional conflicts than they would in the face of a Soviet invasion.[7]

Furthermore, U.S. intervention in local conflicts where the offending power was a Soviet ally could not but take into account the possibility of Soviet involvement — a consideration that might inhibit both the local states from seeking U.S. help and the U.S. President from providing it. Finally, most domestic or intra-regional threats, rooted in complex social, economic, religious, ethnic, and political factors, would not lend themselves to military solutions. The presence and intervention of foreign military forces in such situations could aggravate the resentment of the local population and, rather than stabilizing domestic strife, would expedite the downfall of a regime that relied upon outside help.[8]

It was perhaps with these considerations in mind that the Pentagon outlined a cautious approach to Gulf crises not directly involving the Soviet Union. In his FY 1983 report to Congress, Defense Secretary Casper Weinberger stated that in so far as non-Soviet threats were concerned, U.S. intervention would, in most cases,

> include economic, technical, political, and security assistance programs. U.S. military participation would necessarily be affected by the political sensitivities involved and could range from the provision of training, material and security assistance to the employment of third-party assistance or the tailored use of military force.[9]

Contingency Planning and Response

The constraints on U.S. military intervention in a non-Soviet contingency in the Gulf was particularly evident in the U.S. policy toward the Iran–Iraq War, the most serious threat to Gulf security during the period covered in this study. The U.S. response to the war was based largely on arms transfers to Saudi Arabia designed to bolster its capability against Iran, economic and political backing of Iraq to prevent an Iranian victory in the war, and an over-the-horizon military presence meant to reassure the GCC states of U.S. resolve to prevent a spillover of the war into the Arab side of the Gulf. As part of its overall strategy in the Gulf, the United States also encouraged 'third-party assistance', by endorsing and supporting efforts by its European allies, Britain and France, and its regional allies, Jordan and Pakistan, to develop a capability to assist the GCC states in a crisis. In addition, the United States used arms sales to the GCC countries to realize the twin objectives of enhancing the latter's capabilities against local threats and increasing its leverage with their individual as well as collective security policies. The following sections will look at these elements of the U.S. strategy in some detail.

Response to the Gulf war: 1980 – 84

As noted earlier, in the aftermath of the Iranian revolution and the Soviet invasion of Afghanistan, the United States viewed its security challenges in the Gulf mainly in terms of a possible collapse of the Saudi regime and Soviet expansionism. In the end, however, both fears proved to be unfounded. The most crucial test for the new U.S. strategy in the region came in the shape of armed confrontation between the Gulf's two most powerful states, Iran and Iraq.

When the war broke out in September 1980, the United States found itself in an unenviable position. Coming after successive debacles in Iran and Afghanistan, this conflict threatened U.S. interests further. Looming in Washington were the fears of yet another oil shock and the possible engulfment of the remaining conservative regimes by a spillover of the conflict. Yet, while the stakes were so serious, the United States had little ability to influence the course of events. It lacked diplomatic relations with both sides. The newly formed RDJTF was irrelevant as far as the belligerents were concerned.[10] Cooperation with the Iranian side

Contingency Planning and Response

was impossible in view of the continuing hostage crisis. Washington's room for manoeuvre was restricted by a fear that any help it might extend to either side could backfire dangerously by pushing the other towards Moscow, whose contacts with both sides far exceeded Washington's. This concern was especially grave with respect to Iran, where the revolution already appeared to have opened up tempting opportunities for the Soviets. Finally, the United States also feared that a clear victory for either side would jeopardize its interests even further. An Iraqi victory might have led to the disintegration of Iran and invited Soviet intervention in that country. Besides, whichever country emerged as a clear winner would have been well placed to extend its domination over the Arabian Peninsula and force its own brand of radical anti-Westernism on the existing pro-Western outlook of the conservative regimes.[11]

The shape of U.S. policy towards the war was influenced by these considerations. The policy had four basic objectives: (1) to seek a dynamic balance of power between the warring sides so that neither achieved victory; (2) to ensure that the Soviets did not exploit the conflict to gain a dominant position in either country; (3) to prevent the war from undermining the survival of the conservative regimes; and (4) to ensure the continued flow of oil from the Persian Gulf.[12]

The Carter administration's first reaction to the war was to declare its neutrality and non-involvement. But before clarifying its response, it also sought similar assurances from Moscow. Washington was lucky because Moscow, too, could ill afford to take sides. Open and all-out support for Baghdad, as would have seemed logical in view of Baghdad's status as an ally under their Treaty of Friendship, meant the loss of any conceivable opportunity to befriend the new regime in Iran — an objective the Kremlin clearly cherished. On the other hand, support for Iran would have meant abandoning its long-established alliance with Iraq and setting a dangerous example to other Soviet allies in the Third World. Thus, it was not surprising that when Secretary of State Edmund Muskie met his Soviet counterpart, Andrei Gromyko, in New York in September 1980, he reportedly received Moscow's pledge of neutrality in the Iran – Iraq War.[13]

But while professing neutrality, the Carter administration was also keen to avoid any impression of indifference to the outcome of the conflict. As Muskie declared in October 1980: 'to be impartial is not to be inactive; to declare that we will not take sides is not to

Contingency Planning and Response

declare that we have no interests at stake'.[14] The administration's desire to prevent an Iranian collapse at a time when Iraq seemed poised for an overwhelming victory, and its continuing preoccupation with the fate of American hostages in Teheran, led it to propose an 'arms for hostages' deal. Under the terms of the deal, President Carter offered to release about $150 million in armaments (including aircraft spares) negotiated by the Shah but held up by the Carter administration in retaliation against the seizure of American hostages. In return, Teheran was required to free all the hostages. Iran, however, did not see merit in the proposed deal, despite the acute shortage of spares for U.S.-made weapons which was undermining its ability to fend off the Iraqi offensive.[15]

To minimize provocations to Teheran, the Carter administration discouraged Saudi Arabia and other GCC regimes from becoming closely aligned with the Iraqi war effort. In September 1980 planned moves by Iraq to use military bases in the Arabian Peninsula prompted the administration to ask the Gulf States to stay neutral.[16] But mere advice could not reassure the GCC states of U.S. commitment to defend them from Iran's frequent threats to spread the conflict to the Arabian Peninsula. Although seriously depleted, Iran's air force still had the capability to create panic in the GCC states through bombing raids. Thus, for the United States and the Arab Gulf States, containment of the Gulf war meant assisting the latter's defences against the Iranian air force.

Soon after the war broke out, the Saudis, according to Brzezinski, asked 'for American military protection' on an emergency basis, including 'deployment of American AWACS, enhanced air defense, and greater intelligence support'.[17] The Saudi request was prompted by fears of imminent Iranian air strikes (in retaliation against planned Iraqi moves to use Saudi, Omani, and Kuwaiti bases for attacks against Iran). After a brief but heated inter-agency debate, during which the State Department opposed the deployment on the ground that it would compromise U.S. neutrality (at least in Soviet eyes), President Carter approved immediate deployment of four AWACS early warning aircraft accompanied by 300 U.S. Air Force crew and ground support personnel. On October 5 the Pentagon announced plans to send another 100 personnel, this time to accompany ground radar and communication equipment.[18] Although in the end Iraq did not use GCC facilities, that did not prevent Pentagon officials from claiming that it was the presence of American AWACS that 'discouraged the Iranians from acting out of desperation'.[19]

Contingency Planning and Response

The AWACS deployment, apart from serving as a powerful symbol of U.S. commitment to Saudi security, was a considerable boost to the latter's air defence capability. Conventional ground radar, with limited range, could not give the Saudi Air Force sufficient warning time to intercept any attacking Iranian aircraft before it reached vital targets close to the Gulf coast. The AWACS, with a range of more than 200 miles, eliminated this deficiency. A dramatic illustration of the AWACS' early warning capability was provided in May 1984, when Saudi-piloted F-15s (some reports have claimed that the pilots were Pakistani) using information supplied by the AWACS (operated by a U.S. crew), destroyed at least one Iranian F-4 plane near Jubail.[20] Iranian air operations near that area ceased thereafter. Later the information collected by the AWACS was made available to other GCC states and possibly to Iraq.[21]

Brzezinski and Brown also advocated sending U.S. F-15 squadrons to Saudi Arabia along with the AWACS in order to reinforce Saudi air defence assets.[22] As with the AWACS, the State Department opposed the proposal, arguing that such actions were likely to prove even more provocative to Moscow, although the AWACS deployment could at least pass as a defensive measure. Although U.S. interceptors were not eventually deployed to the region, Washington was secure in the knowledge that if need arose F-14 interceptor squadrons from the aircraft carrier *Eisenhower*, then operating in the Indian Ocean, could be flown to Saudi Arabia in 'less than two hours'.[23]

While assisting the air defence capability of the GCC states, the Carter administration also threatened the use of military force to keep the Strait and the Gulf open to shipping. 'It is imperative that there be no infringement of the freedom of ships to and from the Persian Gulf region', declared President Carter in September 1980.[24] The administration sought to back up its pledge through reinforced naval deployments. For example, 32 U.S. ships, including the aircraft carriers *Eisenhower* and *Midway*, were deployed in the western Indian Ocean in October 1980. This powerful flotilla maintained a patrol over the Strait, ready to 'sweep any mines laid by Iran, assist tankers hit in any attack or confront any Iranian vessels that tried to harass oil ships'.[25] To reinforce its own presence, the United States sought contributions from its two principal European allies, Britain and France. Britain organized a 'Gulf patrol' near the Strait of Hormuz to escort British tankers in the Gulf.[26] The French presence in the region

129

Contingency Planning and Response

was much more substantial, including 20 ships in the western Indian Ocean region, 1,200 paratroopers on Réunion Island, and about 3,500 marines and legionnaires in Djibouti. Both Britain and France expressed a commitment to the freedom of navigation in the Gulf, although France turned down a U.S. proposal for a joint Western naval force in the Gulf. But informal consultations and coordination between allied naval forces in the region took place, and this became an important aspect of the U.S. policy toward the Gulf war.[27]

By the time the Carter administration left office, the essential elements of the U.S. response to the war were already in place. The Reagan administration's policy toward the war during its first term differed little from that of its predecessors. The Reagan administration reaffirmed the Carter principle that its neutrality in the conflict did not mean indifference to its outcome. The new Secretary of State, Alexander Haig, announced the U.S. determination to protect 'its friends and interests that are endangered by the continuation of hostilities' in the Gulf.[28] The Reagan administration also stressed that it wanted neither Iran nor Iraq to win the war. A 'victory by either side', the State Department warned, was 'neither militarily achievable or strategically desirable because of its destabilizing effect on the region'.[29]

Two important developments marked the Reagan administration's policy toward the war during its first term in office. The first was an increased commitment to Saudi security and a strengthening of U.S.–Saudi military cooperation. The centrepiece of this development was the sale of the AWACS package at a total price of $5 billion. Although linked more to the long-term U.S. strategy in the region (to be discussed later in the chapter) than to the immediate requirements of the administration's policy toward the Gulf war (which had been met by its predecessor's deployment of USAF AWACS to the Kingdom), the AWACS sale none the less became a symbol of growing U.S. concern over the potentially destabilizing consequences of the Gulf war. It also provided an opportunity for Reagan to add a corollary to the Carter Doctrine, stressing U.S. commitment to Saudi internal stability. In the course of his intensive personal lobbying to secure congressional approval for the sale, President Reagan declared on 1 October 1981: 'Saudi Arabia we won't permit to be an Iran.' Explaining the meaning of this statement, Defense Secretary Caspar Weinberger stated, 'We would not stand by in the event of Saudi requests, as we did before with Iran, and allow a government that

Contingency Planning and Response

has been totally unfriendly to the United States and to the Free World to take over.'[30] Whether or not this commitment to Saudi Arabia would be extended to other GCC states, especially Kuwait, in the event of an Iranian attack, was not confirmed. But at least some administration officials were contemplating greater U.S. military involvement in the Gulf. A secret State Department memorandum, written in mid-1984 by Admiral John Howe, then director of Political-Military Affairs, sketched five 'thresholds' in the war which, if crossed, might lead to escalating U.S. intervention in support of the GCC states. The deployment of the AWACS in response to Saudi requests put the United States at 'threshold 3'. Threshold 4 entailed active involvement of the U.S. Navy, using escort ships, carriers, and fighter patrols, to protect shipping in the Gulf and vital installations in Kuwait or Saudi Arabia. Threshold 5, which would be crossed if U.S. personnel involved in the previous threshold were killed by Iranians, would, according to Howe's scenario, trigger full-scale U.S. military retaliation involving 'an active use of American forces to take out targets in Iran'.[31]

Like its predecessor, the Reagan administration also resorted to emergency transfers of arms to the Saudi Kingdom in response to anticipated Iranian air attacks. In May 1984, when shipping in the Persian Gulf came under severe threat following repeated hits scored by both Iran and Iraq, the Saudis requested immediate delivery of Stinger missiles [shoulder-fired anti-aircraft missiles]. The Reagan administration, fearing inevitable election-year congressional opposition to the sale, sought to bypass it by invoking a presidential waiver. It approved the immediate transfer of 400 Stinger missiles and 200 Stinger launchers, along with the deployment by the CENTCOM of a KC-10 tanker aircraft. It also accelerated the delivery of 12 sets of conformal fuel tanks (purchased earlier) needed to extend the range of Saudi F-15s. Justifying the presidential waiver before Congress, the State Department claimed that the move had 'sent a signal across the Gulf to Teheran', thereby preventing 'a potential emergency from getting larger'.[32] It has since been revealed by the congressional investigation into Irangate that in return for this help as well as for the sale of the AWACS aircraft in 1981, the Saudis agreed, in an informal *quid pro quo*, to provide financial assistance to the Nicaraguan contras.[33]

The second major development in the Reagan administration's policy toward the war was the beginnings of a U.S. tilt towards

Contingency Planning and Response

Iraq. The official posture of 'neutrality' was never abandoned. But a conspicuous improvement in U.S. – Iraqi relations was evident, partly influenced by the administration's 'victory for neither side' objective. For it was Iraq that was now on the defensive, following Iran's success in recapturing Khorramshar in May 1982. As Iraqi fortunes in the war plummetted, U.S. – Iraqi relations began to thaw.

An important part in this development was played by a shift in the Iraqi approach to the war during its third year, when frustrated by Iran's refusal to come to any kind of ceasefire agreement with the Hussein regime, the latter decided to take the war to the waters of the Persian Gulf. The Iraqi objectives were twofold: first, to incapacitate Iran economically and second, to raise the stakes of the outside world, particularly the United States, in a quick end to the conflict. The new Iraqi tactics were to attack Iranian oil terminals in the Gulf and tankers taking crude deliveries from Iranian ports. To carry out the attack, Iraq requested France, its main source of Western arms, to supply it with super-Etendard attack planes capable of launching Exocet anti-ship missiles. In May 1983, when Iraqi foreign minister Tariq Aziz went to Paris to negotiate the deal, he also met U.S. Secretary of State George Shultz.[34] Four months later, the Iraqi Deputy Foreign Minister travelled to Washington to offer prospects for improved relations with the U.S. if the Reagan administration acted to organize an international boycott of arms sales to Iran while tolerating third-party transfer of U.S.-made weapons to Iraq.[35] The United States had earlier sought to dissuade France from selling the super-Etendard planes to Iraq, but by October the objections had been dropped. The official Iraqi paper, *Ath-Thawra*, claimed in October 1983 that the U.S. position in the war had shifted towards 'acceptance of a decisive Iraqi action against Iranian oil installations', an action Iraq claimed would cripple Iran's war-making ability and force Khomeini to the negotiating table.[36]

During 1984 the Reagan administration's support for Iraq became more concrete and substantial. Although Washington condemned the Iraqi use of chemical weapons in the war, Iraq was removed from the list of unfriendly states, which included countries practising 'state-sponsored terrorism'. In May 1984 Iraq claimed that it had received assurances from the United States to increase its efforts to persuade its European allies to stem the flow of arms to Iran.[37] And the United States for the first time publicly blamed Iran for the continuation of the war. Shortly before the

Contingency Planning and Response

London Economic Summit, Reagan himself praised Iraq for 'playing by the rules of the game' while accusing Teheran as being 'the one who seems to resist any effort' to bring the conflict to an end.[38] The United States also voted in favour of UN resolutions condemning Iran's refusal to negotiate a truce with Baghdad.

The political/diplomatic support for Iraq was complemented by economic measures. Almost $1 billion in U.S. commodity credits was made available to Iraq for the purchase of U.S. agricultural products. The administration also backed efforts by Iraq to build a new pipeline to the Jordanian port of Aqaba. Iraq had launched the pipeline project in a bid to increase its oil exports, which had been severely curtailed by the destruction of its oil terminals in the Gulf and the closure of its pipeline through Syria, which backed Iran in the Gulf war. In June 1984 the U.S. Ex-Im Bank, under political pressure from Reagan officials, extended credit guarantees to cover 85 per cent of the construction budget of the pipeline of $570 million. The administration justified this assistance as a 'necessary element' of its victory-for-neither-side policy, which necessitated avoiding the 'economic collapse' of Iraq.[39]

Following the establishment of full diplomatic relations between the two countries in November 1984, the Reagan administration's support for Iraq was apparently extended into the strategic arena. This included intelligence information, in the form of photos taken by U.S. satellites and reconnaissance aircraft, on Iranian positions and installations which were or would be, targets of Iraqi bombing missions.[40] Later, the CIA established a direct secret link between Baghdad and Washington to improve the communication channels transmitting U.S. intelligence information. The former Director of Central Intelligence, William Casey, reportedly encouraged Iraq to carry out more raids on Iranian installations.[41]

While U.S. – Iraqi relations continued to improve, the Reagan administration maintained its tough but largely rhetorical stance with regard to the freedom of navigation in the Gulf. At the height of the tanker war in 1984, Iran threatened to close the Strait of Hormuz in response to the Iraqi acquisition of super-Etendard planes. This was largely an empty threat. Iran clearly lacked the means to mine the Strait, and, contrary to popular belief, at no point is the Gulf narrow or shallow enough to be blocked by sinking a tanker.[42] But this did not deter Reagan from publicly committing U.S. forces to keep the Strait open to shipping. A special Cabinet-level group was set up at the White House to co-ordinate contingency planning. Naval forces in the Gulf of Oman

133

Contingency Planning and Response

were increased, and in February the administration hinted that ground troops might also be sent to the Gulf if naval forces proved inadequate.[43] According to a congressional estimate, some 10,500 U.S. military personnel were deployed aboard U.S. naval ships in the Gulf and the Arabian Sea in May 1984, in addition to 1,000 U.S. personnel stationed in the GCC states.[44] From this time, the U.S. Navy began the practice of escorting U.S.-flag oil tankers in the Gulf, a practice that later led the former White House spokesman, Larry Speakes, to assert: 'The U.S. has been prepared to protect U.S. shipping and prepared to keep the Straits open, and has done so by using its military.'[45]

The Reagan administration, like its predecessor, recognized both the limitations of military force and the importance of political and economic instruments in its policy towards the Gulf war. None the less, both administrations believed that while U.S. forces could not be used to dictate the outcome of the war itself, they could play a crucial role in protecting U.S. interests in the neighbourhood: by keeping the sea lanes open and sending a strong signal to Teheran that the United States would not be indifferent to its efforts to spread the war to the GCC states. The U.S. resolve was never seriously tested by Iran, and it is unlikely that the stand taken by the Carter and Reagan administrations was not a factor in Teheran's calculations. But although the United States managed to emerge from the first four years of the conflict with its interests in the Gulf largely intact, it failed to realize its declared objective of bringing the conflict to an end. The Gulf war continued to cast a shadow over the future of oil supplies from the region and regime security in the GCC states.

Arms sales

Security assistance and arms transfers played a major role in the evolution of the post-Shah U.S. military strategy in the Gulf, despite the controversy over arms sales to the Shah. But the United States viewed arms sales as a cost-effective and practical adjunct to its interventionist posture. A Pentagon assessment in 1980 concluded that while the conservative Gulf States facing an uncertain future in the wake of the Iranian revolution did not have the 'capability to defend against a full-scale Soviet or Soviet-instigated invasion, . . . for lesser contingencies their capabilities now range from fair to good and will improve given timely and appropriate

Contingency Planning and Response

U.S. military assistance'.[46] By helping the GCC states to defend themselves, the United States could avoid politically risky and potentially counter-productive intervention in low-level conflicts in the Gulf. Thus, U.S. security assistance to the regional countries could be 'complementary' to the RDJTF, not a 'substitute' (see Table 6.1).[47]

Table 6.1: U.S. security assistance to the Gulf Cooperation Council States (in millions U.S. dollars)

			Country			
Type of assistance	Bahrain	Kuwait	Oman	Qatar	Saudi Arabia	United Arab Emirates
FMS Cash sales						
(1975–87)	481.6	1,533	—	0.8	59,974[b]	1,159.5
FMS Guaranteed						
(1975–87)	—	—	190[a]		254[b]	—
Total no. of military students trained						
(1983–87)	78	1,196	81	50	3,646	342

Source: Statement of General George B. Crist, Commander-in-Chief, U.S. Central Command before the Defense Policy Panel of the House Armed Services Committee, March 17, 1987.
[a]Figures are for the 1974–87 period.
[b]Figures are for the 1979–87 period.

Restraint on arms sales to the developing countries was one of the many casualties among the Carter administration's early foreign policy principles following the Shah's overthrow. Nowhere was this change in greater evidence than in the Gulf region. Immediately after the Shah's downfall, Defense Secretary Harold Brown toured the Middle East to discuss the administration's desire to boost security assistance to the pro-Western regional states as part of its new 'regional cooperative security framework'.[48] Acting on Brown's recommendation, Carter himself confirmed this policy in late February 1979.[49] After it was put to the test during the Yemeni crisis in the following month (when the administration rushed F-5 combat planes and M-60 tanks to North Yemen to fight an alleged South Yemeni attack), the Carter administration made a substantial review of the existing policy on weapon sales to the smaller Gulf monarchies. In the 1970s, when

Contingency Planning and Response

U.S. arms sales to Saudi Arabia and Iran rose phenomenally in accordance with the Nixon Doctrine, the smaller Gulf States had been discouraged (with the minor exceptions of Kuwait and Oman) from buying 'offensive' or 'sophisticated' weaponry — including fixed-wing aircraft. In 1977, for example, the United States had turned down a UAE request for TOW missiles, offering instead the M-16 rifle. In 1980 the Carter administration made a 'thorough reexamination' of existing policy and decided on an 'enhanced defense supply relationship' with the smaller states. The list of weapons that could be sold to these states now came to include M-60 tanks, FX (F-20) combat aircraft, the TOW missile, and improved Hawk anti-aircraft missile systems.[50]

The Reagan administration carried this liberalization process further in terms of both policy guidelines and actual sales, reflecting its total rejection of the early Carter policy of reducing America's conventional arms trade. Carter's half-hearted and half-pursued moralism on the issue was replaced by the new Reagan rhetoric that dubbed arms transfers as an 'essential element' of U.S. 'global defense posture and an indispensable component of its foreign policy'.[51] The Reagan approach was reflected in initiatives such as the elimination of the last of the Carter restraints, including the so-called 'Leprosy Letter', which had prohibited U.S. diplomatic missions abroad from assisting U.S. defence manufacturers in negotiating sales. It also increased by 30 per cent the U.S. security assistance programs for FY 1982 and created a Special Defense Acquisition Fund to purchase arms in anticipation of future urgent FMS requests which otherwise might have to wait for some time due to the long lead times involved in manufacturing. Finally, the Reagan administration raised the dollar threshold at which arms sales proposals were required to obtain congressional approval from $7 million to $14 million for weapons and from $25 million to $50 million for other defence articles and services.[52]

In the Gulf, although the smaller GCC states, such as Bahrain and Oman, benefitted from the new U.S. policy on arms sales (see Table 6.2), Saudi Arabia continued to be the largest buyer of U.S. equipment by a substantial margin. The most important deal concluded between the two countries during this period was the 'AWACS Package' (see Table 6.3) in 1981, which the Reagan administration described as an 'important part of a comprehensive U.S. strategy for the Southwest Asia region'.[53] The objectives of the deal were threefold.

Contingency Planning and Response

Table 6.2: Major identified arms agreements between the United States and the GCC States, 1979–85

Recipient	Date of agreement	Weapon systems	Quantity
Bahrain	Dec 1981	Improved Hawk SAM	—
	Jan 1982	Bell 412 transport helicopters	2
	Apr 1982	F-5E fighter aircraft	4
		F-5F training aircraft	2
		TOW ATGW	2,000
	Feb 1983	F-4J Phantom fighter	12 +
	Feb 1985	F-5E/F fighter/support aircraft	6
		AIM-9P3 Sidewinder AAM	—
	Nov 1985	M-60A-3 MBT	54
Kuwait	Sept 1979	Improved Hawk SAM	—
	Oct 1980	M-113 A2 APC	52
		M-113 APC/Ambulance	29
		M-113 SP TOW ATGW AFV	6
		M-577 A2 command post	14
		M-125 A2 mortar carrier	2
	Jun 1981	Improved Hawk SAM	60
	Mar 1982	M-113 A2 APC	16
		M-901 Improved TOW vehicle	56
		Improved TOW ATGW	4,800
	Dec 1981	Improved Hawk SAM launcher	27
		Improved Hawk SAM	164
	Jan 1982	L-100-30 transport aircraft	4
	July 1984	Sedan patrol boats	20
	August 1984	V-150/300 APC	20/62
Oman	Oct 1979	Sidewinder AAM	250
	Oct 1980	C-130H transport aircraft	1
		M-60 medium tank	6
	Mar 1981	C-130H transport aircraft	1
	Nov 1981	C-130H transport aircraft	2
	May 1983	Bell-214 ST helicopter	6
	Sept 1985	AIM-9P4 Sidewinder AAM	300
Saudi Arabia	July 1979	M-60 A1 medium tanks	32
	Oct 1979	Dragon ATGW launchers	172
		Dragon ATGW	1,292
	Nov 1979	Maverick ASM	916
		Sidewinder AAM	660
		TOW ATGW	1,000
		TOW ATGW launchers	50
	Feb 1981	V-150 Commando AFV	579
	Oct 1981	KC-135 tanker aircraft	6
		AIM-9L Sidewinder AAM	1,177
		E-3A AWACS	5

Contingency Planning and Response

Table 6.2 — continued

Recipient	Date of agreement	Weapon systems	Quantity
	Feb 1982	M198 155mm towed howitzer	18
	May 1982	RF-5E reconnaissance aircraft	10
		F-5F training aircraft	5
	May 1983	KC-707 tanker aircraft	6 +
		AIM-7F Sparrow AAM	1,000
	Jun 1984	FIM-92A Stinger SAM	200
	1984	M-198 Howitzer	30
	Mar 1985	AIM-9P4 AAM	671
		AIM-9L AAM	995
		Harpoon ASM	100
UAE	Jun 1981	C-130H transport aircraft	2
	Nov 1981	TOW ATGW launchers	54
		Improved Hawk SAM launchers	7 batteries
		Improved Hawk SAM	343
	Jan 1983	C-130 H-30 transport aircraft	1

Source: *The military balance* (London: International Institute for Strategic Studies) for years 1980–81, 1981–82, 1982–83, 1983–84, 1984–85, 1985–86, 1986–87.

Some of the agreements are subject to cancellation or changes.

Abbreviations: ATGW, anti-tank guided weapon; AAM, air-to-air missile; AFV, armoured fighting vehicle; ASM, air-to-surface missile; AWACS, airborne warning and control system; APC, armoured personnel carrier; SAM, surface-to-air missile; TOW, tube-launched, optically tracked, wire-guided.

The first was to enhance Saudi capabilities against Iranian air attacks. Since most of Saudi Arabia's important locations — population centres, oil production and export facilities, military installations — are either on or close to the coast, early warning ground radar could not be placed in locations forward enough to provide sufficient warning time to intercept attacking aircraft. For example, low-flying Iranian aircraft approaching the oil fields in the Eastern Province could not be detected by existing ground radar until they were less than 2 to 4 minutes from the target. This warning time would be insufficient for scrambling Saudi F-15s to intercept. The AWACS, on the other hand, can detect low-flying aircraft at ranges of about 200 miles, thereby giving the Saudi Air Force enough time to scramble and intercept the attacker.[54]

The second objective behind the AWACS deal was 'the development, with U.S. backing, of a regional air defense system for the entire Gulf region'.[55] In such a system, the Pentagon stated, the Gulf 'air defense networks could be linked, data transmitted, and

Table 6.3: The AWACS package, 1981

Element	Quantity	Cost	Delivery schedule	Deployment location	Manpower requirement
E-3A AWACS (including 3 years spares, technical data, support equipment and training		$3.7 billion	Beginning 48 months after approval	Riyadh for approximately 1 year, then Al Kharij	170 aircrew, 2 cockpit and mission crews for each aircraft; 360 maintenance crew for total 5 aircraft. This would allow one 24-hour AWACS orbit for 7 days
Ground defence environment	22 major system elements of hardened command and control facilities, data-processing and display equipment, new radars, and ground entry stations	$2.1 billion	6 years		
KC-707 (including 3 years of initial spares, support equipment, continental U.S. training, 3 years of contractor aircraft maintenance and training)	6 with an option to buy two more	$2.4 billion	Beginning 40–44 months after approval	Riyadh for 1 year, later Al-Kharij	96 aircrew, 320 initial contractor personnel support
Conformal fuel tanks (CFTS)	101 sets	$110 billion	27 months after contract award	RSAF F-15 operation bases: Dhahran, Taif and Khamis, Mushayt	
AIM-9L air-to-air missiles	1177	$200 million	30 months	RSAF F-15 operation bases: Dharan, Taif and Khamis, Mushayt	9 U.S. contractor personnel

Source: 'U.S. proposes air defense package for Saudi Arabia' (Background Paper, August 24, 1981), *Department of State Bulletin* (October 1981): 52–57; Anthony H. Cordesman, *The Gulf and the search for strategic stability* (Boulder, CO: Westview Press, 1984): 306.

air defense interceptors controlled'.[56] Under the terms of the agreement with Saudi Arabia, any expansion of the AWACS cover would require U.S. permission as well as full technical involvement. Thus, 'the U.S. would be assured of a key role in the development of any regional air defense system and of continuing participation in its operations'.[57]

Soon after the AWACS deal was concluded, the GCC states began a serious drive to build a regional air defence network. Kuwait, the UAE, Bahrain, and Qatar purchased Hawk anti-aircraft missile batteries, which could be linked to the Saudi air defence system, with the Saudi AWACS as the centrepiece. Saudi Arabia announced that it would build a command control, communications, and intelligence system which would have the capacity to link the air defence systems, including Hawk missiles and interceptors, of the other GCC states. According to one report, when the Saudis complete their system in 1990, 'it will provide a Gulf-wide defence network able to coordinate between 100 to 150 fighter planes purchased by the other GCC states'.[58]

The third important aspects of the AWACS deal was to be its contribution to U.S. capability for direct intervention in the Persian Gulf. With the AWACS and the F-15 enhancements, the United States provided 'an extensive logistics base and support infrastructure, including spare parts, facilities, trained personnel, and specialized test and maintenance equipment'. This infrastructure would be 'fully compatible' with the needs of the RDJTF/CENTCOM units.[59] The AWACS itself would play a key role during the early phase of a U.S. intervention in the Gulf. As General P. X. Kelly told Congress,

the most critical period of any deployment of forces is the initial arrival, i.e., before adequate air superiority is established. The in-place AWACS aircraft could provide the RDF with an immediate air surveillance capability which would be compatible with the establishment of an effective air defense network.[60]

While the AWACS deal was a major breakthrough in U.S.–GCC security relations, the U.S. policy of assisting the GCC's self-defence capability faced a major challenge from pro-Israeli groups within the United States, which succeeded in persuading Congress to block some important deals due to fears of their impact on Israeli security. The GCC states were frustrated by the

Contingency Planning and Response

Israeli ability, through pro-Israel groups within the United States, to 'veto', water down, or impose insulting conditions and restraints on major U.S. arms sales proposals for the Arab countries.[61] Such lingering frustration could partly explain the subsequent Saudi decision to negotiate massive arms deals with European suppliers, such as an air defence system from France and Tornado combat aircraft from Britain. A good example of the problems caused by the pressure from the Jewish lobby was the Reagan administration's refusal to sell Stinger air defence missiles to Kuwait in 1984. Kuwait, the GCC member seemingly least willing to cooperate with the U.S. strategy, had requested the missiles to defend itself against Iranian air attacks. In making the request, the Kuwaiti regime had softened its traditional rhetoric against U.S. regional military policies. Its need for such defence was even more urgent than Saudi Arabia's, since Iranian warplanes had already bombed Kuwait on several occasions. The U.S. refusal, while granting a similar Saudi request, was thus a shock to the Kuwaiti leadership. In protest the Kuwaiti foreign minister immediately travelled to Moscow to conclude an arms deal worth over $100 million.[62]

'Third party' assistance

Another option given serious consideration by the United States in dealing with intra-regional contingencies in the Gulf was third-party assistance. Two countries whose security role received special recognition in the U.S. strategy were Pakistan and Jordan. Other potential sources of support included Britain and France, both of which possess a capability for long-range military intervention.

Following the renewal of the U.S.–Pakistani strategic partnership with a $3 billion aid package in 1981, there was considerable speculation on a Pakistani role in the U.S. strategy in the Persian Gulf. Although the Reagan administration described the objective of its aid as being 'to create a stronger, more self-reliant Pakistan as it confronts Soviet power in neighbouring Afghanistan',[63] a subsequent report by the Senate Foreign Relations Committee stressed that 'a common commitment to stability in the Persian Gulf' provided another 'important basis' for the renewed and revitalized U.S.–Pakistani security relationship.[64] In this respect, Pakistan's expected role in U.S. strategy seemed to centre around

Contingency Planning and Response

two possibilities. One was the provision of access to its military bases to U.S. forces. The other was Pakistan's potential as a source of 'third-party assistance' to the GCC states.[65]

Indeed, Pakistan seemed well suited for the second role. It already had a significant military presence in the Arabian Peninsula. It had for long been a major source of manpower (Baluchi) for the Omani army; Pakistani military advisory groups were active in all the conservative Gulf States.[66] Pakistan's security ties with Saudi Arabia were especially close. As the aforementioned Senate Foreign Relations Committee report noted: 'the United States and Pakistani contributions to Saudi stability are complementary — the United States is the major source of high technology Saudi weapons while Pakistan is probably the biggest supplier of personnel'.[67] The security ties between the two countries became stronger following the outbreak of the Gulf war, when Pakistan agreed to deploy as many as 20,000 of its elite troops in the Kingdom,[68] to assist its external defence as well as the protection of the royal family. While Pakistani manpower was a key factor in offsetting Saudi manpower shortages, Saudi aid played a key role in the modernization of the Pakistani military, especially when the Kingdom financed the Pakistani purchase of F-16 aircraft from the United States in 1981.

The large and well-trained Pakistani armed forces could not only spare manpower for deployment to the Gulf; Pakistan also had the potential to assist in other areas. As *Middle East* magazine pointed out, Pakistani air defence assets, especially the F-16 fighter/ground attack aircraft purchased with U.S. FMS credit, could be used for air defence operations in the GCC states by operating from 'a string of air bases along the Gulf and in Baluchistan which could be interchangeable in a crisis'. By 1984 Pakistan had already launched projects to develop such airbases in Baluchistan.[69] In addition, Pakistani forces, experienced in crowd control operations at home and more apolitical (when they are in Saudi or other GCC territory) than most non-indigenous Arab personnel employed by GCC military establishments, could be particularly useful in dealing with domestic disorders — situations in which the U.S. forces would be least effective.[70]

It should be emphasized that to date little direct evidence has emerged of a Pakistani role in the Gulf within the framework of the U.S. military strategy. The governments of both countries have been categorical in denying any such role. Pakistan is extremely sensitive to being seen as an American surrogate in the Gulf.

142

Contingency Planning and Response

Instead, Islamabad has claimed that its security involvement in the Gulf predates the new U.S. strategy and is based on its own national interests. The latter include a stake in the stability of the Arabian Peninsula, a major market for Pakistani exports and a place where a large number of Pakistanis have earned their living since the Gulf oil boom. At the same time, however, Pakistani and U.S. strategic interests in the Gulf are highly complementary. Although Pakistan has every incentive and reason to undertake a military effort to assist the GCC states without being prodded by the United States, the latter's assistance, particularly in providing logistics, transport, and communications support might be essential to any large-scale Pakistani force projection into the Gulf. Moreover, Pakistan might not dare send troops to the Gulf without a U.S. guarantee for protection from possible Iranian or Soviet reprisals, as might be the case. Indeed, Iran's emergence as the main threat to the GCC states might have undermined Pakistan's security role in the Gulf. Fear of Iranian subversion within its own Shi'ite population would discourage Pakistan from intervening in support of the GCC countries facing Iranian aggression.

Like Pakistan, Jordan figured prominently in the U.S. strategy in the Gulf. Jordan had already established substantial security linkages with the GCC states and Iraq, 'supplying officers . . . , military intelligence personnel and infrastructure and training missions throughout the peninsula'.[71] In the case of Oman, Jordan could point to a 'proven record' of intervention in support of a conservative regime, having assisted Sultan Qaboos in his fight against the Dhofari rebels in the early 1970s. Unlike Pakistan, Jordan was far less reticent in acknowledging its desire and ability to play a contingency assistance role in the Gulf. King Hussein himself emphasized this point in 1982: 'We Arabs, alone, can help each other if there is trouble. . . . A superpower can only intervene if another has already done so, and then it is too late.'[72] The Jordanian chief-of-staff claimed that Jordan had the ability to send a battalion, or a brigade, of paratroops at short notice to a Persian Gulf trouble spot. The King was reported to have discussed the possibility of Jordanian contingency deployments to the Gulf during a visit to Bahrain shortly after an abortive coup attempt there in late 1981.[73]

As an Arab state, Jordan's role in assisting GCC states facing a domestic threat could be politically less disruptive than Pakistan's. Indeed, following the outbreak of the Iran–Iraq War, an important factor favouring Jordan's security role in the Persian

143

Gulf was the unusual combination of Saudi and Iraqi endorsement. Iraq became a major beneficiary of Jordanian involvement in Gulf security, receiving King Hussein's strong backing, including help from Jordanian 'volunteer' troops, in its war against Iran. King Hussein's diplomatic and material support supplemented the contributions made by the GCC states in financing Baghdad's war effort. Saudi endorsement of Jordan's contingency role in the Gulf was indicated by its willingness to finance the purchase of Jordan's air defence systems.

While U.S. security assistance to Pakistan was stated by both sides to be unrelated to the latter's capability to act as a source of 'third-party assistance' to the GCC states, in the case of Jordan the United States undertook a specific but secret project to facilitate Jordanian intervention in the Gulf. Recognizing that the greatest obstacle to the latter would be Jordan's lack of transport and equipment, the United States initiated the Jordanian Logistics Plan (JLP; the so-called Jordanian Rapid Deployment Force). The project was said to have originated following the seizure of the Grand Mosque in 1979, although the Reagan administration gave it the real push. Under the plan, the United States proposed to train 8,000 Jordanian troops (2 brigades) as a contingency force equipped with C-130 transport aircraft, TOW anti-tank missiles, Stinger surface-to-air missiles, DIVAD anti-aircraft guns, and satellite communications equipment — all supplied by the United States. This force would have been available to support pro-Western regimes in the Middle East, especially in the Persian Gulf. To finance the project, the Reagan administration had managed to secure Senate agreement to put about $200 million into a classified section of the FY 1984 defence authorization bill.[74]

The project ran into trouble, however, following its disclosure to the public — Israeli radio breaking the story. Jewish groups in the United States set into motion a campaign to deny the JLP congressional approval and funding. The campaign dampened the administration's enthusiasm for the project, especially in view of the approaching presidential elections. A subsequent rejection of a Jordanian request for Stinger anti-aircraft missiles, also resulting from Jewish lobby pressures, evoked a bitter condemnation of U.S. policy by the King, creating a crisis in the bilateral relationship. Little has been heard of the JLP since then.

Unlike those of Jordan and Pakistan, the strategic roles of Britain and France in the Gulf are to a large extent based upon arms sales. France and Britain have traditionally supplied most of

Contingency Planning and Response

the weapons purchased by the smaller Gulf States — Kuwait, Qatar, Bahrain, and the UAE. Considerable arms have also been sold by both to Saudi Arabia, Iraq, Pakistan, and Egypt. French arms sales to Iraq, estimated to exceed some $5 billion during the 1980–85 period, were a major factor in reducing Baghdad's dependence on Moscow and permitting Iraq to develop a more pro-Western outlook.

In the early 1980s, both France and Britain took steps to enhance their capabilities for rapid long-range intervention. France set up a Forces d'Action Rapide (FAR) with the mission to 'deploy large conventional forces . . . both in and outside Europe, within a very short time'.[75] The 47,000-strong FAR was assigned five combat divisions, three of which could be used for distant power projection. Its airborne component, the 11th Parachute Division, would be kept in a 'constant alert status, and within 24 hours could proceed to the Middle East or Africa'.[76] The British program was more modest than France's, but not totally insignificant. In 1980 the Defence Ministry announced that a parachute battalion was available for overseas deployment at 7 days' notice.[77] Three years later, Britain announced the formation of a 5,000-strong 'quick-strike force'. The lead element of this force was the 5th Airborne Brigade, consisting of 1,800 paratroopers, an artillery regiment, a light helicopter squadron, and logistics units. If necessary, this force could be supplemented by the 3rd Royal Marine Commando Brigade, which has an amphibious capability. The British RDF project also involved the modification of half the C-130 transport aircraft fleet to increase their paratroop-carrying capacity by 50 per cent and creation of a headquarters to undertake deployment planning and execution.[78]

The long-range intervention capabilities of France and Britain, while modest compared to that of the United States, have none the less proved to be effective in low-level conflicts in the Third World. Examples include the reported French involvement in ending the seizure of the Grand Mosque in Mecca in December 1979 and the performance of British troops in the Falklands/Malvinas campaign in 1982. France has repeatedly backed regimes in Francophone Africa by intervening on their behalf in domestic conflict situations. What is more uncertain is whether France would be willing to work within the framework of the U.S. strategy in the Gulf in making use of its intervention capabilities. In the past it has refused to do so, particularly at the beginning of the Iran–Iraq War, when it rejected a U.S. proposal for a combined Western

145

Contingency Planning and Response

naval force in the Gulf to protect shipping. Differences between the United States and its European allies over a host of political and strategic issues in the Middle East, including the Palestinian issue, are well known. While the United States and its West European allies share the same interests and objectives in the Gulf, and the latter could find it in their own interest to come to the rescue of the GCC states, this might not be in the shape of joint operations with U.S. forces.[79]

The 'worst case' threat

Notwithstanding the attention given to non-Soviet contingencies, the most important consideration shaping the evolution of the RDJTF/CENTCOM's operational planning was the requirement to deter and defeat the 'worst-case' threat. The focus on this threat, generally defined as an all-out Soviet invasion of Iran,[80] was the subject of a great deal of controversy. To begin with, strategic analysts, including those in the Pentagon, viewed this scenario as the least likely of all contingencies that might threaten U.S. interests in the Gulf. Secondly, critics argued that focus on the worst-case threat could undermine the RDJTF's ability to cope with the more likely lesser threats. A force designed primarily for use against the Soviets would, in the words of one critic, need to be 'massive, firepower-oriented, logistically cumbersome, and land-dependent'.[81] Such a force would not be suitable for countering intra-regional threats in which the enemy might remain dispersed and elusive.[82] To defeat local threats, the United States would require a light and highly mobile force logistically independent of land bases.

But the Pentagon responded to such criticisms with the following arguments. To begin with, while the threat of a direct Soviet invasion of Iran was unlikely, it was so only in a relative context and could not be regarded as absolutely improbable.[83] Moreover, emphasis on the worst-case threat made political and strategic sense in so far as regional and Soviet perceptions of U.S. power and credibility were concerned. A military strategy that wrote off the Soviet threat and focused exclusively on domestic and intra-regional contingencies could, in the Pentagon's view, increase the risk of Soviet miscalculation, give credence to suspicions that the RDJTF was designed primarily to interfere in the domestic affairs of the regional states, and create a poor image of U.S. power in the

Contingency Planning and Response

region. As one Pentagon official put it, 'It is only when those countries feel that they have a sufficient guarantee of security against the worst case, that we are likely to make substantial progress in [obtaining their cooperation in] other scenarios.'[84]

The Pentagon also rejected arguments that its focus on the Soviet threat would undermine the RDJTF's ability to counter lesser contingencies. 'The "big scenario" ', according to one official, was 'needed for planning and programming of force structure because it is the big scenario that stresses our capabilities as opposed to our operational planning'.[85] The latter was not driven by any one scenario, but designed for flexibility.[86] Thus, according to the Pentagon, 'if we have the capability of posing a credible deterrent to that worst case, then we believe that we have the capability of meeting lesser contingencies'.[87]

In defining the worst-case threat, the Pentagon took into account several possible scenarios of a Soviet attack on the Gulf. One was a Soviet airborne 'leapfrog' into Saudi oil fields, which, from the U.S. point of view, could be the most damaging threat to Western interests. But it could not be regarded as the most difficult to defend against. Soviet forces would lack an effective overland approach, and the air and sea lanes of communication would be long and vulnerable to U.S. interdiction. The Soviet airborne forces would be easy targets for destruction in the absence of tactical fighter cover and an early link-up with ground forces.[88] On the other hand, a Soviet push into northern Iran (Azerbaijan) using airborne and ground units would probably be the most difficult threat to which to respond. Enjoying overland supply routes and tactical air cover, the Soviet forces would be impossible to evict. But that threat would not affect the West's 'vital' interests, which would lie to the south in the oil fields.

The possibility of a Soviet invasion of the Gulf from Afghanistan was also considered in U.S. contingency planning. But such an invasion by itself would be less demanding than an invasion through northern Iran. The Iranian oil fields are even more distant from Afghanistan than from the Soviet southern border. There are fewer roads. The terrain through which the invasion would have to pass, especially the Khorassan desert, is at least as forbidding as that in northern Iran. The climate is extremely hot, water very scarce. The wind and dust conditions would increase the rate of mechanical breakdowns. Moreover, since the Soviet forces currently stationed in Afghanistan were dispersed and bogged down in fighting the rebels, an invasion through Afghanistan

Contingency Planning and Response

could not be launched without moving forces from their peacetime locations in the southern and other military districts. This, however, would stretch the supply lines and give the United States more warning time.[89]

Thus, Pentagon officials concluded that a Soviet threat to the Gulf would not be worst case unless spearheaded by ground units moving through the northern Iranian land corridors. While such an invasion would most certainly involve participation of airborne and naval forces and might be complemented by a push through Afghanistan, the basic purpose of the latter would be to support the southward ground offensive, which would be the main feature of the overall threat.

In its initial years, the RDJTF was regarded by its many critics as nothing more than a 'tripwire', meant to deter a Soviet attack by underlying the threat of U.S. nuclear retaliation. In fact, some critics, such as Kenneth Waltz, suggested that given the existing inadequacies in the RDJTF's force structure and strategic lift capabilities, the Pentagon could realistically plan its defence against the Soviet threat by openly adopting a tripwire strategy (in Waltz's term an 'asset-seizing, deterrent' force). Such a strategy would aim at seizing, at the first hint of trouble, the Gulf oil fields and deter any further Soviet advance by threatening nuclear retaliation.[90]

But the credibility of a tripwire strategy in the Gulf was open to question. The state of nuclear parity between the superpowers would limit the prospects of either side achieving deterrence of conventional attacks by threatening to go nuclear. In Western Europe, where American stakes were regarded as higher than in the Gulf, and where American response to a Soviet attack would be automatic (the same could not be said of the Gulf), the credibility of NATO's tripwire strategy (or 'massive retaliation') had become increasingly dubious as the Soviets bridged the nuclear gap.[91] Many of the important theatre conditions and strategic assumptions sustaining nuclear deterrence in Europe were absent in the Persian Gulf. In the Gulf, unlike in Europe, the United States did not have a permanent, land-based military presence — destruction of which can be treated as the Soviet snapping of the tripwire. Unlike in Europe, deterrence in the Persian Gulf could not be extended uniformly within the region — Saudi Arabia, for example, would always be regarded as more vital to the United States than northern Iran.[92]

While Carter administration officials later admitted considering

148

Contingency Planning and Response

use of the nuclear weapons to deter the worst-case threat in the Gulf, in 1980 the Pentagon insisted that conventional deterrence and defence were 'feasible' objectives.[93] None the less, the Carter administration left the escalation option open. As Harold Brown put it: 'any direct conflict between American and Soviet forces carries the risk of intensification and geographical spread of the conflict'. The United States, according to Brown, 'could not concede to the Soviets full choice of the arena or the actions'.[94] The Reagan administration decided to make a substantially greater investment on the RDJTF/CENTCOM so as to enhance its conventional war-fighting capabilities. But it too did not rule out escalation, especially horizontal escalation.

The Pentagon's declared strategy to counter the worst-case threat consisted of 'three time dimensions'. The first stage would *precede* the actual Soviet attack. U.S. forces would deploy following warning signals, in a 'preemptive' mode. The second stage, which would follow if preemption failed to deter the enemy attack, would involve defensive war-fighting, designed to harass, blunt, and further discourage the Soviet advance. The difference between preemption and defence lay in the fact that while in the former speed would be more important than force size, in the latter, the balance of force projection capabilities would become the most crucial variable. In 1981 the Pentagon explained 'three time dimensions' in the following terms:

> First, given warning and timely political decisions, we would move forces as close as possible to the area of potential conflict. This would signal to the Soviets that we consider vital Western interests at stake and that further movement on their part would risk war between the two superpowers. Should deterrence fail, the second dimension involves our ability to fight in the region. We must deploy forces rapidly to interdict and blunt a Soviet attack, although we would not be compelled to respond only at the Soviet point of attack. Thirdly, this strategy must take into account how we would cope with the potential for a wider war. Conflict with the Soviets may not be contained to the region and the United States would have to be prepared for a global confrontation.[95]

Contingency Planning and Response

The preemptive strategy

The RDJTF/CENTOM's strategy stressed preemptive deployments, or the ability to get to the scene of conflict first.[96] The key principle in a preemptive deployment would be the ability to become 'firstest with the mostest', although the emphasis would be distinctly on speed rather than force size or firepower. As Harold Brown described the RDJTF's preemptive strategy in 1980:

> What is important is the ability rapidly to move forces into the region with the numbers, mobility, and firepower to preclude initial adversary forces from reaching vital points. It is not necessary for our initial units to be able to defeat the whole force an adversary might eventually have in place. It is also not necessary for us to await the firing of the first shot or the prior arrival of hostile forces; many of our forces can be moved upon strategic warning and some upon receipt of even very early and ambiguous indication.[97]

Indeed preemption was viewed as the key to the U.S. ability not only to deter or defeat, but more importantly to its being able to respond at all, to a Soviet attack on Iran. In any superpower conflict, the risks and uncertainties are so great that they inhibit each side from initiating an attack on the other. As such, the side that would reach the theatre second would be at a distinct disadvantage, because to continue military action it would have to remove the forces of the other side by *firing the first shot*. Thus, the greater danger of being preempted by the Soviets, as analyst Richard Betts pointed out, would not lie in 'the force-multiplying edge it can give the Soviet Union in determining the outcome of battle'; rather, it would be 'the danger that by being slow on the draw, Washington may be deterred from any engagement at all'.[98]

If the American forces managed the first entry, then the risks of counter-intervention would pass to the Soviets, who must then seriously rethink their plan before striking first at the forces of the other superpower. Such a prospect might be enough to deter the Soviets. In 1981 the Pentagon confidently asserted that 'early arrival of even a few forces could be determinant in deterring an attack on oil producers in the first place, or in dissuading an attacker from pressing his aggression'.[99]

The Pentagon suggested that apart from deterrence, a preemptive deployment could be used 'to occupy key positions' in the

Contingency Planning and Response

crisis area.[100] One category of 'key positions' would be the airfields and ports of the threatened country and neighbourhood, which would be absolutely crucial for receiving reinforcements and supplies. The RDJTF commander revealed that if necessary, U.S. forces would seize theatre airfields and ports to facilitate reinforcement of the 'cutting edge' forces.[101] The other category of positions that a preemptive force might occupy would be the oil fields, since preemption would be the best way of securing them before they were damaged by enemy attack or sabotage. Besides, such a move would ensure that even if the rest of the territory of the threatened country fell into enemy hands, the most critical parts, in which the West's vital interests are located, would remain under U.S. control.[102] Secret Pentagon documents leaked to the press indicated that U.S. forces would be prepared to seize the oil fields if the Iranian regime of the day failed to 'invite' U.S. troops in the face of a massive Soviet attack.[103] According to a report in the *New York Times*, the Joint Chiefs' 'Defense Guidance' had established that U.S. forces in the Gulf must be 'ready to force their way in, if necessary, and not to wait for an invitation from a friendly government'.[104]

But getting there first assumed the availability of ample warning time and a prompt decision on the part of the President to commit U.S. forces. In 1982 the commander of the RDJTF predicted that the worst-case threat could provide at least one month's warning time[105] because of the low readiness status of most of the Soviet forces stationed in the southern military districts. More than 60 per cent of those divisions were of category III readiness status, that is possessing most of their weapons (though probably not the latest models) but manned at about 25 to 30 per cent of their total strength.[106] Mobilizing them to their full strength, providing them with enough trucks, and equipping and training them for their demanding mission would take time. Indeed, indications of the Soviet build-up for the invasion of Czechoslovakia and Afghanistan were apparent three months before the actual operation.

Between 1979 and 1984 the RDJTF/CENTCOM's force projection capability to the Gulf increased significantly in respect to both force size and speed of deployment. In 1980 the Congressional Budget Office (CBO) estimated that 24,200 troops could be projected to the Persian Gulf within 16 days of mobilization. This figure, the CBO predicted, would be more than doubled (to 49,200 troops) when the readiness and strategic lift enhancement programs then being undertaken had been completed. This

151

Days from mobilization	1980 without Rapid Deployment Force			With Rapid Deployment Force		
	Number of troops	Peacetime base	Means of transport	Number of troops	Peacetime base	Means of transport
First	1,000 (Airborne)	Vicenza, Italy	Airlift	1,000 (Airborne)	Vicenza, Italy	Airlift
Second	1,000 (Airborne)	Ft. Bragg, North Carolina	Airlift	1,000 (Airborne)	Ft. Bragg, North Carolina	Airlift
Ninth	2,200 (Airborne)	Afloat in Mediterranean	Sealift	14,200 (12,000 Marine) (2,000 Marine)	U.S.-based Afloat in Mediterranean	Airlift Sealift
Sixteenth	20,000 (12,000 Marine) (8,000 Army, mechanized)	Okinawa, Japan Ft. Stewart, Georgia	Sealift Airlift	33,000 (12,000 Marine) (16,000 Army, mechanized) (5,000 Army, airborne)	Okinawa, Japan Ft. Stewart, Georgia Ft. Bragg North Carolina	Sealift Sealift Airlift
Total	24,200			49,200		

Source: Congressional Budget Office, *U.S. ground forces: design and cost alternatives for NATO and non-NATO contingencies* (1980).

Contingency Planning and Response

force would include two marine amphibious brigades and a mechanized division (see Table 6.4).[107] Another analyst predicted in 1982 that 'by the latter part of 1983, the RDJTF Commander could have the capability to commit the equivalent of five divisions to Southwest Asia in less than 30 days'.[108]

The Pentagon's official *interim* goal was a capability to deploy, assuming no simultaneous contingency in Europe, 'a joint task force and required support forces to SWA within six weeks'. The long-term goal was to be able to concurrently reinforce all theatres including NATO, Southwest Asia, and the Pacific within that period.[109] The deployment of U.S. forces would begin with 'air defense forces followed by light ground forces and reinforced by heavy forces'.[110] Apart from tactical aircraft consisting of carrier-based aviation, the CENTCOM could, with Saudi cooperation, deploy 2 squadrons of F-15 fighters within 2 days, assuming a CONUS mobilization time of 3 days during the warning period. AWACS early warning and control aircraft would be ready, operating from Saudi Arabia. B-52 bombers of the Strategic Projection Force (SPF) could be deployed within 48 hours, and a combat-ready brigade (5,000 men) of the 82nd Airborne Division from the U.S. East Coast within 48 to 72 hours. Combat elements of the entire division (16,500 men) would take less than two weeks to arrive in the Gulf, although arrival of support units would take a few more days.

One marine amphibious brigade (about 12,000 men and 40 attack aircraft), using equipment pre-positioned off Diego Garcia, could be deployed to the Gulf in about a week. The DOD estimated that a full marine amphibious force (MAF) — a division plus air wing — could be deployed in about four weeks. The 101st Airborne Division, deployed by sea but not using the SL-7 ships, could take 30 to 35 days to close. When the strategic mobility enhancement programs undertaken by the Carter and Reagan administrations were completed, the United States would probably have enough airlift to deploy both the 82nd and the 101st by air, assuming, of course, no simultaneous demand for airlift operations to other theatres. Finally, the 24th Infantry (Mechanized) Division could be brought in within five to six weeks, although the DOD claims that the SL-7 ships could move a heavy division to the Gulf within 14 to 16 days via the Suez Canal.[111]

But the above estimates in most cases assumed best-case conditions. Needless to say, reaction times and force sizes would

Contingency Planning and Response

vary significantly depending on a number of factors apart from warning. It would depend upon the size and type of threat expected, the mix of U.S. troops and equipment to meet the threat, access to regional facilities, and the possibility of simultaneous contingencies elsewhere in the world. Other conditions that could affect the RDJTF/CENTCOM's response time would include the level of enemy attrition of its airlift and sealift operations, and availability of en route access in the territory of allied countries.

The preemptive strategy developed by the RDJTF/CENTCOM assumed exceptional political courage and quick decision-making ability on the part of the American President. Critics argued that since public opinion might not appreciate the significance of strategic warning, the United States might be cast as the aggressor for being the first side to send in its troops. Also, the deterrent value of preemption was openly questioned since the Soviet leadership would surely have taken into account the prospect of an American preemptive presence in the crisis theatre before launching their attack. Once the decision to attack was made, the Soviets would be unlikely to be deterred by the prospect of an encounter with light CENTCOM forces.[112]

The power projection balance

Thus, a conventional preemptive strategy would be credible only if it was backed by a capability to rapidly and substantially reinforce the early arrival of U.S. forces. These forces must be able to make the Soviet advance as difficult as possible, with the hope that the Kremlin would find an invasion too costly to sustain. While the RDJTF/CENTCOM officials did not doubt the Soviet Union's ability to put a formidable force structure in Iran within a short time, they believed that the United States could pursue a credible defensive strategy by exploiting Soviet vulnerabilities arising from technological inferiority and the difficult terrain conditions in Iran. It should be noted here that while the analysis in this chapter covers the 1980–84 period, many of the problems confronting Soviet forces as outlined below should apply today, despite some Soviet technological advances in recent years.

Like that of Czechoslovakia or Afghanistan, a Soviet invasion of Iran might be spearheaded by its airborne forces. The Soviet Union possesses the world's largest airborne force[113] (a total of 7

154

Contingency Planning and Response

active divisions). In 1984–85 Soviet airlift capability[114] was estimated to be sufficient to transport one airborne division to about 1,000 miles and two divisions to a range of 600 miles.[115] These forces would enjoy superior power and better battlefield mobility than their U.S. airborne counterparts. However, Soviet fighter aircraft operating from southernmost home bases (Kirovabad and Askhabad) or Afghanistan (Shindand) lacked the range (although this may no longer be the case since the Soviets have begun deploying MiG-29 and SU-27 fighters in the Southern Theatre) to provide cover for operations in the oil fields in Khuzestan, Saudi Arabia, and the Strait of Hormuz. Without fighter cover, transport aircraft, being large and with little manoeuvrability, would be vulnerable. U.S. land- and carrier-based tactical aircraft, which could be on scene in a matter of hours, could intercept the airlifters and disrupt airborne insertions into many targets. The former JCS Chairman, David Jones, noted in 1980 that a Soviet airborne assault into the Iranian oil fields 'would be an easy operation to interdict. . . . A few AWACS and a few fighters could just devastate an airborne operation.'[116]

Pentagon officials viewed the combat potential of the Soviet navy's Indian Ocean squadron with far less seriousness. Although the peacetime Soviet Indian Ocean fleet averaged between 20 and 25 ships (of which about seven or eight are combatants, the rest supports), this would need augmentation in order to operate in a combat situation. But these additional units would have to traverse great distances from their home fleets: 3,300 miles from the Black Sea fleet anchorages; 8,000 miles from the Pacific fleet; 10,800 miles from the Baltic fleet; and 11,200 from the northern fleet. The likely denial of passage through the Suez Canal would increase the distances for ships deployed from the Mediterranean side. Apart from the time consumed, Soviet fleet movements to the Indian Ocean would require passage through chokepoints, such as the Greenland–Iceland–Faroes Gap and the Malacca–Sunda–Lombok Staits. This would be a very significant vulnerability. The former Chief of Naval Operations, Admiral Thomas Hayward, claimed at a congressional hearing in 1981 that the U.S. Navy would have a 'very significant capability to interdict the Soviet navy's own efforts to reinforce their Indian Ocean fleet'.[117]

The Soviet Union's lack of adequate naval support facilities in the Indian Ocean littoral could be another major constraint on its war-fighting capability. By the early 1980s the Soviet Union was reportedly enjoying 'unrestricted access' to Aden, Socotra Island

155

Contingency Planning and Response

(both in the PDR Yemen), and Dhalak Island (Ethiopia). Yet U.S. officials conceded that Dhalak Island housed nothing more than a 'minor repair facility' for the Soviet Indian Ocean squadron.[118] Besides, Soviet ships operating from Dhalak Island would lend themselves to interception by Western (French or U.S.) forces based in Djibouti and could be 'rather easily bottled in narrowly confined areas by mining'.[119] In the PRDY, U.S. officials admitted that Socotra had 'rudimentary facilities sufficient only to provide for limited maritime support activity and exercises'.[120] Although the extent of Soviet access to Aden was not clear (in 1980 Under Secretary of Defense Robert Komer called Aden 'more a facility than a base since the Soviets do seem to move in and out of there'),[121] the availability of only one 'base' was inherently a limiting factor — allowing no room for redundancy. Chastened by past experience in Somalia and Egypt, where costly and exclusive facilities had to be abandoned in the wake of their expulsion from these countries, the Soviets, noted the Pentagon, had chosen to 'minimise their capital investment in overseas facilities'.[122]

Pentagon officials viewed the Soviet ground forces as presenting the most difficult challenge to U.S. forces in the Gulf. In addition to about 30 divisions stationed in the southern theatre, including the four deployed in Afghanistan, the Soviets could draw upon the KGB border guards, about 50,000 of whom were deployed in the southern theatre. The Soviet border guards are impressively mechanized (possessing tanks, armoured fighting vehicles, and self-propelled artillery), and are trained to operate outside national boundaries as well as inside (which is their primary mission).

Numbers apart, the Soviet ground forces would have an overwhelming superiority in firepower and armour. Although the Soviets had only one tank division in the southern districts, their motor rifle divisions carry more tanks per soldier than corresponding U.S. mechanized divisions. A Soviet tank division contains 1,000 men and 335 tanks, while a Soviet motorized rifle division contains 14,000 troops and between 216 to 266 tanks. In contrast, the 24th Mechanized Division would have a total of 216 battle tanks.

On the other hand, U.S. military planners recognized that any large-scale movement of heavy ground forces through the mountainous terrain in northern Iran would confront the latter with significant vulnerabilities. From the Soviet border the distances to the Iranian oil fields are long (some 300 miles to Teheran and 650

156

Contingency Planning and Response

miles to Abadan). In covering this distance, the Soviet ground forces would have to cross two formidable mountain ranges. The first, comprising the Qareh Dagh, Elbruz, and Golul Dagh ranges, lie on the Soviet–Iranian border. The second is the Zagros Mountains, between Teheran and the oil fields on the Persian Gulf Coast. The roads that pass through these mountains are narrow and difficult, crossing bridges, running through several tunnels, and clinging to the sides of many gorges. As a consequence, the Soviet forces would have to negotiate some 300 'chokepoints' — a very significant vulnerability, exploitable to great effect by a clever defender. Other problems include extreme and inhospitable weather, scarce water supplies, and a total absence of supply depots and maintenance shops along the routes.[123] Thus the difficult operational environment in Iran would make the advance of Soviet invasion forces slow, painstaking, and decidedly vulnerable. As the U.S. Joint Chiefs of Staff noted:

> Soviet commanders would find it difficult to mass their forces. Iran is a big country with formidable terrain. Ground units and resupply would be moved predominantly by road over routes vulnerable to military action and natural impediments such as snow and floods. With limited frontages, long axes of attack, and the need to maintain security of the LOCs [lines of communications], Soviet forces could become strung out and separated. A large portion of the force would be absorbed in rear-area security and mutual support between axes would be difficult; air defense would be scattered and spread thin. Soviet aircraft would be operating without low-level ground-controlled intercept radar or fast-reaction interceptor aircraft coverage and, in later stages of the conflict, would operate from minimum-capability airfields in Iran. The appearance of overwhelming numbers of Soviet forces could be dissipated in the long defiles of the Zagros Mountains.[124]

In defending against the Soviet advance, the U.S. strategy emphasized air interdiction operations.[125] While interdiction might not be enough to halt a Soviet invasion permanently, it could be expected to delay their advance sufficiently to permit the build-up of a strong U.S. position round the oil fields. Such operations could be supplemented by the use of airborne, airmobile, and Special Operation Forces in the mountains. As the former Army Chief of Staff General Edward Meyer pointed out, the use of the

157

Contingency Planning and Response

light airborne force in restricted terrain would present 'significant advantages over the heavy, mechanized, road-bound Soviet force'.[126] Airmobile units could delay the Soviets at the chokepoints and destroy a large number of Soviet tanks.[127] Light infantry forces would be effective in ambushing and killing Soviet troops without suffering major losses.

Thus, Pentagon officials hoped that in a confrontation in Iran between Soviet and U.S. forces, the latter would have a clear naval superiority and their capability to interdict a Soviet airborne seizure of Iranian oil fields would be quite significant. The United States could also have air superiority around the oil fields, especially if bases in Oman and Turkey remain available and the Saudis granted contingency access. The invading Soviet ground forces could be subjected to considerable harassment and damage. U.S. forces could almost certainly delay the Soviet advance and *reduce* their size and firepower by destroying tanks and killing troops. Pentagon officials confidently asserted that a Soviet invasion of Iran 'would not be a blitzkrieg, but rather a land war fought laboriously through narrow defiles, mountain pass after mountain pass'.[128]

But would this actually deter the Soviets from continuing their advance further toward the oil fields and persuade them to terminate the conflict? What if the Soviets were to take the losses and still persist in their attack by pouring in additional resources? While few doubted the RDJTF/CENTCOM's ability to *delay* and *blunt* the attack, serious questions remained as to whether it could also *defeat* and *roll back* a determined Soviet effort. Pentagon officials could talk about an ability to 'deter' and 'dissuade', but not 'defeat'. As General David Jones testified:

> The Soviets would have greater difficulty than many people appreciate. . . . An interdiction program could give them a great deal of trouble. . . . I am assuming that the Soviets would be willing to rob from other parts of the world and sustain an effort in Southwest Asia. . . . I can see some circumstances where we could have the force to stop them. But if they made a sustained and significant effort, that would be a different circumstance.[129]

Contingency Planning and Response

Escalation: nuclear or horizontal?

If a conventional defence of Iran against the worst-case threat did not prove to be feasible, then one obvious option for the United States would be to escalate, either by resorting to nuclear weapons or by initiating attacks on the Soviets from strategic vantage points elsewhere in the globe. The issue of escalation was one of the most controversial aspects of the U.S. military strategy in the Gulf. Carter's National Security Advisor, Zbigniew Brzezinski, confirmed in his memoirs that he had instructed the military 'to develop options involving both "horizontal and vertical escalation" in the event of a Soviet military move toward the Persian Gulf', so that the United States 'would be free to choose either the terrain or the tactic or the level of our response'.[130] Shortly after the President's State of the Union address, official consideration of nuclear options in the Persian Gulf was indicated in leaked Pentagon documents, especially a report entitled 'Capabilities in the Persian Gulf'. The report, prepared in the Office of the Secretary of Defense, examined various options available to the United States for countering a Soviet offensive in Iran. After detailing the mismatch between the force projection capabilities of both sides, it concluded: 'To prevail in an Iranian scenario, we might have to threaten or make use of tactical nuclear weapons.'[131]

Several elements in the force structure of the RDJTF/ CENTCOM were 'dual-capable', that is capable of launching both conventional as well as nuclear warheads. Such systems included aircraft carriers with onboard nuclear weapons; the B-52H bomber squadrons of the Strategic Project Force (SPF); nuclear-capable artillery pieces, howitzers, and anti-submarine aircraft; plus many other tactical nuclear delivery systems integrated into Army, Navy, and Air Force units.[132] While the SPF was set up ostensibly for the purpose of conducting conventional long-range bombing operations, classified documents leaked by columnist Jack Anderson suggested that it was also oriented to a 'Limited Nuclear Option' (LNO), with the aim being to 'significantly degrade Soviet capabilities to project military power in the Middle East – Persian Gulf region for a period of at least 30 days'.[133] Another possibility concerned Atomic Demolition Munitions (ADM), which as the DOD's Program Analysis and Evaluation Office noted in a study, 'alone could quickly seal all avenues of approach into Iran'.[134]

Contingency Planning and Response

Of course, any decision to escalate the conflict to tactical nuclear levels needed to be very carefully weighed against the risks involved. Apart from setting a precedent and arousing worldwide protests, it could provoke Soviet retaliation in kind. Faced with a nuclear attack the Soviet Union might well seek to destroy the sources of U.S. strikes, especially aircraft carriers or regional bases. This would carry the potential of uncontrolled escalation. Since sunk carriers and lost regional facilities would mean the end of the CENTCOM theatre conventional war-fighting capabilities, the American President would be left in the unenviable position of having to choose between withdrawal or further escalation.

The risks associated with nuclear escalation would seem to make horizontal escalation a more attractive option. In simple terms, horizontal escalation involves taking the conflict to other geographic theatres where the enemy is perceived to be at a disadvantage, so that his superiority in the original theatre of conflict may be offset. This strategy had considerable appeal to the Reagan administration during the early phase of its first term.[135]

Several potential horizontal targets were identified. One category of targets included Soviet 'surrogates' — Cuba, Libya, Vietnam. Another option called for targeting Soviet personnel abroad or even Soviet territory — such as the Soviet 'brigade' in Cuba or the Soviet Asian land mass.[136] Also, some 'Maritime Strategists' advocated hitting Soviet naval targets. Navy Secretary John Lehman stated that the goal of the U.S. Navy would be 'to put the Soviet fleet on the bottom if they attempt to inderdict our lifelines, and nothing less'.[137]

But like nuclear weapons, a horizontal escalation strategy was fraught with major problems and risks. The U.S. force structure and equipment inventory, already stretched thinly, was clearly inadequate to support a war-widening strategy. The cost of building up the additional force structure would be immense. Furthermore, a war-widening strategy within existing or planned force levels would involve a serious diversion of the already scarce resources that had been committed to the Gulf. The consequent weakening of the U.S. ability to defend the Gulf with conventional assets would increase the pressure toward vertical escalation, thereby eroding the very rationale for choosing horizontal escalation as a preferable alternative to nuclear confrontation.

Another problem lay in choosing the right horizontal target. In selecting a target, the United States would need to ensure, on the one hand, that it had sufficient strategic value for the Soviets so

Contingency Planning and Response

that if threatened, the Soviets would be induced to make concessions. On the other hand, the target would not have to be important enough to the Soviets that its destruction invited Soviet nuclear retaliation.[138] It was difficult to find a target that could meet either criterion fully. There could be no basis to believe that the Soviet surrogates — Cuba, Libya, or Vietnam — would enjoy greater importance in Moscow's eyes than Persian Gulf oil; Moscow might be tempted to trade off Cuba for the control of the West's lifeline. On the other hand, actions such as putting 'the Soviet fleet to the bottom' or hitting the Soviet Far East could be exceedingly risky. Such actions might well drive the Soviets into a comparable response of using nuclear weapons to destroy the U.S. fleet. In other words, horizontal escalation would be no guarantee that the risk of nuclear warfare could be entirely avoided.

To sum up, there were no easy options in the planned U.S. response to the threat of a massive Soviet attack on Iran. While a preemptive strategy alone might not be enough to deter the Soviets, a strategy relying mainly on escalation would offer no assurance of success at an acceptable cost to the United States. Thus, a combination of preemption, defence, and escalation was seen by the Pentagon as the most credible way of countering the worst-case threat, despite the major uncertainties and risks associated with each of the three elements.

Notes

1. *A discussion of the Rapid Deployment Force with Lt. General P. X. Kelly* (Washington D.C.: American Enterprise Institute for Public Policy Research, 1980): 4.

2. U.S. Congress. House. Committee on Appropriations. *Military construction appropriations for fiscal year 1984*, Part 5: 102.

3. U.S. Congress. Senate. Committee on Armed Services. *Department of Defense authorization for appropriations for fiscal year 1981*, Part 1: 445; House. Committee on Foreign Affairs. *U.S. interests in, and policies toward, the Persian Gulf* (1980): 81.

4. U.S. Congress. Senate. Committee on Armed Services. *Department of Defense authorization for appropriations for fiscal year 1983*, Part 6: 3719. It is interesting that the qualifying phrase 'aided and directed by outside powers' was something of an afterthought. It was absent in an earlier draft of his prepared statement which was distributed to the Committee members. West admitted at the hearings that he had added these words. Ibid., p. 3755.

5. Congressional Budget Office, *U.S. ground forces, design and cost alternatives for NATO and non-NATO contingencies* (1980): 59

Contingency Planning and Response

6. Jimmy Carter, *Keeping faith: memoirs of a President* (Boston, MA: Little, Brown, 1983): 438.

7. See Gordon Edgin, 'The War Powers Act and the Rapid Deployment Joint Task Force: a game plan for the President', *Joint Perspectives* (Fall 1981): 101.

8. For a discussion, see *Rapid Deployment Forces: reassurance or threat to American security interests?* Report of the staff of members of Congress for Peace Through Law, *Congressional Record*, June 27, 1980: S8704.

9. Department of Defense, *Annual report to Congress, FY1983*: III – 101.

10. *Washington Post*, September 25, 1980: A36 – 37.

11. U.S. Congress. Senate. Committee on Foreign Relations. *War in the Gulf* (1984): 9.

12. Ibid., pp. 8 – 10; *Department of State Bulletin* (December 1980): 2 – 3; U.S. Congress. House. Committee on Foreign Affairs and Joint Economic Committee. *U.S. policy toward the Persian Gulf* (1982): 7; House. Committee on Foreign Affairs. *Development in the Persian Gulf, June 1984* (1984): 3 – 8.

13. Zbigniew Brzezinski, *Power and principle: memoirs of the National Security Advisor, 1977 – 1981* (New York: Farrer, Straus and Giroux, 1983): 452.

14. *Department of State Bulletin* (December 1980): 3.

15. Gary Sick, *All fall down: America's fateful encounter with Iran* (London: I. B. Tauris & Co., 1985): 314.

16. Brzezinski, *Power and principle*, p. 452.

17. Ibid., pp. 452 – 3.

18. *New York Times*, October 12, 1980: 1, 22.

19. Ibid.

20. U.S. Congress. Senate. Committee on Armed Services. *War in the Gulf* (1984): 14.

21. Joe Stork and Martha Wenger, 'U.S. ready to intervene in the Gulf war', *Merip Reports* (July – September 1984): 46.

22. Ibid., p. 45.

23. *New York Times*, October 12, 1980: 22.

24. Cited in Congressional Research Service, *Petroleum imports from the Persian Gulf: use of U.S. armed force to ensure supplies* (1981): 23.

25. *Washington Post*, October 16, 1980: A1, A30 – 1.

26. *Strategic survey, 1980 – 81* (London: International Institute for Strategic Studies, 1981): 20.

27. For a discussion of the outcome of such efforts see Amitav Acharya, 'NATO and "out-of-area" contingencies: the Gulf experience', *International Defense Review* (May 1987): 569 – 76.

28. *Middle East Economic Digest*, June 11, 1982: 36.

29. U.S. Congress. House. Committee on Foreign Affairs. *Developments in the Persian Gulf, June 1984*: 5.

30. Cited in Congressional Research Service, *Arms sales to Saudi Arabia: AWACS and the F-15 enhancements* (1982): 27.

31. *Washington Post*, August 25, 1984: G13.

32. U.S. Congress. House. Committee on Foreign Affairs. *Developments in the Persian Gulf, June 1984*: 7, 10, 15, 26 – 7.

33. *International Herald Tribune*, February 5, 1987: 1.

Contingency Planning and Response

34. Dilip Hiro, 'Chronicle of the Gulf war', *Merip Reports* (July–September 1984): 11.

35. *Middle East International*, September 30, 1983: 13.

36. *Middle East International*, October 28, 1983: 7.

37. *Middle East International*, June 29, 1984: 13.

38. Ibid.

39. U.S. Congress. Senate. Committee on Foreign Relations. *War in the Gulf* (1989): 9–10; House. Committee on Foreign Affairs. *Developments in the Persian Gulf, June 1985*: 51.

40. This relevation was made by Bob Woodward in the *Washington Post* in December 1986. Reproduced in the *West Australian*, December 16, 1986: 7. See also *International Herald Tribune*, November 11, 1986: 4; *Middle East International*, December 19, 1986: 8.

41. *West Australian*, December 16, 1986: 7.

42. *The Times* (London), March 2, 1984: 18.

43. *Middle East International*, March 9, 1984: 14.

44. U.S. Congress. Senate. Committee on Foreign Relations. *War in the Gulf* (1984): 9.

45. *The Australian*, May 14, 1986: 6.

46. U.S. Congress. Senate. Committee on Appropriations. *Department of Defense appropriations for fiscal year 1981*, Part 1: 430.

47. U.S. Congress. Senate. Committee on Armed Services. *Department of Defense authorization for appropriations for fiscal year 1983*, Part 6: 3723.

48. *New York Times*, February 12, 1979: A4; *New York Times*, February 13, 1979: A1; *New York Times*, February 19, 1979: A3.

49. *Public papers of the Presidents of the United States: Jimmy Carter, 1979, Book I* (Washington, D.C.: U.S. Government Printing Office, 1980): 312–13.

50. U.S. Congress. House. Committee on Foreign Affairs. *U.S. security interests in the Persian Gulf. Report of a staff study mission* (1981): 26; House. Committee on Foreign Affairs. *U.S. policy toward the Persian Gulf* (1982): 94.

51. *World armaments and disarmament: SIPRI Yearbook, 1982* (Stockholm: Stockholm International Peace Research Institute, 1982): 179; *Department of State Bulletin* (July 1981): 51–53; Department of State, *Middle East Regional Security*, Current Policy no. 270 (March 23, 1981).

52. Andrew Pierre, 'Arms sales: the new diplomacy', *Foriegn Affairs* (Winter 1981–82): 277–8.

53. U.S. Congress. Senate. Committee on Armed Services. *Military and technical implications of the proposed sale to Saudi Arabia of airborne warning and control system (AWACS) and F-15 enhancements* (1981): 4.

54. Ibid., pp. 5–6; *Department of State Bulletin* (October 1981): 54–55; Congressional Research Service, *Arms sales to Saudi Arabia: AWACS and the F-15 enhancements* (1982): 6–11.

55. *Washington Post*, November 1, 1981: A12.

56. U.S. Congress. Senate. Committee on Armed Services. *Military and technical implications*, p. 85.

57. 'Gulf Council viability linked to AWACS', *Aviation Week and Space Technology*, October 26, 1981: 20–21.

58. *Middle East International*, May 30, 1986: 15.

Contingency Planning and Response

59. *Department of State Bulletin* (October 1981): 57.

60. U.S. Congress. Senate. Committee on Armed Services. *Military and technical implications*, p. 84.

61. See for a discussion John Duke Anthony, 'The Gulf Cooperation Council', *Orbis* (Fall 1984): 447–50; Cheryl A. Rubenberg, 'The conduct of U.S. foreign policy in the Middle East in the 1983–84 Presidential election season', *American–Arab Affairs* (Summer 1984): 28–30.

62. U.S. Congress. Senate. Committee on Foreign Relations. *War in the Gulf* (1984): 23, 30–31; Mohammed al-Rumaihi, 'Kuwaiti–American relations: a case of mismanagement', *American–Arab Affairs* (Summer 1984): 77–80.

63. *Department of State Bulletin* (November 1981): 82.

64. U.S. Congress. Senate. Committee on Foreign Relations. *United States security interests in South Asia* (1984): 17.

65. See for example Claudia Wright, 'A risky bet on General Zia', *The Atlantic* (June 1981): 29.

66. U.S. Congress. House. Committee on Foreign Affairs. *Security and economic assistance to Pakistan* (1981): 223.

67. U.S. Congress. Senate. Committee on Foreign Relations. *United States security interests in South Asia* (1984): 17.

68. U.S. Congress. Senate. Committee on Foreign Relations. *United States security interests in South Asia* (1984): 17; *The military balance 1984–1985* (London: International Institute for Strategic Studies, 1984); David Khalid, 'Pakistan's relations with Iran and the Arab states', *Journal of South Asian and Middle Eastern Studies* (Spring 1982): 21.

69. 'Zia's new role in the Gulf', *The Middle East* (April 1983): 33; see also Jamal Rashid, 'Pakistan and the Central Command', *Middle East Report* (July–August 1986): 28–34; Lawrence Lifschultz, 'From the U-2 to the P-3: the U.S.–Pakistan relationship', *New Left Review* (September–October 1986): 71–80.

70. Shirin Tahir-Kheli and William O. Staudenmaier, 'The Saudi–Pakistani military relationship: implications for U.S. policy', *Orbis* (Spring 1982): 159–60.

71. Joe Stork and Jim Paul, 'Arms sales and the militarization of the Middle East', *Merip Reports* (February 1983): 9.

72. Patrick Seale, 'Hussein offers to become Gulf's policeman', *The Bulletin*, March 16, 1982: 88.

73. *International Herald Tribune*, March 27–28, 1982: 1.

74. *New York Times*, October 22, 1983: 1, 4; *Washington Post*, March 9, 1984: A28; *Middle East International*, February 10, 1984: 7–8.

75. Giovanni de Briganti, 'Forces d'Action Rapide: France's Rapid Deployment Force', *Armed Forces Journal International* (October 1984): 122.

76. Andre L. Rilhac, 'Armour in French Rapid Assistance Forces', *Armour* (September–October 1982): 21.

77. David A. Brown, 'Rapid Deployment Force contemplated by British', *Aviation Week and Space Technology*, July 7, 1980: 18.

78. *The Age* (Melbourne), November 16, 1983: 8; Major General T. A. Boam, 'Defending Western interests outside NATO: the United Kingdom's contribution', *Armed Forces Journal International* (October 1984): 118.

Contingency Planning and Response

79. For a discussion, see Amitav Acharya, 'NATO and "out-of-area" contingencies: the Gulf experience', *International Defense Review* (May 1987): 569 – 76.

80. U.S. Congress. Senate. Committee on Armed Services. *Department of Defense authorization for appropriations for fiscal year 1982*, Part 4: 1714 – 15.

81. Jeffrey Record, 'The RDF: is the Pentagon kidding?' *Washington Quarterly* (Summer 1981): 43.

82. Remarks by Senator William Cohen in U.S. Congress. Senate. Committee on Armed Services. *Department of Defense authorization for appropriations for fiscal year 1982*, Part 4: 1994.

83. Ibid., p. 1966.

84. Ibid., p. 1733.

85. Paul K. Davis, *Observations on the Rapid Deployment Joint Task Force: origins, direction, and mission* (Santa Monica, CA: Rand Corporation, June 1982): 30. Mr. Davis is a former Director of Special Regional Studies at the Pentagon.

86. U.S. Congress. Senate. Committee on Armed Services. *Department of Defense authorization for appropriations for fiscal year 1982*, Part 4: 1715 – 16; General P. X. Kelly, 'Rapid Deployment: a vital trump', *Parameters* (March 1981): 52.

87. U.S. Congress. House. Committee on Armed Services. *Hearings on H.R. 1816 (H.R. 2972), FY1984*: 987.

88. Congressional Budget Office, *U.S. ground forces: design and cost alternatives for NATO and non-NATO contingencies* (1980): 53 – 54.

89. See the testimony by the Defense Intelligence Agency, U.S. Congress. Senate. Committee on Armed Services. *Department of Defense authorization for appropriations for fiscal year 1981*, Part 5: 3141; Thomas L. McNaugher, *Balancing Soviet power in the Gulf*, manuscript (Washington, D.C., 1984): 51 – 53; Joshua M. Epstein, 'Soviet vulnerabilities in Iran and the RDF deterrent', *International Security* (Fall 1981): 148 – 9.

90. Waltz's views are presented in 'A strategy for the Rapid Deployment Force', *International Security* (Spring 1981): 49 – 73. A 'tripwire' force is generally defined as a force that has 'no realistic hope itself of defeating an enemy force but which, if defeated, would irrevocably commit the strategic forces of the parent nation'. *The Rapid Deployment Force* (Greenwich, CT: Defense Marketing Service, 1980): viii.

91. Albert Wohlstetter, 'Meeting the threat in the Persian Gulf', *Survey* (Spring 1980): 164.

92. *Challenges for U.S. national security. Assessing the balance: defense spending and conventional forces. A preliminary report*, Part II (Washington, D.C.: Carnegie Endowment for International Peace, 1981): 157.

93. *Department of State Bulletin* (May 1980): 65.

94. Ibid. The Reagan administration's declaratory policy on vertical escalation was similar to that of its predecessor.

95. Statement by Francis J. West, Assistant Secretary of Defense for International Security Affairs, U.S. Congress. Senate. Committee on Armed Services. *Department of Defense authorization for appropriations for fiscal year 1983*, Part 6: 3723. This was echoed by Deputy Secretary of Defense Frank C. Carlucci at another hearing: U.S. Congress. Senate. Committee

165

Contingency Planning and Response

on Appropriations. *Department of Defense appropriations fiscal year 1983*, Part 3: 280.

96. Long before the RDJTF was set up, National Security Advisor Zbigniew Brzezinski had told *New Yorker* magazine reporter Elizabeth Drew: 'We ought to contemplate getting there first, . . . This is going to put a premium on preemption because who gets there first has command of the situation.' Cited in Jan Austin and Banning Garrett, 'Quick strike', *Inquiry*, July 24, 1978: 15. He reaffirmed the need for preemption in December 1979. See *Washington Post*, December 20, 1979: A22.

97. *Department of State Bulletin* (May 1980): 65. At a Pentagon press briefing in June 1980, General P. X. Kelly was reported by the *New York Times* correspondent to have 'asserted . . . that he was ready to move troops into the Middle East or the Persian Gulf should he be ordered to launch a pre-emptive strike to seize threatened ground before the Russians got there'. *New York Times*, June 19, 1980: A15.

98. Richard K. Betts, *Surprise attack: lessons for defense planning* (Washington, D.C.: Brookings Institution, 1982): 262. General Kelly made the same point: U.S. Congress. House. Committee on Armed Services. *Hearings on military posture and H.R. 6495 (H.R. 6974), FY1981*, Part 3: 129.

99. U.S. Congress. Senate. Committee on Armed Services. *Department of Defense authorization for appropriations for fiscal year 1982*, Part 4: 1755. See also *Transcript of the news briefing by General P. X. Kelly USMC, Commander RDJTF* (DOD/PAO: June 18, 1980).

100. Department of Defense, *Annual report to Congress, FY1983*: III – 92.

101. U.S. Congress. House. Committee on Armed Services. *Hearings on military posture and H.R. 6495 (H.R. 6974), FY1981*, Part 3: 132.

102. Stansfield Turner, 'Toward a new defense strategy', *New York Times Magazine*, May 10, 1980: 16.

103. *Washington Post*, January 3, 1981: C9; *Washington Post*, February 3, 1981: 18.

104. *New York Times*, May 30, 1982: 12. A report by the Congressional Research Service made the same point: '[defence] guidance documents . . . say that the forces must be capable of coercive entry without waiting for an invitation.' Congressional Research Service, *Rapid Deployment Force* (1984): 4.

105. U.S. Congress. Senate. Committee on Appropriations. *Department of Defense appropriations for fiscal year 1983*, Part 3: 226.

106. Keith A. Dunn, 'Toward a U.S. military strategy for Southwest Asia', in Alvin Z. Rubinstein (ed.), *The great game: rivalry in the Persian Gulf and South Asia* (New York: Praeger, 1983): 226. These views are supported by most analysts, including the London-based International Institute for Strategic Studies. See *The Military Balance* for relevant year. In 1981 some increases in the readiness status of Soviet Southern District forces were reported. This created a certain degree of alarm in Washington. But overall no dramatic upgrading followed.

107. Congressional Budget Office, *U.S. ground forces: design and cost alternatives for NATO and non-NATO contingencies* (1980): p. 47.

108. Maxwell O. Johnson, *The military as an instrument of U.S. policy in Southwest Asia: the Rapid Deployment Join Task Force, 1979 – 1982* (Boulder, CO: Westview Press, 1983): 104.

Contingency Planning and Response

109. Department of Defense, *Annual report to Congress, FY1983*: III–92; Department of Defense, *Annual report to Congress, FY1984*: 209.

110. U.S. Congress. Senate. Committee on Armed Services. *Department of Defense authorization for appropriations for fiscal year 1984*, Part 6: 3142.

111. These deployment times for the different force components are derived from: H.Q. Rapid Deployment Joint Task Force, *Fact sheet* (April 1981): 5; U.S. Congress. Senate. Committee on Foreign Relations. *U.S. security interests and policies in Southwest Asia* (1980): 325; House. Committee on Foreign Affairs. *U.S. interests in, and policies toward, the Persian Gulf* (1980): 64; Senate. Committee on Appropriations. *Department of Defense appropriations for fiscal year 1983*, Part 3: 226; Senate. Committee on Armed Services. *Department of Defense authorization for appropriations for fiscal year 1983*, Part 6: 3730; John M. Collins, *U.S. –Soviet military balance: concepts and capabilities, 1960–1980* (New York: McGraw-Hill, 1980): 386–7; U.S. Congress. House. Committee on Foreign Affairs. *Developments in the Persian Gulf, June 1984*: 59–60; M. Rich, W. Stanley and S. Anderson, *Improving U.S. Air Force readiness and sustainability*, R-3113/1-AF (Santa Monica, CA: Rand Corporation, 1984); Anthony H. Cordsman, *The Gulf and the search for strategic stability* (Boulder, CO: Westview Press, 1984): 810, 857.

112. John M. Collins, 'Rapid Deployment Forces: facts versus fantasy', *Marine Corps Gazette* (February 1981): 69.

113. Department of Defence, *Soviet military power 1985*: 62–63, 66.

114. For a discussion of the evolution of the Soviet airlift capability, see Peter Borgart, 'The Soviet transport air force: aircraft and capabilities', *International Defense Review* (June 1979): 945–50; Collins, *U.S. –Soviet military balance*, pp. 274–6; William Schneider, 'Soviet military airlift: key to rapid power projection', *Air Force Magazine* (March 1980): 80–86.

115. McNaugher, *Balancing Soviet power* (manuscript), p. 20; Congressional Research Service, *Rapid Deployment Force* (1985): 8; Collins, *U.S. –Soviet military balance*, p. 276.

116. *Washington Post*, June 17, 1980: A1.

117. U.S. Congress. House. Committee on Armed Services. *Hearings on military posture and H.R. 2970 (H.R. 3519), fiscal year 1982*, Part 1: 1123.

118. U.S. Congress. Senate. Committee on Armed Services. *Department of Defense authorization for appropriations for fiscal year 1984*, Part 6: 2975. During the 1979–84 period, Dhalak Island had been visited by an average of about 70 Soviet ships per year. Apart from the Soviet Indian Ocean squadron, it has also catered to ships from the Soviet Mediterranean fleet. The floating drydock displaces 8,500 tons and services Ethiopian vessels as well. Department of Defense, *Soviet military power, 1984*: 125–6.

119. Keith A. Dunn, 'Constraints on the U.S.S.R. in Southeast Asia: a military analysis', *Orbis* (Fall 1981): 620–1.

120. U.S. Congress. House. Committee on Foreign Affairs. *U.S. policy toward the Persian Gulf* (1982): 110.

121. U.S. Congress. Senate. Committee on Foreign Relations. *U.S. security interests and policies in Southwest Asia* (1980): 301.

122. Department of Defense, *Soviet military power, 1984*: 124–5.

123. Joshua Epstein analyzes Soviet difficulties in the Iranian terrain

167

Contingency Planning and Response

in the light of a 1941 Soviet Command Study of Iran. See his 'Soviet vulnerabilites', op.cit., pp. 130 – 7.

124. U.S. Congress. House. Committee on Appropriations. *Military construction appropriation for 1984*, Part 5: 374.

125. U.S. Congress. Senate. Committee on Armed Services. *Department of Defense authorization for appropriations for fiscal year 1981*, Part 5: 3149; House. Committee on Appropriations. *Department of Defense appropriations for 1982*, Part 4: 377.

126. U.S. Congress. Senate. Committee on Armed Services. *Department of Defense authorization for appropriations for fiscal year 1982*, Part 4: 1991.

127. General Hamilton H. Howze (Rtd.), 'Confrontation in the Middle East', *Army* (August 1980): 25.

128. U.S. Congress. House. Committee on Appropriations. *Department of Defense appropriations for 1982*, Part 1: 389.

129. U.S. Congress. House. Committee on Armed Services. *Hearings on military posture and H.R. 2970 (H.R. 3519), fiscal year 1982*, Part 1: 1132 – 3.

130. Brzezinski, *Power and principle*, p. 445.

131. A summary of the report appeared in the *New York Times*, February 3, 1980.

132. Testimony by the Director of the Center for Defense Information, Admiral Gene LaRocque USN (Rtd.): U.S. Congress. House. Committee on Armed Services. *Hearings on H.R. 1816 (H.R. 2972), fiscal year 1984*: 1068 – 9. For a detailed discussion of the nuclear delivery systems in the RDF, see Christopher Paine, 'On the beach: the Rapid Deployment Force and the nuclear arms race', *Merip Reports* (January 1983): 3 – 11, 30.

133. *Washington Post*, September 24, 1980: C27.

134. Cited in Epstein, 'Soviet vulnerabilities', p. 132.

135. U.S. Congress. House. Committee on Appropriations. *Department of Defense appropriations for 1982*, Part 1: 274 – 5.

136. *Washington Post*, July 17, 1981: A1, A11.

137. Cited in Keith A. Dunn and William O. Staudenmaier, *Strategic implications of the continental – maritime debate, Washington Papers*, no. 107 (New York: Praeger, 1984): 29.

138. Joshua M. Epstein, 'Horizontal escalation: sour notes of a recurrent theme', *International Security* (Winter 1983 – 84): 19 – 31; see also Dunn and Staudenmaier, *Strategic implications of the continental – maritime debate*, pp. 29 – 30.

168

7

Conclusion

The crises in Iran and Afghanistan were a turning point in the U.S. global strategic posture in general and its Persian Gulf policy in particular. They marked the erosion, both in a political and a strategic sense, of the so-called Vietnam syndrome and ushered in a mood of geopolitical assertiveness. This transition was reflected, first and foremost, in the domestic arena where the critics of the Vietnam War began losing, for the first time in over a decade, the debate on the use of force in support of U.S. foreign policy goals. The Carter administration's early efforts to put the post-Vietnam U.S. foreign policy on a new moral footing was abandoned in the face of rising domestic disapproval. In foreign policy the transition was evident in superpower relations, where it led to the demise of detente and created renewed tensions. In terms of U.S. dealings with the Third World, it produced a greater appreciation of the utility of military force as a policy instrument.

That this remarkable transition in U.S. foreign policy was catalysed by events in and around the Persian Gulf was perhaps not surprising or odd. During the 1970s no other region outside of traditional U.S. alliances came to be regarded as so vital to the security of the United States and its allies. No other region displayed so many conditions adversely affecting the pursuit of Western interests. U.S. and Western interests in the Gulf (access to oil, containment of Soviet influence, and the preservation of conservative regimes) had evolved steadily since the end of World War II. But the importance of these interests telescoped during the 1970s as the result of a number of factors — the increasingly critical dependence of the Western consumer nations on Persian Gulf oil as the result of rising consumption and shrinking domestic

169

Conclusion

reserves, the British withdrawal from east of Suez and the perceived threats to U.S. regional interests. Fears of a possible collapse of the conservative order in the Gulf from the pressures of rapid socioeconomic change were aggravated by the potential for increased competition from the Soviet Union backed by its growing naval capability. The new solidarity among the producer nations, determined to wrest control of their oil resources from Western multinationals and subject their availability to the satisfaction of their economic (price) and political demands, added to the uncertainties facing the managers of U.S. interests. The demonstrated willingness and ability of the Arab Gulf States to use oil as a political weapon ended the hitherto successful effort by U.S. policymakers to keep the issue of oil supply from the Gulf separate from the Arab–Israeli conflict and forced them to take greater cognizance of Saudi Arabia's sensitivity toward U.S. support for Israel. While this realization was beginning to take hold, the October War and the accompanying oil price hike led to a considerable strengthening of U.S. economic stakes in the Gulf. The emergence of the Gulf States as significant financial powers with huge reserves of surplus revenues, which could be recycled to the West either in the form of import of goods and services or investments in Western financial markets, became another factor in the emergence of the Gulf from the backwaters of international politics to the forefront of the U.S. global strategic agenda.

If the Arab oil embargo underscored threats to U.S. access to Persian Gulf oil posed by *deliberate action* by the producers, the Iranian revolution and the Soviet invasion of Afghanistan highlighted, in the American mind, the threats of *disruption* which might be caused by domestic instability and external intervention. But the impact of the twin crises on American strategic perceptions touched more than the question of a cutoff in the flow of oil. The U.S. view of the events of 1979 in Southwest Asia was marked by an unprecedented degree of alarm and pessimism. The fall of the Shah was a major setback to the U.S. regional, indeed, global position, undermining basic economic and strategic interests of the Western nations. Besides, the Iranian revolution aggravated the Carter administration's fears about the possible collapse of pro-Western regimes in the so-called arc of crisis. The 'threats' posed by the Afghanistan crisis aroused similar speculation concerning the possibility of Soviet expansion into the Gulf. The invasion reinforced perceptions of an alleged Soviet 'geopolitical offensive' aimed at eventual domination of the whole region and control

Conclusion

of Western access to raw materials.

The U.S. response to these problems and crises was marked by increasing emphasis on military force as the instrument for protecting Western interests. The Nixon Doctrine, which had been applied to the Gulf in a situation where alternative options were severely restricted by the Vietnam debacle, survived as the basic framework of U.S. policy in the aftermath of the 'first oil crisis' (embargo and the price hike). But at the same time it became clear that the United States was not averse to changes in its strategy as it concerned the use of military force in pursuit of its regional goals. The Ford administration's threats to retaliate against embargos with military action represented the first important move away from the policy of relying on local surrogates. But continued adherence to the Nixon Doctrine became further complicated, as a result of the growing resentment within the U.S. policymaking organization against the Shah's 'hawkish' stand on oil prices, and the congressional and media disapproval of the official policy of liberal compliance with the Shah's persistent quest for American weapons. These factors led to the undermining of the 'twin-pillar' approach even before the Iranian revolution.

In this sense, the Nixon Doctrine can be more properly described as a stop-gap arrangement forced on the United States by the Vietnam predicament. Of course, United States policymakers might not have perceived it as such at the time of the British withdrawal. But the fact remains that the Vietnam syndrome did not prevent the Nixon administration from carrying out a major build-up of U.S. naval power in the Indian Ocan and the Congress from eventually approving, after some resistance within the Senate, the Diego Garcia military base. The Vietnam syndrome did not discourage the Ford administration's statements concerning the seizure of Gulf oil fields; nor did it dissuade the allegedly moralistic Carter administration from developing the blueprint for a global intervention force, with the Persian Gulf as a specially identified focus. The Vietnam syndrome did show up in preventing a speedy translation of this blueprint into reality, but it is clear that it applied much less to the Persian Gulf than to Southeast Asia, where, unlike the Gulf, the United States had no genuine 'vital' interests.

The Iranian revolution, along with the hostage crisis and the Soviet invasion of Afghanistan, completed the evolution of U.S. strategic policy in the Gulf from one of reliance on the British to reliance on local surrogates to reliance, at least in a declaratory

Conclusion

sense, on its own military interventionist capability. Emphasis on building this capability came to dominate the Carter and Reagan administrations' strategic policy on the Gulf. The Carter administration revived a rapid-deployment strategy conceived years ago and gave it an exclusive Gulf focus. It assembled a 'central reserve' of combat units, including ground forces, which could be deployed at short notice for combat operations in the Gulf. To remove the deficiencies that initially undermined the credibility of this enterprise, the Carter and Reagan administrations made significant investments in improving the readiness, strategic mobility, and war-fighting ability of the forces that were earmarked for a Persian Gulf mission. A network of regional support facilities was negotiated and built, and a new unified command for the Gulf/Southwest Asia region was established.

But while the CENTCOM could no longer be dismissed as a paper tiger, the projection of U.S. power into the Gulf remained beset with several major constraints. One set of problems concerned the organizational aspect and the human and technological resources that affect military capability. These problems were evident in the continuing readiness problems of the CENTCOM's constituent units, their dual commitment, and their apparent weaknesses against the armour-heavy, firepower-intensive opponent forces in the Gulf region and its vicinity. There was no major initiative to raise additional forces to meet the demands of a simultaneous conflict in the Gulf and elsewhere, beyond marginal 'compensatory measures' undertaken by the NATO allies. In another respect, while the creation of the CENTCOM with a specific geographic responsibility removed much of the complexity and the apparent tentativeness of the RDJTF and the intense inter-service rivalry it aroused, the CENTCOM suffered from the same problem of lack of day-to-day control over its assigned forces as its predecessors. And despite considerable investment, the CENTCOM could not overcome the gaps in strategic mobility, especially in the critical area of aircraft, which fell short of the requirement set by the congressionally mandated mobility study (CMMS).

A second set of factors affecting the projection of U.S. power into the Gulf related to the contribution of America's Southwest Asian and NATO allies. In the wake of setbacks in Iran and Afghanistan, U.S. policymakers hoped that a strong response, backed by a capability to protect its interests and those of its allies from varied threats, would win back the confidence of the regional

Conclusion

allies and induce their positive response and cooperation. Such cooperation, in turn, would be a necessary condition for the effectiveness of the U.S. strategy, which depended on access to regional military bases that otherwise would be politically destabilizing. The recognition of this mutually reinforcing linkage between regional cooperation and the RDJTF/CENTCOM was the central basis behind such ideas as the 'regional cooperative security framework' (Carter–Brzezinski) or 'strategic consensus' (Reagan–Haig).

But the response of the regional states, especially Saudi Arabia and the fellow Gulf monarchies, to the U.S. strategy was ambivalent and did not lead to the degree of cooperation expected by U.S. policymakers. While the United States scored important successes in securing access to military bases and facilities in countries such as Oman, Egypt, Kenya, and Saudi Arabia, in several cases the agreements highlighted the problems and complications in the strategic relationship between the two countries rather than a spirit of cooperation. With the exception of Diego Garcia, the United States was not able to secure assured, timely, and exclusive use of regional military installations. The pro-Western states in Southwest Asia showed little inclination to accept anything more than an 'over-the-horizon' U.S. presence, thereby undermining the credibility of the U.S. strategy.

The failure of U.S. efforts to build a 'regional cooperative security framework' or 'strategic consensus' could be attributed to several factors. In a general sense, it was linked to the differing strategic priorities of the United States and the regional countries. While the United States, for reasons relating to political expediency and the broader strategic concerns of a superpower, put a great deal of emphasis on the Soviet threat, the regional states were preoccupied with more limited and local threats — for example, Somalia against Ethiopia, Israel against Syria, Pakistan against India, and Oman against South Yemen. Such differences created gaps in the strategic understanding between the United States and its regional friends. They also made the United States wary of a closer security relationship with some of the friendly regional states for fear of becoming unnecessarily involved in local disputes. Furthermore, antagonisms between pro-Western regional countries frustrated U.S. efforts to bring them together under a security umbrella dominated by its interventionist capability; this was most strikingly evident in the case of the failed attempt to cement a 'strategic consensus' between Israel and the Arab friends.

173

Conclusion

The United States faced major obstacles in winning meaningful support from the conservative Gulf States for its interventionist strategy. This was largely due to the latter's desire to limit superpower rivalry in the region, their suspicion that the RDJTF/CENTCOM could be used to seize their oil fields as well as to protect them from enemies, and their disapproval of the U.S. policy towards the Arab–Israeli conflict. The Gulf States deplored the American failure to supplement its military strategy with a diplomatic initiative aimed at a political settlement of the Arab–Israeli problem, recognizing the Palestinian right to self-determination. If anything, the new U.S. security posture in the Gulf was accompanied by a marked reduction in U.S. efforts to seek a solution to the Arab–Israeli conflict. This was evident from the Carter administration's failure to live up to the expectations initially raised at Camp David, Haig's attempts to sidestep the Palestinian issue and focus on other regional security problems, and the Reagan administration's subsequent failure to push strongly for Israeli concessions to its own peace plan. Such failures might reflect the general intractability of the issues complicating a solution. But they gave the impression that emphasis on a military instrument could undermine the role of diplomacy in solving the region's major security problems.

America's NATO allies generally agreed that a capability for military intervention should be a part of any Western strategy to protect access to Gulf oil. But translating this approval into concrete supportive measures was not easy. The allies were unable, because of financial and political pressures, to devote additional resources to offset the impact of a possible wartime diversion of U.S. resources from Europe to the Gulf. The compensatory measures adopted were inadequate, especially in the key areas of manpower (both combat and support) and strategic mobility. In so far as direct force contribution by allies was concerned, a British interventionist role in the Gulf could not be more than symbolic (although this did not diminish its political value for the United States), while the French resisted the kind of coordination between their forces and those of the United States that would maximize the overall effectiveness of a Western military effort.

An evaluation of the U.S. strategy in the Gulf would have to consider how its intervention capability was, or might have been, put to use. This study reveals that in the period between the 1973–74 oil crisis, when the need for such a capability was recognized for the first time since the British withdrawal from the

Conclusion

region, and 1984, by which time the basic elements of the capability were already in place, declaratory U.S. policy on the Gulf indicated the possibility of intervention in four different scenarios: (a) an oil embargo with severe economic consequences for the West (Ford administration); (b) a Soviet military intervention in the Gulf (Carter administration); (c) severe domestic instability in Saudi Arabia (Reagan administration); and (d) an Iranian attempt to close the oil lanes and the related prospect of a direct spillover of the Iran–Iraq War to the GCC states.

The Carter and Reagan administrations carefully avoided any talk of using force to break an oil embargo, which was first indicated by the Ford administration. But the new U.S. military strategy in the Gulf envisaged a forcible seizure of the Iranian oil fields in the event of a Soviet invasion of Iran.

With the exception of the Iran–Iraq War, the Pentagon's contingency planning for the Gulf remains untested. But despite the impressive build-up under Carter and Reagan in preparation for these contingencies, U.S. policymakers faced considerable uncertainty in deciding whether military force could be an appropriate and effective option in many of them. There was justified scepticism over the ability of the RDJTF/CENTCOM to deter and repel a Soviet attack on Iran, even though the U.S. strategy carried the threat of escalating such a conflict to a global nuclear confrontation between the superpowers. Recognition that a U.S. intervention in non-Soviet contingencies might be ineffective or counterproductive was evident from the nature of the Pentagon's planning for such threats.

The Gulf war, which extended beyond the first Reagan administration, proved to be the most significant challenge to the U.S. strategy during the period covered by this study. The war itself demonstrated that the most likely threats to regional security in the Gulf were likely to be intra-regional, rather than Soviet-inspired. It also showed the limitations of U.S. military power in bringing the conflict to an end. The U.S. response to the conflict recognized these limitations. Although the stand taken by the United States against Iran's frequent threats to close the Strait of Hormuz might have been a factor in Teheran's failure to carry the threat out, the latter's behaviour continued to pose a threat to the GCC and to U.S. interests in the region.

In sum, the U.S. military strategy in the Gulf during the period under investigation faced several challenges including problems relating to force structure, logistics and limited access to regional

Conclusion

military bases, failure to win significant support from the regional countries, and the outbreak and continuation of the Iran–Iraq War. Efforts by the Carter and Reagan administrations to overcome these constraints did not produce expected or required outcomes. This demonstrated a major credibility problem for the U.S. security role in the region, despite the commitment of significant resources by the two administrations to repair the damage to U.S. standing caused by the fall of the Shah.

Bibliography

A. U.S. Government sources

A.1 Congressional hearings and reports
(Washington, D.C.: U.S. Government Printing Office)

A.1.1. House of Representatives

Committee on Appropriations. Subcommittee on the Department of Defense. *Supplemental Appropriation Bill, FY1980.* Hearings, Part 4. 96th Congress, 2nd Session, 1980.

Committee on Appropriations. Subcommittee on the Department of Defense. *Department of Defense Appropriations for 1981.* Hearings. Part 5 96th Congress, 2nd Session, 1980.

Committee on Appropriations. Subcommittee on the Department of Defense. *Department of Defense Appropriations for 1982.* Hearings. Part 1. 97th Congress, 1st Session, 1981.

Committee on Appropriations. Subcommittee on the Department of Defense. *Department of Defense Appropriations for 1982.* Hearings. Part 2. 97th Congress, 1st Session. 1981.

Committee on Appropriations. Subcommittee on the Department of Defense. *Department of Defense Appropriations for 1982.* Hearings. Part 4. 97th Congress, 1st Session, 1981.

Committee on Appropriations. Subcommittee on the Department of Defense. *Department of Defense Appropriations for 1983.* Hearings. Part 6. 97th Congress, 2nd Session, 1982.

Committee on Appropriations. Subcommittee on the Department of Defense. *Department of Defense Appropriations for 1984.* Hearings. Part 6. 98th Congress, 1st Session, 1983.

Committee on Appropriations. Subcommittee on the Department of Defense. *Department of Defense Appropriations for 1985.* Hearings. Part 1. 98th Congress, 2nd Session, 1984.

Committee on Appropriations. Subcommittee on the Department of Defense. *Department of Defense Appropriations for 1985.* Hearings. Part 2. 98th Congress, 2nd Session, 1984.

Committee on Appropriations. Subcommittee on the Department of Defense. *Department of Defense Appropriations for 1985.* Hearings. Part 7. 98th Congress, 2nd Session, 1984.

Committee on Appropriations. Subcommittee on Military Construction Appropriations. *Military construction appropriations for 1981.* Hearings. Part 4. 96th Congress, 2nd Session, 1980.

Committee on Appropriations. Subcommittee on Military Construction Appropriations. *Military construction appropriations for 1982.* Hearings. Part 5. 97th Congress, 1st Session, 1981.

Committee on Appropriations. Subcommittee on Military Construction

Bibliography

Appropriations. *Military construction appropriations for 1982.* Hearings. Part 6. 97th Congress, 1st Session, 1981.

Committee on Appropriations. Subcommittee on Military Construction Appropriations. *Military construction appropriations for 1982.* Hearings. Part 1. 97th Congress, 2nd Session, 1982.

Committee on Appropriations. Subcommittee on Military Construction Appropriations. *Military construction appropriations for 1983.* Hearings. Part 3. 97th Congress, 2nd Session, 1982.

Committee on Appropriations. Subcommittee on Military Construction Appropriations. *Military construction appropriations for 1983.* Hearings. Part 5. 97th Congress, 2nd Session, 1982.

Committee on Appropriations. Subcommittee on Military Construction Appropriations. *Military construction appropriations for 1984.* Hearings. Part 5. 98th Congress, 1st Session, 1983.

Committee on Appropriations. Subcommittee on Military Construction Appropriations. *Military construction appropriations for 1985.* Hearings. Part 4. 98th Congress, 2nd Session, 1984.

Committee on Appropriations. Subcommittee on Military Construction Appropriations. *Military construction appropriations for 1985.* Hearings. Part 6. 98th Congress, 2nd Session, 1984.

Committee on Appropriations. *Military construction appropriation bill, 1981.* House Report 96-1097. 96th Congress, 2nd Session, 1980.

Committee on Appropriations. *Making appropriations for military construction, Department of Defense, fiscal year 1981.* Conference Report on H.R. 7592. 96th Congress, 2nd Session, 1980.

Committee on Appropriations. *Military construction appropriation bill, 1982.* House Report 97-193. 97th Congress, 1st Session, 1981.

Committee on Appropriations. *Military construction appropriation bill, 1983.* House Report 97-726. 97th Congress, 2nd Session, 1982.

Committee on Appropriations. *Making appropriations for military construction for the Department of Defense for fiscal year ending September 30, 1983.* Conference Report on H.R. 6968. 97th Congress, 2nd Session, 1982.

Committee on Appropriations. *Military construction appropriation bill, 1984.* House Report 98-238. 98th Congress, 1st Session, 1983.

Committee on Appropriations. *Military construction appropriation bill, 1985.* House Report 98-850. 98th Congress, 2nd Session, 1984.

Committee on Armed Services. *Military posture briefings.* 87th Congress, 1st Session, 19761.

Committee on Armed Services. *Hearings on military posture and H.R. 9751 to authorize appropriations during fiscal year 1963.* 87th Congress, 2nd Session, 1962.

Committee on Armed Services. *Hearings on military posture and H.R. 4016 to authorize appropriations during fiscal year 1966.* 89th Congress, 1st Session, 1965.

Committee on Armed Services. *Hearings on military posture and a bill (H.R. 9240) to authorise appropriations during the fiscal year 1968.* 90th Congress, 1st Session, 1967.

Committee on Armed Services. *Hearings on military posture and an Act (S. 3293) to authorize appropriations during the fiscal year 1969.* 90th Congress, 2nd Session, 1968.

Bibliography

Committee on Armed Services. *Report of the special subcommittee to inspect facilities at Berbera, Somalia, to the Committee on Armed Services.* 94th Congress, 1st Session, 1975.

Committee on Armed Services. *The posture of military airlift.* A report by the Research and Development Subcommittee of the Committee on Armed Services. 94th Congress, 2nd Session, 1976.

Committee on Armed Services. *Report of the delegation to the Indian Ocean area.* 96th Congress, 2nd Session, 1980.

Committee on Armed Services. *Hearings on military posture and H.R. 6495 (H.R. 6974), Department of Defense authorization for appropriations for FY1981.* Part 3. 96th Congress, 2nd Session, 1980.

Committee on Armed Services. *Department of Defense Authorization Act, 1981.* House Report 96-916. 96th Congress, 2nd Session, 1980.

Committee on Armed Services. *Department of Defense Authorization Act, 1981.* Conference report on H.R. 6974. 96th Congress, 2nd Session, 1980.

Committee on Armed Services. *Hearings on military posture, H.R. 2614 and H.R. 2970 (H.R. 3519), Department of Defense authorization for appropriations for FY1982.* Part 1. 97th Congress, 1st Session, 1981.

Committee on Armed Services. *Hearings on military posture and H.R. 2970 (H.R. 3519), Department of Defense authorization for appropriations for FY1982.* Part 3. 97th Congress, 1st Session, 1981.

Committee on Armed Services. *Hearings on military posture and H.R. 2970 (H.R. 3519) and H.R. 745, Department of Defense authorization for appropriations for FY1982.* Part 5. 97th Congress, 1st Session, 1981.

Committee on Armed Services. *Report of the delegation to the Middle East and Africa.* Committee print no. 18 (May 28, 1982). 97th Congress, 2nd Session, 1982.

Committee on Armed Services. *Hearings on military posture and H.R. 5968 (H.R. 6030), Department of Defense authorization for appropriations for FY1983.* Part 4. 97th Congress, 2nd Session, 1982.

Committee on Armed Services. *Hearings on military posture and H.R. 5968 (H.R. 6030), Department of Defense authorization for appropriations for FY1983, and H.R. 5639 to authorize appropriations for civil defense programs for FY1983–FY1984.* Part 7. 97th Congress, 2nd Session, 1982.

Committee on Armed Services. *Defense Department authorization and oversight. Hearings on H.R. 5167, FY1985.* Part 3. 98th Congress, 2nd Session, 1984.

Committee on Armed Services. Subcommittee on military installations and facilities. *Hearings on H.R. 1816 (H.R. 2972) to authorize certain construction at military installations for FY1984.* 98th Congress, 1st Session, 1983.

Committee on Budget. *Military readiness and the Rapid Deployment Joint Task Force.* Hearings. 96th Congress, 2nd Session, 1980.

Committee on Foreign Affairs. *Foreign assistance legislation for fiscal year 1981.* Hearings. Part 1. 96th Congress, 2nd Session, 1980.

Committee on Foreign Affairs. *U.S. security interests in the Persian Gulf.* Report of a staff study mission to the Persian Gulf, Middle East, and Horn of Africa (March 16, 1981). 97th Congress, 1st Session, 1981.

Bibliography

Committee on Foreign Affairs. Subcommittee on the Near East and South Asia. *U.S. interest and policy toward the Persian Gulf.* Hearings. 92nd Congress, 2nd Session, 1972.

Committee on Foreign Affairs. Subcommittee on the Near East and South Asia. *New perspectives on the Persian Gulf.* Hearings. 93rd Congres, 1st Session, 1973.

Committee on Foreign Affairs. Subcommittee on the Near East and South Asia. *The Persian Gulf, 1974: money, politics, arms and power.* Hearings, 93rd Congress, 2nd Session, 1974.

Committee on Foreign Affairs. Subcommittee on Europe and the Middle East. *U.S. policy toward Iran, January 1979.* Hearings. 96th Congress, 1st Session, 1979.

Committee on Foreign Affairs. Subcommittee on Europe and the Middle East. *Review of recent developments in the Middle East, 1979.* Hearings. 96th Congress, 1st Session, 1979.

Committee on Foreign Affairs. Subcommittee on Europe and the Middle East. *U.S. interests in, and policies toward, the Persian Gulf, 1980.* Hearings. 96th Congress, 2nd Session, 1980.

Committee on Foreign Affairs. Subcommittee on Europe and the Middle East. *NATO after Afghanistan.* Report prepared by the Congressional Research Service. 96th Congress, 2nd Session, 1980.

Committee on Foreign Affairs. Subcommittee on Europe and the Middle East. *U.S. – Western European relations in 1980.* Hearings. 96th Congress, 2nd Session, 1980.

Committee on Foreign Affairs. Subcommittee on Europe and the Middle East. *Saudi Arabia and the United States: the new context in an evolving 'special relationship'.* Report prepared by the Congressional Research Service. 97th Congress, 1st Session, 1981.

Committee on Foreign Affairs. Subcommittee on Europe and the Middle East. *NATO's future role.* Hearings. 97th Congress, 2nd Session, 1982.

Committee on Foreign Affairs. Subcommittee on Europe and the Middle East. *Developments in the Persian Gulf, June 1984.* Hearings. 98th Congress, 2nd Session, 1984.

Committee on Foreign Affairs. Subcommittee on Europe and the Middle East. *Developments in the Middle East, April 1985.* Hearings. 99th Congress, 1st Session, 1985.

Committee on Foreign Affairs. Subcommittee on Europe and the Middle East and the Joint Economic Committee. *U.S. policy toward the Persian Gulf.* Hearings. 97th Congress, 2nd Session, 1982.

Committee on Foreign Affairs. Subcommittee on Europe and the Middle East and the Subcommittee on Asian and Pacific Affairs. *Soviet Role in Asia.* Hearings. 98th Congress, 1st Session, 1983.

Committee on Foreign Affairs. Subcommittee on International Security and Scientific Affairs and Subcommittee on International Economic Policy and Trade and Subcommittee on Asian and Pacific Affairs. *Security and economic assistance to Pakistan.* Hearings. 97th Congress, 1st Session, 1981.

Committee on Foreign Affairs. Subcommittee on International Security and Scientific Affairs and Subcommittee on Africa. *Review of U.S. policy*

Bibliography

toward the conflict in the Western Sahara. Hearings. 98th Congress, 1st Session, 1983.

Committee on International Relations. *United States arms policies in the Persian Gulf and the Red Sea areas: past, present, and future.* Report of a staff survey mission to Ethiopia, Iran and the Arabian Peninsula. 95th Congress, 1st Session, 1977.

Committee on International Relations. Special Subcommittee on Investigations. *The Persian Gulf, 1975: the continuing debate on arms sales.* Hearings. 94th Congress, 1st Session, 1975.

Committee on International Relations. Special Subcommittee on Investigations. *Oil fields as military objectives: a feasibility study.* Prepared by the Congressional Research Service. Hearings. 94th Congress, 1st Session, 1975.

Committee on Government Operations. Subcommittee on Commerce and Monetary Affairs. *Operations of Federal agencies in monitoring, reporting on, and analyzing foreign investments in the U.S. Part 2: OPEC investments in the U.S.* Hearings. 96th Congress, 1st Session, 1979.

Committee on Interstate and Foreign Commerce. Subcommittee on Energy and Power. *The energy factbook.* Prepared by the Congressional Research Service. 96th Congress, 2nd Session, 1980.

A.1.2 Senate

Committee on Appropriations. *Department of Defense appropriations for FY1968.* Hearings. Part 1. 90th Congress, 1st Session, 1967.

Committee on Appropriations. *Department of Defense appropriations for FY1981.* Hearings. Part 6. 96th Congress, 2nd Session, 1980.

Committee on Appropriations. *Military construction appropriation bill, 1981.* Senate Report 96-931. 96th Congress, 2nd Session, 1980.

Committee on Appropriations. Subcommittee on Military Construction Appropriations. *Military construction appropriations for fiscal year 1982.* Hearings. 97th Congress, 1st Session, 1981.

Committee on Appropriations. *Department of Defense appropriations for FY1983.* Hearings. Part 3. 97th Congress, 2nd Session, 1982.

Committee on Appropriations. *Military construction appropriation bill, 1983.* Senate Report 97-572. 97th Congress, 2nd Session, 1982.

Committee on Appropriations. Subcommittee on Military Construction Appropriations. *Military construction appropriations for fiscal year 1984.* Hearings. 98th Congress, 1st Session, 1983.

Committee on Armed Services. Subcommittee on Procurement Policy and Reprogramming. *Civil Reserve Air Fleet (CRAF) enhancement program.* Hearings. 96th Congress, 1st Session, 1979.

Committee on Armed Services. *Department of Defense authorization for appropriations for fiscal year 1981.* Hearings. Part 1. 96th Congress, 2nd Session, 1980.

Committee on Armed Services. Subcommittee on Research and Development. *Department of Defense authorization for appropriations for fiscal year 1981.* Hearings. Part 5. 96th Congress, 2nd Session, 1980.

Committee on Armed Services. Subcommittee on Sea Power and Force

Bibliography

Projection. *Department of Defense authorization for appropriations for fiscal year 1982.* Hearings. Part 4. 97th Congress, 1st Session, 1981.

Committee on Armed Services. *Europe and the Middle East: strains on key elements of America's vital interests.* Report on a study mission by Senator S. Cohen (R. Maine), Chairman of the Subcommittee on Sea Power and Force Projection, to the Wehrkunde Conference, Munich, West Germany, and to Egypt, Israel, Bahrain, and Oman. 97th Congress, 2nd Session, 1982.

Committee on Armed Services. *Military and technical implications of the proposed sale to Saudi Arabia of airborne warning and control system (AWACS) and F-15 enhancements.* Hearings. 97th Congress, 1st Session, 1981.

Committee on Armed Services. *Department of Defense authorization for appropriations for fiscal year 1983.* Hearings. Part 2. 97th Congress, 2nd Session, 1982.

Committee on Armed Services. Subcommittee on Sea Power and Force Projection. *Department of Defense authorization for appropriations for fiscal year 1983.* Hearings. Part 6. 97th Congress, 2nd Session, 1982.

Committee on Armed Services. Subcommittee on Sea Power and Force Projection. *Department of Defense authorization for appropriations for fiscal year 1984.* Hearings. Part 6. 98th Congress, 1st Session, 1983.

Committee on Armed Services. *Department of Defense authorization for appropriations for fiscal year 1985.* Hearings. Part 2. 98th Congress, 2nd Session, 1984.

Committee on Armed Services. Subcommittee on Sea Power and Force Projection. *Department of Defense authorization for appropriations for fiscal year 1985.* Hearings. Part 8. 98th Congress, 2nd Session, 1984.

Committee on Armed Services. *Department of Defense authorization for appropriations for fiscal year 1986.* Hearings. Part 3. 99th Congress, 1st Session, 1985.

Committee on Armed Services. Subcommittee on Military Construction and Stockpiles, with Subcommittee on Military Construction Appropriations of Senate Appropriations Committee. *Military construction authorization fiscal year 1981.* 96th Congress, 2nd Session, 1980.

Committee on Armed Services. Subcommittee on Military Construction. *Military construction authorization fiscal year 1982.* Hearings. 97th Congress, 1st Session, 1981.

Committee on Armed Services. Subcommittee on Military Construction and Committee on Appropriations. *Military construction authorization and appropriations fiscal year 1983.* Hearings. 97th Congress, 2nd Session, 1982.

Committee on Armed Services. Subcommittee on Military Construction. *Military construction authorization fiscal year 1984.* Hearings. 98th Congress, 1st Session, 1983.

Committee on Energy and Natural Resources. *Access to oil: the United States relationship with Saudi Arabia and Iran.* Report. 95th Congress, 1st Session, 1977.

Committee on Energy and Natural Resources. *Project interdependence: U.S. and world energy outlook through 1990.* Report prepared by the Congressional Research Service, 95th Congress, 1st Session, 1977.

Committee on Energy and Natural Resources. *Geopolitics of oil.* Hearings.

Bibliography

Two parts. 96th Congress, 2nd Session, 1980.

Committee on Foreign Relations. *U.S. military sales to Iran.* A staff report to the Subcommittee on Foreign Assistance. 94th Congress, 2nd Session, 1976.

Committee on Foreign Relations. *United States foreign policy and overseas military installations.* Report prepared by the Congressional Research Service, 96th Congress, 1st Session, 1979.

Committee on Foreign Relations. Subcommittee on Near Eastern and South Asian Affairs. *U.S. security interests and policies in Southwest Asia.* 96th Congress, 2nd Session, 1980.

Committee on Foreign Relations. *Persian Gulf situation.* Hearings. 97th Congress, 1st Session, 1981.

Committee on Foreign Relations. *NATO today: the Alliance in evolution.* A report to the Committee on Foreign Relations. 97th Congress, 2nd Session, 1982.

Committee on Foreign Relations. *The Middle East.* A report by Senator Charles Percy (R-Illinois) on a study mission to the Middle East. 97th Congress, 2nd Session, 1982.

Committee on Foreign Relations. *Fiscal year 1983 security assistance.* Hearings. 97th Congress, 2nd Session, 1982.

Committee on Foreign Relations. *Hidden war: the struggle for Afghanistan.* A staff report. Senate Print 91-181. 98th Congress, 2nd Session, 1984.

Committee on Foreign Relations. *War in the Gulf.* A staff report. Senate Print 98-225. 98th Congress, 2nd Session, 1984.

Committee on Foreign Relations. *United States security interests in South Asia.* A staff report. Senate Print 98-189. 98th Congress, 2nd Session, 1984.

A.1.3 Joint Economic Committee

The U.S. role in a changing world political economy: major issues for the 96th Congress. A compendium of papers submitted to the Joint Economic Committee. 96th Congress, 1st Session, 1979.

Economic consequences of the revolution in Iran. A compendium of papers submitted to the Joint Economic Committee. 96th Congress, 1st Session, 1979.

The political economy of the Middle East: 1973–78. A compendium of papers submitted to the Joint Economic Committee. 96th Congress, 2nd Session, 1980.

The Persian Gulf: are we committed? At what cost? A dialogue with the Reagan administration on U.S. policy. 97th Congress, 1st Session, 1981.

A.2 Congressional Research Service (Library of Congress, Washington, D.C.)

Iran: Executive and congressional reactions and roles. Issue Brief no. IB80001: by Mark M. Lowenthal and Ellen C. Collier (January 31, 1981).

Iran in crisis. Issue Brief no. IB79009: by Clyde R. Mark (updated, September 1979).

Arms sales to Saudi Arabia: AWACS and the F-15 enhancements. Issue Brief no. IB1078: by Richard F. Grimmett (updated, May 1982).

Bibliography

Iran: confrontation with the United States. Issue Brief no. IB79118: by Iran Task Force (updated, December 1980).

Afghanistan: Soviet invasion and U.S. response. Issue Brief no. IB80006: by Richard P. Cronin (updated, February 1982).

Regional support facilities for the Rapid Deployment Force. Report no. 82-53F: by James P. Wootten (March 1982).

Amphibious assault and the crisis in Iran. By John Stocker (December 1979).

Petroleum imports from the Persian Gulf: use of U.S. armed force to ensure supplies. Issue Brief no. IB79046: by John M. Collins, Clyde R. Mark, and Elizabeth A. Severns (updated, January 1982).

U.S. –Soviet relations after Afghanistan. Issue Brief no. IB80080: by Stuart Goldman (updated, November 1980).

Soviet policy towards the Third World. Issue Brief no. IB79102: by William H. Cooper (updated, May 1980).

Rapid Deployment Force. Issue Brief no. IB80027: by James P. Wootten (updated, May 1985).

A.3 Congressional Budget Office (Washington, D.C.)

U.S. projection forces: requirements, scenarios and options (1978).

The economic impact of oil import reductions (1978).

U.S. airlift forces: enhancement alternatives for NATO and non-NATO contingencies (1979).

The Marine Corps in the 1980s: prestocking proposals, the Rapid Deployment Force and other issues (1980).

U.S. ground forces: alternatives for NATO and non-NATO contingencies (1980).

Resources for defense: a review of key issues for fiscal years 1982 – 1986 (1981).

Rapid Deployment Forces: policy and budgetary implications (1983).

Improving strategic mobility: the C-17 program and alternatives (1986).

A.4 General Accounting Office (Washington, D.C.)

Information on the requirement for strategic airlift (June 1976).

Further information needed in Navy's oversight and management of contracting for facilities construction on Diego Garcia. GAO/NSIAD-84-62 (May 1984).

Performance capabilities of the C-5 and C-17 cargo aircraft. GAO/NSIAD-84-119 (July 1984).

A.5 Department of Defense, Washington, D.C. (including the Organization of the Joint Chiefs of Staff, Department of Navy [Marine Corps], Army and Air Force)

Department of Defense. *Annual report to Congress.* FY1962 – FY1988.

Department of Defense. *Report on Allied contribution to common defense.* 1982 – 1984.

Organization of the Joint Chiefs of Staff. *United States military posture.* 1980 – 1988.

Bibliography

Department of Defense. *Soviet military power*. 1982–1987.
Joint Chiefs of Staff (Historical Section). *The rapid deployment mission* (February 1981.)

A.6 Department of State (Washington, D.C.)

Department of State Bulletin. 1970–1986.
Current Policy Series (Bureau of Public Affairs): 1981–1982, nos. 270, 304, 306, 307, 310, 312, 313, 320, 323, 324, 325, 326, 332, 395.

A.7 Published interviews

'After Iran: next turn for U.S. foreign policy'. Interview with Zbigniew Brzezinski, Assistant to the President for National Security Affairs. *U.S. News and World Report*, December 31, 1979: 36–38.
'America's plans to meet Soviet challenge'. Interview with Harold Brown, Secretary of Defense, *U.S. News and World Report*, February 11, 1980: 33–36.
A discussion of the Rapid Deployment Force with Lt. General P. X. Kelly (Washington, D.C.: American Enterprise Institute for Public Policy Research, 1980).
'Interview with Lt. Gen. Robert C. Kingston, Commander-in-Chief, U.S. Central Command', *Armed Forces Journal International* (July 1984); 67–73.
'Initially . . . it's all airlift'. Interview with commander, RDJTF, *Airlift* (Fall 1982): 2–6.
'Interview with General George B. Crist, Commander-in-Chief, U.S. Central Command', *Marine Corps Gazette* (December 1986): 30–37.

A.8 Other

Department of Defense, *The RDJTF command decision*, news release (April 24, 1981).
Department of Energy, *1982 annual energy review*. DOE/EIA-0384(82) (Washington, D.C.: Energy Information Administration, April 1983).
Kelly, Lt. General P. X., 'Rapid deployment: a vital trump', *Parameters*, vol. 11 (March 1981): 50–53.
Members of Congress for Peace Through Law, 'Rapid Deployment Forces: reassurance or threat to American security interests', *Congressional Record*, Senate, June 27, 1980: S8702–S8705.
Organization of the Joint Chiefs of Staff, 'Projection of U.S. military power and the Soviet threat', *Asia Pacific Defense Forum*, vol. 6 (fall) 1981): 14–20.
Office of Technology Assessment, *World petroleum availability, 1980–2000: a technical memorandum* (Washington, D.C.: October 1980).
Public papers of the Presidents of the United States: Jimmy Carter, 1979 (Washington, D.C.: U.S. GPO, 1980).

Bibliography

Public papers of the Presidents of the United States: Jimmy Carter, 1980–1981. Book 1, January 1–May 23, 1980 (Washington, D.C.: U.S. GPO, 1981).

Rapid Deployment Joint Task Force, *Fact sheet* (HQ, Rapid Deployment Joint Task Force: Public Affairs Office, April 1981).

Statement of General George B. Crist, USMC, Commander-in-Chief, U.S. Central Command Before the Defense Policy Panel of the House Armed Services Committee on the Status of the United States Central Command, March 17, 1987.

Steadman, Richard C. *The national military command structure.* Report of a study requested by the President and conducted in the Department of Defense (Washington, D.C.: U.S. GPO, July 1978).

United States Central Command, *Fact sheet* (HQ, U.S. Central Command: Public Affairs Office, March 1983).

B. Books and Monographs

Abir, Mordechai and Areyh Yodfat. *In the direction of the Gulf: the Soviet Union and the Persian Gulf* (London: Frank Cass, 1977).

Al-Bahrna, Husain, M. *The legal status of the Arabian Gulf States* (Manchester: University of Manchester Press, 1968).

Alexander, Yonah, and Allan Nanes (eds). *The United States and Iran: a documentary history* (Frederick, MD: University Press of America, 1980).

Amin, S. H. *International and legal problems of the Gulf* (London: Middle East and North African Studies Press, 1981).

Amirie, Abbas (ed.). *The Persian Gulf and Indian Ocean in international politics* (Teheran: Institute for International Political and Economic Studies, 1975).

Amirsadeghi, Hossein (ed.). *The security of the Persian Gulf* (London: Croom Helm, 1981).

Anthony, John Duke. *Arab states of the lower Gulf: people, politics, petroleum* (Washington, D.C.: Middle East Institute, 1975).

Ayoob, Mohammed (ed.). *Conflict and intervention in the Third World* (Canberra: Australian National University Press, 1980).

Beazley, Kim, and Ian Clark. *Politics of intrusion: the superpowers and the Indian Ocean* (Sydney: Alternative Publishing Cooperative, 1979).

Berg, Larry L., Lawrence M. Baird, and Emilio E. Varanini III (eds). *The United States and world energy sources* (New York: Praeger, 1982).

Bezboruah, Monoranjan. *U.S. strategy in the Indian Ocean: the international response* (New York: Praeger, 1977).

Bowie, Christopher J. *Concepts of operations and USAF planning for Southwest Asia,* R-3215-AF (Santa Monica, CA: Rand Corporation, September 1984).

Bowman, Larry W., and Ian Clark (eds). *The Indian Ocean in global politics* (Nedlands: University of Western Australia Press, 1981).

Brzezinski, Zbigniew. *Power and principle: memoirs of the National Security Advisor, 1977–1981* (New York: Farrar, Straus and Giroux, 1983).

Burger, Ethan S. *Eastern Europe and oil: the Soviet dilemma.* P-6368 (Santa Monica, CA: Rand Corporation, October 1979.

Bibliography

Burrell, Robert M. *The Persian Gulf, Washington Papers*, no. 1 (New York: Library Press, 1972).

Busch, Briton C. *Britain and the Persian Gulf, 1894–1914* (Berkeley, CA: University of California Press, 1967).

Carter, Jimmy. *Keeping faith: memoirs of a President* (New York: Bantam Books, 1982).

Chubin, Shahram. *Security in the Persian Gulf: the role of outside powers* (London: Gower Publishers, for the International Institute for Strategic Studies, 1981).

Chubin, Shahram (ed.). *Security in the Persian Gulf: domestic political factors* (London: Gower Publishers, for the International Institute for Strategic Studies, 1980).

Chubin, Shahram, and Sepehr Zabih. *The foreign relations of Iran: a developing state in a zone of great power conflict* (Berkeley, CA: University of California Press, 1971).

Collins, John M. *U.S. –Soviet military balance: concepts and capabilities, 1960–1980* (New York: McGraw-Hill, 1980).

Cordesman, Anthony H. *The Gulf and the search for strategic stability: Saudi Arabia, the military balance in the Gulf, and trends in the Arab –Israeli military balance* (Boulder, CO: Westview Press, 1984).

Cordier, Sherwood S. *U.S. military power and rapid deployment requirements in the 1980s* (Boulder, CO: Westview Press, 1983).

Cottrell, Alvin J. *Military forces in the Persian Gulf, Washington Papers*, no. 60 (Beverly Hills, CA: Sage Publications, 1978).

Cottrell, Alvin J. (ed.). *The Persian Gulf States: a general survey* (Baltimore, MD: Johns Hopkins University Press, 1980).

Cottrell, Alvin J. et al. *Sea power and strategy in the Indian Ocean* (Beverly Hills, CA: Sage Publications, 1981).

Dadant, Philip M. *Improving U.S. capability to deploy ground forces to Southwest Asia in the 1990s*, N-1943-AF (Santa Monica, CA: Rand Corporation, 1983).

Daniel, Marshall E. *Defense transportation organisation: strategic mobility in changing times* (Washington, D.C.: National Defense University, 1979).

Darby, Phillip. *British defence policy east of Suez, 1947–1968* (London: Oxford University Press, 1973).

Davis, Paul K., *Observations on the Rapid Deployment Joint Task Force: origins, direction and mission*, P-6751 (Santa Monica, CA: Rand Corporation, 1981).

Dawisha, Adeed. *Saudi Arabia's search for security, Adelphi Papers*, no. 158 (London: International Institute for Strategic Studies, 1979).

Digby, James F. *The emerging American strategy: application to Southwest Asia*, N-1700-FF (Santa Monica, CA: Rand Corporation, 1981).

El-Azhary, M. S. (ed.). *The Iran –Iraq War* (New York: St. Martin's Press, 1984).

Farid, Abdel Majid (ed.). *Oil and security in the Arabian Gulf* (London: Croom Helm, 1981).

Fukuyama, Francis. *The security of Pakistan: a trip report*, N-1584-RC (Santa Monica, CA: Rand Corporation, 1980).

Fukuyama, Francis. *The Soviet threat to the Persian Gulf*, P-6596 (Santa Monica, CA: Rand Corporation, 1981).

Bibliography

Grummon, Stephen R. *The Iran–Iraq War: Islam embattled, Washington Papers*, no. 92 (New York: Praeger, 1982).

Haffa, Robert P. *The half war: planning U.S. rapid deployment forces to meet a limited contingency, 1960–1983* (Boulder, CO: Westview Press, 1984).

Halliday, Fred. *Arabia without the Sultans* (Harmondsworth: Penguin Books, 1975).

Heard-Bey, Frauke. *From trucial states to United Arab Emirates: a society in transition* (London: Longman, 1982).

Heikal, Mohammed. *The return of the Ayatollah* (London: Andre Deutsch, 1981).

Hudson, Michael C. *Arab politics: the search for legitimacy* (New Haven, CT: Yale University Press, 1977).

Hurewitz, J. C. (ed.). *Diplomacy in the Near and Middle East — a documentary record, 1535–1956*, 2 vols (New York: Octogon Books, 1972).

Ismael, Tareq. *Iraq and Iran: roots of conflict* (Syracuse, NY: Syracuse University Press, 1982).

Johnson, Maxwell O. *The military as an instrument of U.S. policy in Southwest Asia: the Rapid Deployment Joint Task Force, 1979–1982* (Boulder, CO: Westview Press, 1983).

Kauppi, Mark V. and R. Craig Nation (eds). *The Soviet Union and the Middle East in the 1980s* (Lexington, MA: D. C. Heath and Co., 1983).

Kelly, John B. *Britain and the Persian Gulf, 1795–1880* (Oxford: Clarendon Press, 1968).

Kelly, John B. *Arabia, the Gulf and the West* (London: Weidenfeld & Nicolson, 1980).

Khalidi, Rashid, and Camille Mansour (eds). *Palestine and the Gulf* (Beirut: Institute of Palestine Studies, 1982).

Khalizad, Zalmay. *The security of Southwest Asia* (London: International Institute for Strategic Studies, 1984).

Kissinger, Henry A. *White House years* (Boston, MA: Little, Brown, 1979).

Kissinger, Henry A. *The years of upheaval* (London: Michael Joseph, 1982).

Koury, Enver M., and Emile A. Nakleh (eds). *The Arabian Peninsula, the Red Sea, and the Gulf: strategic considerations* (Hyattsville, MA: Institute of Middle Eastern and North African Affairs, 1979).

Kramer, Martin. *Political Islam, Washington Papers*, no. 73 (Beverly Hills, CA: Sage Publications, 1980).

Lawrence, Robert G. *U.S. policy in Southwest Asia: a failure in perspective.* National Security Essay Series 84-1 (Washington, D.C.: National Defense University, 1984).

Lenczowski, George. *Russia and the West in Iran, 1918–1948: a study in big power rivalry* (Ithaca, NY: Cornell University Press, 1949).

Lewis, Kevin N. *Reorganizing U.S. defense planning to deal with new contingencies: U.S. –Soviet conflict in the Third World*, P-6799 (Santa Monica, CA: Rand Corporation, 1982).

Litwak, Robert. *Security in the Persian Gulf: sources of international conflict* (London: Gower Publishers, for the International Institute for Strategic Studies, 1981).

Long, David. *The Persian Gulf: an introduction to its people, politics and economy* (Boulder, CO: Westview Press, 1978).

Bibliography

Longrigg, Stephen H. *Oil in the Middle East* (London: Oxford University Press, 1968).

Mako, William P. *U.S. ground forces and the defense of Central Europe* (Washington, D.C.: Brookings Institution, 1983).

Malik, Hafeez (ed.). *International security in Southwest Asia* (New York: Praeger, 1984).

Marlow, John. *The Persian Gulf in the twentieth century* (London: Cresset Press, 1962).

Martin, Lenore G. *The unstable Gulf: threats from within* (Lexington, MA: D. C. Heath, 1984).

McNaugher, Thomas L. *Arms and oil: U.S. military strategy and the Persian Gulf* (Washington, D.C.: Brookings Institution, 1985).

Meo, Leila (ed.). *U.S. strategy in the Gulf: intervention against liberation* (Belmont, MA: Association of Arab-American University Graduates, 1981).

Miles, S. B. *The countries and tribes of the Persian Gulf* (London: Frank Cass, 1966).

Mughisuddin, Mohammed (ed.). *Conflict and cooperation in the Persian Gulf* (New York: Praeger, 1977).

Munroe, Elizabeth (ed.). *The changing balance of power in the Persian Gulf* (New York: American Universities Field Staff, 1972).

Nakhleh, Emile A. *Arab–American relations in the Persian Gulf* (Washington, D.C.: American Enterprise Institute for Public Policy Research, 1975).

Nakhleh, Emile A. *The Persian Gulf and American policy* (New York: Praeger, 1982).

Nibblock, Tim (ed.). *Social and economic development in the Arab Gulf* (London: Croom Helm, 1980).

Noyes, James H. *The clouded lens: Persian Gulf security and United States policy* (Stanford, CA: Hoover Institution Press, 1979).

Nyrop, R. F. et al. *Area handbook for the Persian Gulf State* (Washington, D.C.: American University, 1977).

Odell, Peter R. *Oil and world power*, 6th edn (Harmondsworth: Penguin Books, 1981).

O'Neill, Bard E. *Petroleum and security: the limitations of military power in the Persian Gulf*. Research directorate monograph 77-4 (Washington, D.C.: National Defense University, 1977).

Peterson, John E. *Oman in the twentieth century* (London: Croom Helm, 1978).

Pierre, Andrew J. *The global politics of arms sales* (Princeton, NJ: Princeton University Press, 1982).

Plascov, Avi. *Security in the Persian Gulf: modernization, political development and stability* (London: Gower Publishers, for the International Institute for Strategic Studies, 1982).

Price, David L. *Oman: insurgency and development* (London: Institute for Study of Conflict, 1975).

Price, David L. *Oil and Middle East security, Washington Papers*, no. 41 (Beverly Hills, CA: Sage Publications, 1977).

Quandt, William B. *Saudi Arabia in the 1980s: foreign policy, security and oil* (Washington, D.C.: Brookings Institution, 1981).

Bibliography

Quinlan, David A. *The role of the Marine Corps in rapid deployment forces*, National Security Essay Series 83–3 (Washington, D.C.: National Defense University Press, 1983).

Ra'anan, Uri, Robert L. Pfalzgraff, and Geoffrey Kemp (eds). *Projection of power: perspectives, perceptions and problems* (Hamden, CT: Archon Books, 1982).

Ramazani, R. K. *The Persian Gulf and the Strait of Hormuz* (Alphen aan den Rijn: Sitjhoff and Noordhoff, 1979).

Ramazani, R. K. *United States and Iran: patterns of influence* (New York: Praeger, 1982).

Record, Jeffrey. *The Rapid Deployment Force and U.S. military intervention in the Persian Gulf*, 2nd edn (Cambridge, MA: Institute of Foreign Policy Analysis, 1983).

Reich, Bernard. *United States and Israel: influence in special relationship* (New York: Praeger, 1984).

Rubin, Barry. *Paved with good intentions: the American experience and Iran* (New York: Oxford University Press, 1980).

Rubinstein, Alvin Z. (ed.). *The great game: rivalry in the Persian Gulf and South Asia* (New York: Praeger, 1983).

Saikal, Amin. *The rise and fall of the Shah, 1941–1979* (Princeton, NJ: Princeton University Press, 1980).

Shaffer, Ed. *The United States and the control of world oil* (London: Croom Helm, 1983).

Shaw, John A., and David Long. *Saudi Arabian modernization. The impact of change on stability, Washington Papers*, no. 89 (New York: Praeger, 1982).

Shwadran, Benjamin. *The Middle East, oil and the great powers* (New York: Praeger, 1955).

Sick, Garry. *All fall down: America's fateful encounter with Iran* (London: I. B. Tauris & Co., 1985).

Sorley, Lewis. *Arms transfers under Nixon: a policy analysis* (Lexington, KY: University of Kentucky Press, 1983).

Stoff, Michael B. *Oil, war, and American security* (New Haven, CT: Yale University Press, 1980).

Sullivan, William H. *Mission to Iran* (London: W. W. Norton, 1981).

Szaz, Z. M. (ed.). *The impact of the Iranian events upon Persian Gulf and United States security* (Washington, D.C.: American Foreign Policy Institute, 1979).

Tahir-Kheli, Shirin (ed.). *U.S. strategic interests in Southwest Asia* (New York: Praeger, 1982).

Tahir-Kheli, Shirin, and S. Ayubi (eds). *The Iran–Iraq War: new weapons, old conflicts* (New York: Praeger, 1983).

Tahtinen, Dale R. *Arms in the Persian Gulf* (Washington, D.C.: American Enterprise Institute for Public Policy Research, 1974).

Thompson, W. Scott (ed.). *National security in the 1980s: from weakness to strength* (San Francisco, CA: Institute for Contemporary Studies, 1980).

Toussaint, Auguste. *History of the Indian Ocean* (Chicago, IL: University of Chicago Press, 1966).

Tritten, James John. *Soviet naval war fighting capabilities*, P-6917 (Santa Monica, CA: Rand Corporation, 1983).

Bibliography

Vance, Cyrus. *Hard choices: critical years in America's foreign policy* (New York: Simon & Schuster, 1983).

Wilson, Arnold T. *The Persian Gulf* (London: Allen & Unwin, 1954).

Yodfat, Areyh. *The Soviet Union and the Arabian Peninsula* (London: Croom Helm, 1983).

Yorke, Valery. *The Gulf in the '80s* (London: Royal Institute for International Affairs, 1980).

C. Articles

Acharya, Amitav. 'The Rapid Deployment Force and the U.S. military build-up in the Persian Gulf region: a critical perspective', *Australian Outlook*, vol. 38 (August 1984): 90–98.

Acharya, Amitav. 'Gulf States' efforts to ensure collective security', *Pacific Defence Reporter*, vol. 12 (April 1986): 11–13.

Acharya, Amitav. 'NATO and "Out-of-Area" contingencies: the Gulf experience', *International Defense Review*, vol. 20 (May 1985): 569–76.

Adams, Jay. 'Assessing Israel as a strategic asset', *Middle East Review* (Fall–Winter 1981–82): 43–54.

Adams, Paul D. 'STRICOM's potentialities', *Army*, vol. 13 (November 1962): 46–50, 92.

Agnew, James B. 'Unilateral corps: is the U.S. turning a new strategic corner?' *Army*, vol. 29 (September 1979): 30–33.

Allard, C. Kenneth. 'Soviet airborne forces and preemptive power projection', *Parameters*, vol. 10 (December 1980): 42–51.

Anthony, John Duke. 'The Gulf Cooperation Council', *Journal of South Asian and Middle Eastern Studies*, vol. 5 (Summer 1982): 3–18.

Austin, Jan, and Banning Garrett. 'Quick strike', *Inquiry*, July 24, 1978: 12–15.

Ayoob, Mohammed. 'Two faces of political Islam: and Pakistan compared', *Asian Survey*, vol. 19 (June 1979): 535–46.

Bates, E. Asa. 'The Rapid Deployment Force — fact or fiction', *RUSI*, vol. 128 (June 1981): 23–33.

Bell, Raymond E. 'The Rapid Deployment Force — how much, how soon?' *Army* (July 1980): 18–24.

Bill, James A. 'Resurgent Islam in the Persian Gulf', *Foreign Affairs*, vol. 63 (Fall 1984): 108–27.

Boam, T. A. 'Defending Western interests outside NATO: the United Kingdom's contribution', *Armed Forces Journal International* (October 1984): 116–20.

Borgart, Peter. 'The Soviet transport air force: aircraft and capabilities', *International Defense Review*, vol. 12 (June 1979): 945–50.

Bowman, Larry W., and Jeffrey A. Lefebvre. 'U.S. strategic policy in Northeast Africa and the Indian Ocean', *Africa Report*, vol. 28 (November–December 1983): 4–9.

Brady, Morris J. 'Rapid Deployment Forces operations', *Signal*, vol. 34 (August 1980): 78–79.

Bussert, Jim. 'Is the RDF a Rapid Deployment Farce?' *Military Electronics/ Countermeasures* (April 1982): 24–28.

Bibliography

Chubin, Shahram. 'U.S. security interests in the Persian Gulf in the 1980s', *Daedalus*, vol. 109 (Fall 1980): 31 – 64.

Chubin, Shahram. 'Gains for Soviet policy in the Middle East', *International Security*, vol. 6 (Spring 1982): 122 – 52.

Cittadino, John C., and Frank McLeskey. 'C³I for the Rapid Deployment Joint Task Force (RDJTF)', *Signal*, vol. 36 (September 1981): 31 – 36.

Clementson, John. 'Diego Garcia', *RUSI*, vol. 126 (June 1981): 33 – 39.

Clementson, John. ' "Mission imperative": the Rapid Deployment Joint Task Force', Parts I and II, *Armed Forces* (July – August 1983): 304 – 8, 260 – 5.

Collins, F. C. 'Near-term pre-positioned ship force', *U.S. Naval Institute Proceedings* (September 1980): 117 – 18.

Collins, John M. 'Rapid Deployment Forces: facts vs fantasy', *Marine Corps Gazette*, vol. 65 (February 1981): 68 – 69.

Cooley, John K. 'Iran, the Palestinians, and the Gulf', *Foreign Affairs*, vol. 57 (Summer 1979): 1018 – 34.

Cover, Martin L. 'FMF for the RDF', *U.S. Naval Institute Proceedings*, vol. 108 (June 1982): 51 – 55.

Dawisha, Karen. 'Moscow's moves in the direction of the Gulf — so near and yet so far', *Journal of International Affairs*, vol. 34 (Fall – Winter 1980 – 81): 219 – 33.

de Briganti, Giovanni. 'Forces d'Action Rapide: France's Rapid Deployment Force', *Armed Forces Journal International*, vol. 122 (October 1984): 122 – 3.

DeForth, Peter W. 'U.S. naval presence in the Persian Gulf: the Mideast force since World War II', *Naval War College Review*, vol. 28 (Summer 1975): 28 – 38.

DeHaven, Oren E. 'Strategic mobility: requirements and future trends', *Airlift*, vol. 4 (Fall 1982): 9 – 15.

Denarie, Paul. 'Maximum air mobility for the Force D'Action Rapide', *Defence Today* (April 1984): 135 – 8.

Dicker, R. J. L. 'RDF sealift programs — the long-term maritime pre-positioning force takes shape', *International Defense Review*, vol. 16 (July 1983): 956 – 8.

Dunn, Keith A. 'Constraints on the USSR in Southeast Asia. A military analysis', *Orbis*, vol. 25 (Fall 1981): 607 – 29.

Edgin, Gordon R. 'The War Powers Act and the Rapid Deployment Force: a game plan for the President', *Joint Perspectives*, vol. 2 (Fall 1981): 94 – 105.

Eilts, Herman F. 'Security considerations in the Persian Gulf', *International Security*, vol. 5 (Fall 1980): 79 – 113.

Epstein, Joshua M. 'Soviet vulnerabilities in Iran and the RDF deterrent', *International Security*, vol. 6 (Fall 1981): 126 – 58.

Epstein, Joshua M. 'Horizontal escalation: sour notes of a recurrent theme', *International Security*, vol. 8 (Winter 1983 – 84): 19 – 31.

Fabyanic, Thomas A. 'Conceptual planning and the Rapid Deployment Joint Task Force', *Armed Forces and Society*, vol. 7 (Spring 1981): 343 – 65.

Fahetry, Joe. 'The Rapid Deployment Joint Task Force', *Airlift*, vol. 4 (Fall 1982) 7 – 8.

Bibliography

Feith, Douglas J. 'The oil weapon de-mystified', *Policy Review* (Winter 1981): 19–39.

Foot, Peter. 'The Rapid Deployment Force and NATO', *ADIU Report*, vol. 3 (March–April 1981): 1–3.

Friedman, Norman. 'Maritime aspects of the Rapid Deployment Forces', *Naval Forces*, vol. 3, no. 3 (1982): 18–23.

Frisbee, John L. 'Command lines for combat forces', *Defense/81* (August 1981): 9–17.

Gail, Bridget (pseud.). 'The world oil crisis and U.S. power projection policy: the threat becomes a grim reality', *Armed Forces Journal International* (January 1980): 25–30.

Gordon, Michael R. 'The Rapid Deployment Force — too large, too small or just right for its task', *National Journal*, vol. 14 (March 13, 1982): 451–5.

Halliday, Fred. 'The arc of crisis and the new cold war', *Merip Reports* (October–December 1981): 14–25.

Hanks, Robert J. 'Rapid deployment in perspective', *Strategic Review*, vol. 9 (Spring 1981): 17–23.

Hansen, James H. 'Soviet projection forces — their status and outlook', *Armed Forces Journal International* (October 1981): 76–88.

Hartshorn, J. E. 'From Tripoli to Teheran and back: the size and meaning of the oil game', *World Today*, vol. 27 (July 1971): 291–301.

Hickman, William F. 'Soviet naval policy in the Indian Ocean', *U.S. Naval Institute Proceedings*, vol. 105 (August 1979): 43–52.

Hoagland, Jim and J. P. Smith. 'Saudi Arabia and the United States: security and interdependence', *Survival*, vol. 20 (March–April 1978): 80–83.

Holden, David. 'The Persian Gulf: after the British Raj', *Foreign Affairs*, vol. 49 (July 1971): 721–35.

Hollingsworth, James F., and Allan T. Wood. 'The light armored corps — a strategic necessity', *Armed Forces Journal International* (January 1980): 20–24.

Holzbauer, Joseph R. 'RDF — valid and necessary, but some negative implications', *Marine Corps Gazette*, vol. 64 (August 1980): 33–38.

Howe, Joseph B. 'Communications for Rapid Deployment Forces', *Signal*, vol. 34 (August 1980): 82–84.

Howze, Hamilton H. 'Confrontation in the Middle East', *Army*, vol. 30 (August 1980): 22–26.

Ignotus, Miles (pseud.). 'Seizing Arab oil', *Harper's Magazine*, vol. 250 (March 1975): 45–62.

Iungerich, Raphael. 'U.S. Rapid Deployment Forces — USCENTCOM — what is it? Can it do the job', *Armed Forces Journal International* (October 1984): 88–106.

Jefferies, Cris L. 'NATO and oil: conflict and capabilities', *Air University Review*, vol. 31 (January–February 1980): 35–46.

Johnson, Thomas M., and Raymond T. Barret. 'The Rapid Deployment Joint Task Force', *U.S. Naval Institute Proceedings* (November 1980): 95–98.

Jones, Rodney W., and Brad Roberts. 'Pakistan and regional security',

193

Bibliography

Journal of South Asian and Middle Eastern Studies, vol. 6 (Spring 1983): 3–19.

Jordan, Kevin B. 'Naval diplomacy in the Persian Gulf', *U.S. Naval Institute Proceedings*, vol. 107 (November 1981): 27–31.

Joyner, Christopher C., and S. A. Shah. 'The Reagan policy of "strategic consensus" in the Middle East', *Strategic Review*, vol 9 (Fall 1981): 15–24.

Jukes, Geoffrey. 'The Middle East — the view from Moscow', *World Review*, vol. 21 (August 1982): 83–91.

Kechichian, Joseph A. 'The Gulf Cooperation Council: search for security', *Third World Quarterly*, vol. 7 (October 1985): 853–81.

Kelly, James F. 'Naval deployments in the Indian Ocean', *U.S. Naval Institute Proceedings*, vol. 109 (May 1983): 174–89.

Kennedy, Edward M. 'Persian Gulf arms race or arms control?' *Foreign Affairs*, vol. 54 (October 1975): 14–35.

Kennedy, Floyd. 'The Rapid Deployment Force: Sealift is the key', *National Defense*, vol. 65 (August 1980): 12–14, 32.

Klare, Michael T. 'The power projection gap', *The Nation*, vol. 228 (June 9, 1979): 671–6.

Klare, Michael T. 'Have RDF, will travel', *The Nation* (March 8, 1980): 262–6.

Klare, Michael T. 'An army in search of a war', *The Progressive* (February 1981): 18–23.

Koehl, Stuart L., and Stephen P. Glick. 'The Rapid Deployment Farce', *The American Spectator* (January 1981): 18–21.

Komer, Robert W. 'Maritime strategy vs coalition defense', *Foreign Affairs*, vol. 60 (Summer 1982): 1124–44.

Krulak, Victor H. 'The Rapid Deployment Force: criteria and imperatives', *Strategic Review*, vol. 8 (Spring 1980): 39–43.

Kyle, Deborah M. 'U.S. sealift: dwindling resources vs. rising need', *Armed Forces Journal International* (May 1981): 35–37.

Kyle, Deborah M. 'New assets for amphibious lift', *Armed Forces Journal International* (July 1983): 78–80.

Lacouture, John E. 'Seapower in the Indian Ocean: a requirement for Western security', *U.S. Naval Institute Proceedings*, vol. 105 (August 1979): 30–41.

Larus, Joel. 'Diego Garcia: political clouds over a vital U.S. base', *Strategic Review*, vol. 10 (Winter 1982): 44–55.

Lenczowski, George. 'The Soviet Union and the Persian Gulf: an encircling strategy', *International Journal*, vol. 37 (Spring 1982): 307–27.

Levy, Walter J. 'Oil and the decline of the West', *Foreign Affairs*, vol. 58 (Summer 1980): 909–1015.

Liggett, William R. 'Long-range combat aircraft and Rapid Deployment Forces', *Air University Review*, vol. 33 (July–August 1982): 72–81.

Long, David E. 'The United States and the Persian Gulf', *Current History*, vol. 76 (January 1979): 27–30, 37–38.

Lopez, Ramon. 'The United States Marine Corps in the 1980s', *International Defense Review*, no. 4 (1981): 433–8.

Lopez, Ramon. 'The U.S. Army's future light infantry division — a key

Bibliography

element of the RDF', *International Defense Review*, no. 2 (1982): 185–92.

Luciano, Peter J. 'Sealift capability: a dwindling defense resource', *Defense Management Journal* (Third Quarter 1982): 11–15.

Luttwak, Edward N. 'The American style of warfare and the military balance', *Survival*, vol. 21 (March–April 1979): 57–60.

MacDonald, Charles G. 'Regionalism and the law of the sea: the Persian Gulf perspective', *Naval War College Review*, vol. 33 (September–October 1980): 73–81.

McDonald, Thomas B. 'RDJTF C4IS support', *Signal*, vol. 37 (November 1982): 35–42.

McNaugher, Thomas L. 'Balancing the Soviet power in the Persian Gulf', *Brookings Review*, vol. 1 (Summer 1983): 20–24.

McNaugher, Thomas L. 'Arms and allies on the Arabian Peninsula', *Orbis*, vol. 28 (Fall 1984): 489–526.

Madeley, John. 'Diego Garcia: an Indian Ocean storm-centre', *The Round Table* (July 1981): 253–7.

Malone, Joseph J. 'America and the Arabian Peninsula: the first two hundred years', *Middle East Journal*, vol. 30 (Summer 1976): 406–24.

Mangold, Peter. 'Force and Middle East oil', *The Round Table*, vol. 66 (January 1976): 93–101.

Manning, Robert. 'Rapid Deployment: force or farce?' *Defense Communications and Security Review*, no. 2 (1983): 17–19.

Medvedko, L. 'The Persian Gulf: a revival of gunboat diplomacy', *International Affairs* (Moscow) (December 1980): 23–29.

Meyer, Deborah G. 'Airlift/sealift: you can't be there till you get there', *Armed Forces Journal International*, vol. 121 (July 1984): 76–91.

Moran, Theodor H. 'Iranian defense expenditures and the social crisis', *International Security*, vol. 3 (Winter 1978–79): 178–92.

Nakhleh, Emile A. 'The Palestinian conflict and U.S. strategic interests in the Persian Gulf', *Parameters*, vol. 11 (March 1981): 71–78.

Nelson, Thomas. 'Long haul communications and the Rapid Deployment Force', *Signal*, vol. 34 (August 1980): 80–82.

Newsom, David B. 'America engulfed', *Foreign Policy* (Summer 1981): 17–32.

Noll, E. P. 'RDF and the RDJTF', *Marine Corps Gazette*, vol. 64 (August 1980): 30–32.

Paine, Christopher. 'On the beach: the RDF and the nuclear arms race', *Merip Reports* (January 1983): 3–11.

Peterson, John E. 'American policy in the Gulf and the Sultanate of Oman', *American–Arab Affairs* (Spring 1984): 117–30.

Posen, Barry R., and Stephen W. Van Evera. 'Overarming and underwhelming', *Foreign Policy* (Fall 1980): 99–118.

Price, David L. 'Moscow and the Persian Gulf', *Problems of Communism*, vol. 28 (March–April 1979): 1–13.

Prina, L. Edgar. 'The Fifth Fleet: a permanent U.S. Indian Ocean Force?' *Sea Power*, vol. 22 (April 1979): 26–29.

Quinlan, David A. 'The Marine Corps as a Rapid Deployment Force', *Marine Corps Gazette*, vol. 64 (March 1980): 32–40.

Ramazani, R. K. 'Iran and the United States: an experiment in enduring friendship', *Middle East Journal*, vol. 30 (Summer 1976): 322–34.

Bibliography

Ramazani, R. K. 'Iran's search for regional cooperation', *Middle East Journal*, vol. 30 (Spring 1976): 173–86.

Ramazani, R. K. 'Security in the Persian Gulf', *Foreign Affairs*, vol. 57 (Spring 1979): 821–35.

Ravenal, Earl C. 'The oil grab scenario', *The New Republic*, vol. 172 (January 18, 1975): 14–16.

Record, Jeffrey. 'The RDF: is the Pentagon kidding?' *Washington Quarterly*, vol. 4 (Summer 1981): 41–51.

Rilhac, Andre L. 'Armor in French Rapid Assistance Forces', *Armor* (September–October 1982): 20–22.

Ross, Donald S. 'Considering Soviet threats to the Persian Gulf', *International Security*, vol. 6 (Fall 1981): 159–80.

Rowe, Donald S. 'Collective security and the Rapid Deployment Joint Task Force', *Joint Perspectives*, vol. 1 (Winter 1981): 3–17.

Rubinstein, Alvin Z. 'The evolution of Soviet strategy in the Middle East', *Orbis*, vol. 24 (Summer 1980): 323–37.

Salameh, Ghassane. 'Political power and the Saudi state', *Merip Reports* (October 1980): 5–22.

'Saudi Arabia and the Gulf — a special report', *Military Technology*, vol. 8 (January 1984): 65–78.

Schlitz, William P. 'The airborne/air force team — spearhead for rapid deployment', *Air Force Magazine*, vol. 63 (February 1980): 38–45.

Schneider, William Jr. 'Soviet military airlift: key to rapid power projection', *Air Force Magazine*, vol. 63 (March 1980): 80–87.

Selassie, Bereket H. 'The American dilemma on the Horn', *Journal of Modern African Studies*, vol. 22 (June 1984): 249–72.

Shapley, Deborah. 'Helpless in the Persian Gulf', *New Republic*, vol. 182 (April 26, 1980): 17–20.

Spiegel, Steven L. 'Israel as a strategic asset', *Commentary* (June 1983): 51–55.

Stern, Jonathan P. 'Soviet prospects: Gulf oil strategy', *Washington Quarterly*, vol. 3 (Spring 1980): 66–72.

Sterner, Michael. 'The Iran–Iraq War', *Foreign Affairs*, vol. 63 (Fall 1984): 128–43.

Stone, Norman L. 'An Indian Ocean fleet — the case and the cost', *U.S. Naval Institute Proceedings*, vol. 107 (July 1981): 54–57.

Stork, Joe. 'The Carter Doctrine and U.S. bases in the Middle East', *Merip Reports* (September 1980): 3–14, 32.

Stork, Joe. 'Saudi Arabia and the U.S.', *Merip Reports* (October 1980): 24–30.

Stork, Joe and Jim Paul. 'Arms sales and the militarization of the Middle East', *Merip Reports* (February 1983): 5–15.

Stork, Joe and Martha Wenger. 'U.S. ready to intervene in Gulf war', *Merip Reports* (July–September 1984): 44–48.

Swearingen, Will D. 'Sources of conflict over oil in the Persian–Arabian Gulf', *Middle East Journal*, vol. 35 (Summer 1981): 315–30.

Szyliowicz, Joseph S., and Bard E. O'Neill. 'The oil weapon and American foreign policy', *Air University Review*, vol. 28 (March–April 1977): 41–52.

Thomas, Raju G. C. 'The Afghanistan crisis and South Asian security',

Bibliography

Journal of Strategic Studies, vol. 4 (December 1981): 415-34.

Thompson, W. Scott. 'The Persian Gulf and the co-relation of forces', *International Security*, vol. 7 (Summer 1982): 157-80.

Toch, Thomas. 'Rapid deployment: a questionable trump', *Parameters*, vol. 10 (September 1980): 89-91.

Tucker, Robert. 'Oil: the issue of American intervention', *Commentary*, vol. 59 (January 1975): 21-31.

Tuttle, Jerry O. 'Intelligence support to the Rapid Deployment Force', *Signal*, vol. 34 (August 1980): 75-78.

Valenta, Jiri. 'From Prague to Kabul: the Soviet style of invasion', *International Security*, vol. 5 (Fall 1980): 114-41.

Van Hollen, Christopher. 'Don't engulf the Gulf', *Foreign Affairs*, vol. 59 (Summer 1981): 1064-78.

Volman, Daniel. 'Commanding the center', *Merip Reports* (July-September 1984): 49-50, 64.

Waltz, Kenneth N. 'A strategy for the Rapid Deployment Force', *International Security*, vol. 5 (Spring 1981): 49-73.

Watt, David C. 'The decision to withdraw from the Gulf', *Political Quarterly*, vol. 39 (1968): 310-21.

Wenger, Martha. 'Central command bases in the Middle East', *Merip Reports* (November-December 1984): 24-26.

West, Francis J. 'Limited U.S.-Soviet conflict and the RDF', *Marine Corps Gazette*, vol. 64 (August 1980): 39-46.

Whitehurst, Clinton H. 'Improving our Rapid Deployment Force capability: can it be done sooner and cheaper?', *Defense Transportation Journal*, vol. 36 (September 1980): 22-30.

Wirsing, Robert G., and James M. Roherty. 'The United States and Pakistan', *International Affairs*, vol. 58 (Autumn 1982): 588-609.

Wohlstetter, Albert. 'Meeting the threat in the Persian Gulf', *Survey*, vol. 25 (Spring 1980): 128-88.

Wright, Claudia. 'Implications of the Iran-Iraq War', *Foreign Affairs*, vol. 59 (Winter 1980-81): 275-303.

Wright, Claudia. 'A risky bet on General Zia', *Atlantic Monthly*, vol. 247 (June 1981): 16-23.

Yorke, Valery. 'Bid for Gulf unity', *World Today*, vol. 37 (July-August 1981): 246-9.

Zakheim, Dov S. 'Towards a Western approach to Indian Ocean', *Survival*, vol. 22 (January-February 1980): 7-14.

D. Miscellaneous

Acharya, Amitav. *The Gulf war and 'Irangate': American dilemmas*, Working Paper no. 130 (Canberra: Strategic and Defence Studies Centre, Australian National University, 1987).

Association of the United States Army, *Strategic mobility: can we get there from here — in time* (Arlington, VA: 1984).

Carnegie Endowment for International Peace, *Challenges for U.S. national security: assessing the balance, defense spending and conventional forces*. A Preliminary Report, Part II (Washington, D.C.: 1981).

Bibliography

Center for Defense Information, 'The oil crisis: is there a military option?' *Defense Monitor*, vol. 8, no. 11 (December 1979).

Center for Strategic and International Studies, Georgetown University, *The Gulf: implications of British withdrawal*. Special Report Series no. 8 (Washington, D.C.: February 1969).

Defense Marketing Service, *Rapid Deployment Force* (Greenwich, CT: DMS, 1980).

Glick, Stephen P. *Israeli medical support for the U.S. Armed Forces*. AIPAC Papers on U.S.–Israel Relations no. 5 (Washington, D.C.: American–Israel Public Affairs Committee, 1983).

McNaugher, Thomas L. *Balancing Soviet Power in the Gulf*, manuscript provided by the author (Washington, D.C.: 1984).

'Rapid Deployment Forces: reassurance or threat to American security interests?' Report of the staff members of Congress for Peace Through Law, *Congressional Record*, vol. 126, Part II (June 27, 1980): S8702–8705.

Rosen, Steven J. *The strategic value of Israel*. AIPAC Papers on U.S.–Israel Relations no. 1 (Washington, D.C.: American–Israel Public Affairs Committee, 1982).

Ziring, Lawrence. *The Middle East political dictionary* (Santa Barbara, CA: ABC-CLIO Information Services, 1984).

E. Newspapers and periodicals

The Age (Melbourne)
Air Force Times
The Australian
Aviation Week and Space Technology
BBC Summary of World Broadcasts
Congressional Quarterly Weekly Report
Defense Week
The Economist
Foreign Broadcast Information Service (FBIS)
Guardian Weekly
International Herald Tribune
International Security Yearbook
Kessing's Contemporary Archives
Los Angeles Times
Middle East Economic Digest
The Military Balance
Newsweek
New York Times
Strategic Survey
Time
The Times (London)
U.S. News and World Report
Washington Post
Washington Star
World Armaments and Disarmament: SIPRI Yearbook.

Index

access to regional facilities
90–2, *93–5*, 96, 113–14,
173
Aden 156
Afghanistan 27
Soviet invasion 10, 14, 43–9,
170
U.S. response to 49–57,
99, 171
Soviet threat to Gulf from
147–8
Air Force, U.S. (USAF) 7,
72–3, 76, 79–81, 96, 99,
153
Airborne Warning and Control
System (AWACS), for
Saudi Arabia 107–8, 128,
130, 136–40, *139*
Amin Hafizullah 44–5
Anderson, Jack 159
Anglo-Iranian Oil Company
3
Arab-Israeli conflict 80, 107–9,
114, 170, 173–4
arms, U.S. for Gulf States 28,
33, 134, *135*, 136, *137–8*
blocked by Jewish lobby
140–1
Saudi Arabia 12–13, 30,
31–2, 136, 138
Atomic Demolition Munitions
(ADM) 159
Azerbaijan crisis 2

Bab al-Mandeb 91, 102
Bahrain 96, 111–12
Bakhtiar, Shapur 38
Baluchistan air bases 142
bases, U.S. 90–2, 173
see also Central Command
support bases
Berbera 102–3
Betts, Richard 150
Britain 1

arms supplies to Gulf States
144–5
'east of Suez' policy 5, 170
quick-strike force 145
role in Gulf 4
British Indian Ocean Territory
97
Brown, Harold 47, 50, 56–7,
89, 91, 129, 135, 149, 150
Brzezinski, Zbigniev 50, 52–3,
55–6, 129, 159
Bush, George 8

Camp David initiative 15, 174
Carter administration 89–90,
107, 123, 127–9, 169,
171–2, 174–6
invasion of Afghanistan and
43–9
Iran and 23, 39–40, 127–30,
134–6, 170
Carter Doctrine 49, 52, 55–7,
80, 114, 130
Casey, William 133
Central Command
(CENTCOM) 172–5
airlift for 80–1, *82*, 153
airpower 72–3
amphibious lift 84, 153
area of responsibility 67, *69*,
69–70
escalation and 160
exercises *78*, 79
force projection capability
151, *152*, 153
force structure 70–9, *71*
forward deployed forces 112
Forward Headquarter Element
112
motorized division 77
nuclear capability 159
'over-the-horizon' role 114
preemptive strategy 150–4
problems 73–8, 154, 158, 172

Index

sealift for 81, *82*, 153
  pre-positioned ships 82 – 4
  support bases 92, *93 – 5*, 96,
    99, 101, 103, 106,
    112 – 13, 173
central reserve approach to force
  projection 63 – 4, 92
Command Middle East Force 4
containment strategy 2 – 3, 5,
  13 – 14, 38, 90
Cuba 160

detente, decline 46, 54 – 5
Dhalak island 156
Diego Garcia 53 – 4, 72, 91 – 2,
  96 – 102, *98*, 153, 171
  projects *100 – 1*
Djibouti 92 – 3
dynastic factionalism 42

Egypt *93*, 103, 105 – 7
escalation 149, 159
  horizontal 160
  nuclear 159 – 61, 175
  uncontrolled 160

Fifth Fleet proposal 51
Ford administration 24 – 5, 171,
  175
forward deployment strategy 63
France
  arms supplies to Gulf States
    144 – 5
  Force d'Action Rapide
    (FAR) 145
  fundamentalism 110, 125

Golan Heights annexation 109
Gulf States
  air defence 138, 140 – 1
  arms aid from USA 28 – 32,
    134, *135*, 136, *137 – 8*
  blocked by Jewish lobby
    140 – 1
  British arms supplies to 144 – 5
  Cooperation Council (GCC)
    110 – 16
  dynastic factions 42
  escalation option, U.S. 148 – 9,
    159 – 60, 175

fears of USSR 115
foreign workers in 42
French arms supplies to 144 – 5
investments in USA 12
Israel and 110 – 11, 114, 174
modernization 41
nuclear defence of 148 – 9
Pakistani activity in 142 – 3
Palestinians in 114
radical opposition in 42, 170
regional cooperation 89 – 92,
  148 – 9, 172 – 4
Soviet threat to 49, 146 – 7,
  148 – 9, 173
U.S. exports to 11
Gwadar 96

Haig, Alexander 114 – 15, 130,
  174
Halloran, Richard 77 – 8
Hormuz Straits 91, 133 – 4
Howe, Admiral John 131
Hussein, Saddam 26

Indian Ocean
  Soviet fleet in 13, 49, 155
  U.S. Fifth Fleet proposal 51
Iran
  Arab states' relations with 27
  armed forces 29 – 32
  in containment strategy 3
  corruption in 31
  hostage crisis 40, 127 – 8, 171
  Soviet invasion problems
    154 – 8
  Soviet threat to 146 – 8, 148,
    150 – 1, 175
  U.S. arms supplies 29 – 30,
    33, 128
  U.S. policy towards 21 – 4
  military aid 4
  withdrawal from CENTO 38
  in World War II 2
Iran-Iraq relations 26
Iran-Iraq war 10, 43, 112, 124,
  175
  French arms for Iraq 132
  Gulf States' neutrality 128
  Jordanian aid to Iraq 144
  Soviet neutrality 127

Index

U.S. response 126–34, 175
  aid for Iraq 132–3
  intervention escalation
    131, 133–4, 175
  Western naval patrols 129–30
Iranian revolution 10, 13,
    32–41, 125
  effect on Gulf States 41–3
  effect on USA 38–40, 170–1
  exports under 38
  U.S. response to 49, 53, 99
Iraq
  Kurdish insurgents 26
  U.S. aid for pipeline to
    Aqaba 133
Israel 93
  Arab conflict with 80,
    107–9, 114, 170,
    173–4
  Gulf view of U.S. backing for
    110
  U.S. criticism of 108–9

Jackson, Henry 53
joint task force (JTF), definition
    65
Jones, David 155, 158
Jordan 143–4

Kelly, General P. X. 52, 71, 73,
    123, 140
Kennan, George F. 44
Kennedy, Edward 55
Kenya 92, 104–5
Khasab 111
Khomeini, Ayatollah 39–41
Kilindini 104
Kissinger, Henry 15, 22, 24,
    32
Komer, Robert 91, 123–4, 156
Kuwait, request for U.S.
  missiles rejected 141

Lehman, John 160
lend-lease to Saudi Arabia 2
Liberia 92
Libya 107, 160
Long, Admiral Robert 99

McNamara, Robert 5, 63–4

Marine Corps 72, 76
Masirah Island 111
Mauritius 101–2
Merchant Marine, U.S. 81
Meyer, General Edward 157–8
Middle East
  defence against radical attacks
    124–5
  Force (MIDEASTFOR)
    111–12
  French forces in 130
  fundamentalism 110, 125
  regional disputes 173
  Soviet threat to 49, 114–15
  U.S. difference with European
    allies on 146, 174
Mogadishu 102–3
Mombasa 104
Morocco 92–3
Mossadeq, Dr Mohammed 3
Mozambique Channel 91, 104
Mubarak, Hosni 105, 107–8
Multinational Force in Sinai 69
Muskie, Edmund 127–8
Mutual Defence Assistance
    Program 4

Nairobi 104
Nanyuki 104
National Liberation Fronts 42
Nicaragua, Saudi Arabian aid
  for contras 131
Nixon Doctrine 21–3, 28, 31,
    136, 171
North Atlantic Treaty
    Organization (NATO)
  massive retaliation strategy
    148
  post-Afghanistan Measures
    75–6
  U.S. Middle East commit-
    ments and 74–6, 174
Noyes, James H. 22–3
nuclear weapons 148–9,
    159–61

OECD nations, Western
  relations with 8
oil
  companies in Gulf area 1

201

Index

crisis 7-8, 11, 171
embargo 9-10, 15, 24, 28, 170
 U.S. military threat 24-5, 175
Gulf
 preemptive strategy and 151
 producers' demands 9
 production 6, 8, 10
 revenues 11-12, 170
 Soviet interest in 47-8
 Soviet threat to 147
Gulf fears of Rapid Deployment Force 115-16, 174
import fall consequences for USA 8, 10
importance to West 5-7, 169
Iranian nationalization 24
multinationals 11
prices 8, 24, 38, 170-1
production, world 5-6, 7, 8-10
security against sabotage 124
U.S. production and needs 6
Oman 96, 113-14
 Dhofar rebellion 26-7
 Jordanian aid against rebels 143
 U.S. bases 111

Pakistan 27, 93, 96
 fears of Shi'ite subversion 143
 role in U.S. strategy 141-4
Palestine issue 174
 Iran and 38
 oil weapon 9-10, 13-15
 U.S. support bases and 114
Palestinians in Gulf States 42
Persian Gulf
 agreements on U.S. presence 54
 Carter doctrine 55-7
 combat conditions 76-8
 communications 77
 hostilities in 132-4, 141
 importance 1-2, 4, 7, 10, 15-16, 169
 Nixon Doctrine and 23

Soviet threat to 124
U.S. force projection capability 151, *152*, 153
U.S. objectives 16
U.S. policy 37
see also Central Command; Gulf States; oil; Gulf; strategy
power projection 172
balance, Soviet-U.S. 154-8
preemptive strategy 150-4, 161

radical attacks against moderate states, U.S. policy 124-5
Rapid Deployment Joint Task Force (RDJTF) 52-7, 65, *66-7*, 84-5, 172-5
 airlift for 80-1, 153
 airpower 72-3
 area of responsibility 67, *68*, 69
 exercises *78*, 79
 force projection capability 151, *152*, 153
 force structure 70-9, *71*
 forward deployed forces 112
 motorized division 77, 153
 nuclear capability 159
 'over-the-horizon' role 114, 173
 preemptive strategy 150-4
 problems 73-8, 158
 Soviet threat and 146-7, 148-9, 154, 158
 strategic mobility 84-5, 153
 support bases 92, *93-5*, 96, 99, 101, 112-13
 tasks 123
Ras Banas 106, 111
Reagan administration 57, 89-90, 124, 172, 175
 Iran-Iraq war and 130-4, 136
 Israel and 107, 109, 141, 144, 174
Reza Pahlavi, Shah 2, 4, 24, 171
 fall of 33, 37-9, 170
 regional security and 22-3, 26-8

202

Index

Sadat, President 105
Sadr, Abol Hassan Bani 32
Saudi Arabia 69, 112
  aid for Nicaraguan contras 131
  aid to Jordan 144
  Airborne Warning and Control System (AWACS) for 106–8, 128, 130, 136–40, *139*
  arms for Europe 141
  defence 2
  insurrection 41–2
  Iran and 27–8
  oil embargo and 15, 24
  Pakistani aid in defence 142–3
  Palestine issue and 114
  seizure of Grand Mosque 41–2, 145
  Soviet threat to 147
  U.S. arms for 12–13, 30, 31–2, 131
  U.S. bases in 3, 96
  U.S. policy towards 23
Saunders, Harold 15–16
Schlesinger, James 24, 32, 50
Shamir, Yitzhak 109
Shatt-al-Arab agreement 26
Shi'a Moslems 41
Sinai 69, 106
Sisco, Joseph 15, 22–3, 45–6
Somalia 92, 102–4
Soviet Union
  airlift capability 154–5
  invasion of Afghanistan 10, 14, 43, 57, 99, 170–1
  Iranian detente with 22
  Middle East objectives 2, 13–14, 45–9
  naval combat potential 155
  relations with USA 46
  threat to Middle East 49, 114–15
    Gulf States 124, 127, 146–51, 170, 173
  see also containment strategy
Soviet-U.S. power projection balance 154–8
Speakers, Larry 134

strategic mobility 79–85
  airlift 79–81, *82*, 153
  amphibious lift 84, 153
  sealift 79–80, 81, *82*, 83–4, 153
Strategic Projection Force 96, 99, 153
  nuclear capability 159
strategy 50, 56–7, 174–5
  access to regional facilities 90–2, *93–5*, 96, 173
  air interdiction 157–8
  challenges to 175–6
  escalation option 149, 159
    horizontal 160–1
    nuclear weapons 159–61
  forward deployment 63
  French attitude to U.S. 145–6, 174
  post-Vietnam 169
  preemptive 150–4, 161
  regional cooperation 89–92, 172–4
  stages in 149
  third party aid in 141–6
  tripwire 148

threats to Gulf security 123, 173
  non-Soviet 123–6
  see also containment policy; Soviet Union
Truman Doctrine 2–3
Turkey 93

Unilateral Corps 53
United Arab Emirates 13, 26, 136

Vance, Cyrus 46
Vietnam 160, 169, 171

Wahhabism 42
Waltz, Kenneth 148
Weinberger, Casper 75–6, 125, 130
West, Francis 124

Yemen PDR 156
Yemeni crisis 50

203